ETHICS IN BUDDHISM

ETHICS IN BUDDHISM

Suraj Vashishth

CYBER TECH PUBLICATIONS
4264/3, Ansari Road, Daryaganj, New Delhi-110002 (India)
Ph.: 011-23244078, 011-43559448 Fax: 011-23280028
E-Mail: cyberpublicationsdelhi@yahoo.com
Website: www.cybertechpublications.com

ETHICS IN BUDDHISM

Suraj Vashishisth

First Edition 2010

Published by : Asian Offset Printers

G.S. Rawat for **Cyber Tech Publications**
4264/3, Ansari Road, Daryaganj, New Delhi-110002 (India)
Ph.: 011-23244078, 011-43559448 Fax: 011-23280028
E-Mail: cyberpublicationsdelhi@yahoo.com
Website: www.cybertechpublications.com

Preface

It is well known that the study of economics has up till now avoided questions of moral values and considerations of ethics, which are abstract qualities. However, it is becoming obvious that in order to solve the problems that confront us in the world today it will be necessary to take into consideration both concrete and abstract factors, and as such it is impossible to avoid the subject of moral values. If the study of economics is to play any part in the solution of our problems, it can no longer evade the subject of ethics. Nowadays environmental factors are taken into account both in economic transactions and in solving economic problems, and the need for ethics in addressing the problem of conservation and the environment is becoming more and more apparent.

In fact, economics is one "science" which most clearly integrates the concrete and the abstract. It is the realm in which abstract human values interact most palpably with the material world. If economists were to stop evading the issue of moral values, they would be in a better position to influence the world in a fundamental way and to provide solutions to the problems of humanity and the world at large. Ideally, economics should play a part in providing mankind with opportunities for real individual and social growth rather than simply being a tool for catering to selfish needs and feeding contention in society, and, on a broader scale, creating imbalance and insecurity within the whole global structure with its innumerable ecosystems.

— *Author*

CONTENTS

1

WHAT IS BUDDHISM?

MEANING AND SCOPE

It seems to be very appropriate and even necessary at the outset to draw a well-defined line of demarcation between what is understood as Hinayana Buddhism and what is known as Mahayana Buddhism.

Most people imagine that there is only one school of Buddhism and that one school is no other than the Buddhism they have learned from the Buddhist books written or compiled or translated by Western Orientalists--Orientalists who are in many respects prejudiced against the doctrine which they propose to study most impartially. Owing to these unhappy circumstances, the outsiders are either generally ignorant or altogether misinformed of the true character of Buddhism. For what is understood by the Western people as Buddhism is no more than-one of its main divisions, which only partially expresses the spirit of its founder.

I said here "divisions," but it may be more proper to say "stages of development." For Buddhism, like so many other religions, has gone through several stages of development before it has attained the present state of perfection among the Oriental nations. And it will be evident to you that if we catch only a glimpse of an object and try to judge the whole from this transient impression, we place ourselves in a most awkward position, and shall be at a loss how to extricate ourselves from it. Therefore, let me try in the beginning to take a comprehensive view of the subject we here propose to expound.

Properly speaking, Hinayana Buddhism is a phase of Mahayana Buddhism. The former is preparatory for the latter. It is not final, but merely a stepping stone which leads the walker to the hall of perfect truth. Hinayanism is therefore more or less pessimistic, ascetic, ethical (to be distinguished from religious), and monastical. It fails to give a complete satisfaction to a man's religious yearnings. It does not fully interpret the spirit of Buddha.

The Buddhism now, prevailing in Ceylon, Burma, and Siam may be considered to be betraying in a certain way a Hinayana tendency. The Buddhism of present Japan, on the other hand, is Mahayanistic. It is more comprehensive, more religious, more humanistic, and more satisfying to the innermost needs of the religious consciousness. It cannot be said to be absolutely free from superstition, error, prejudice, etc., for it is a constantly growing, ever-living faith which knows no ossification or fossilization. Some pious people are apt to consider their religious belief to be absolutely fixed and unchanging since the dawn of human consciousness; but they have forgotten, in my opinion, the fact that the human mind is still keeping on unfolding itself, that it has not yet exhausted all its possibilities, that it is constantly coming to a clearer consciousness as to its own nature, origin, and destiny. But what I firmly believe is that in the Buddhism of Japan today are epitomized all the essential results reached through the unfolding of the religious consciousness during the past twenty or thirty centuries of Oriental culture.

In a word, what has been known in the West as the teaching of Buddha does not represent it in its true, unadulterated colour, for it is Hinayanistic in tendency; that is, it is exclusive and not comprehensive, narrow and limited, and not all absorbing and assimilating. What I propose to expound in this lecture tonight is the Mahayana Buddhism, so called by Buddhist scholars of the East.

Let me point out in this connection what is most characteristic of Buddhism as distinguished from any other religion. I refer to a predominant tendency of Buddhism toward intellectuality, and it seems to me that the reason why Buddhism is always ready to stand before the tribunal of science and let her pass a judgment upon its merits or demerits is due to this intellectual tenor. It goes without saying that the intellect does not constitute the most essential element of religion, but we must not forget that a religious system too much given up to sentimentalism (understanding it in its purely psychological sense) is generally prone to accede to unwarranted mysticism, ignoring altogether the legitimate claim of the intellect. Buddhism is fortunately saved from this grievous blunder, and always endeavours not to give a free rein to the wantonness of imagination and the irrationality of affection. Love without enlightenment excludes, discriminates, and contradicts itself. Love is not love unless it is purified in the mill of spiritual insight and intellectual discrimination.

What are, then, the fundamental teachings of Buddhism? I deem it best to consider it from two standpoints, ethical and philosophical, or practical and speculative, or affective and intellectual. The philosophical or speculative is preparative for the ethical or practical, for religion is not a system of metaphysics which plays with verbalism and delights in sophistry, but its aim is pre-eminently practical and spiritual. It must bear fruit in this our everyday life.

To begin with the metaphysical side of Buddhism:

(1) We Buddhists believe that as far as phenomenality goes, things that exist are all separate and discrete, they are subject to the law of individuation and therefore to that of limitation also. All particular things exist in time and space and move according to the law of cause and effect, not only physically but morally. Buddhism does not, though sometimes understood by Western people to do so, advocate the doctrine of emptiness or annihilation. It most assuredly recognizes the multitudinousness and reality of phenomena. This world as it is, is real, not void. This life as we live it, is true, and not a dream.

(2) We Buddhists believe that all these particular things surrounding us come from one ultimate source which is all-powerful, all-knowing, and all-loving. The world

is the expression or manifestation of this reason or spirit or life, whatever you may designate it. However diverse, therefore, things are, they all partake of the nature of the ultimate being. Not only sentient beings, but non-sentient beings, reflect the glory of the Original Reason. Not only man but even the lower animals and inorganic substances manifest the divinity of their source. To use the Christian term, God, it 1 is visible and audible not only in one of its highest manifestations, whom Christians call Jesus Christ, but also in the meanest and most insignificant piece of stone lying in a deserted field. God's splendour is seen not only in the Biblical lilies, but also in the mud and mire from which they grow. The melody of divine reason is heard not only in the singing of a bird or in the composition of an inspired musician, but also in the "slums of life" as Emerson phrases it.

(3) This recognition of the oneness of things naturally leads to our third belief, that the one is the many and the many is the one. God does not dwell in the heavens. It does not direct its affairs in a closed office situated somewhere outside this world. It did not create heaven and earth out of nothingness. According to Buddhism, it is a serious error to seek God outside this life, outside this universe. It is living right among ourselves and directing the course of things according to its innate destiny. Though Buddhists refuse to have God walk out of us, they do not identify it with the totality of existence, they are not willing to cast their lot with pantheists so called. God is immanent, surely enough, but it is greater than the totality of things. For the world may pass away, the universe may be shaken out of its foundation, but God will remain and will create a new system out of the former ruins. The ashes of existence will never be scattered to the winds, but they will gather themselves in the ever designing hand of God and build themselves up to a new order of things, in which it is ever shining with its serene radiance.

To sum up the first part of this discourse, what may be called the metaphysical phase of Buddhism is to recognize (1) the reality of the phenomenal world, (2) the existence of one ultimate reason, and (3) the immanence of this reason in the universe.

Now to come to the practical side of Buddhism: The aim of Buddhism, to state it briefly, is to dispel the clouds of ignorance and to make shine the sun of enlightenment. We are selfish because we are ignorant as to the nature of self. We are addicted to the gratification of the passions, because we are ignorant as to the destiny of humanity. We are quarrelsome and want to make ourselves powerful and predominant at the expense of our fellow-beings, because we are ignorant of the ultimate reason of the universe.

Buddhists do not recognize any original sin, but acknowledge the existence of ignorance, and insist on its total removal as the surest means of salvation. Let us, therefore, all be enlightened as to the statement made before. Let us know that we are all one in the reason of the universe, that the phenomenal world is real only to the extent it manifests reason, that egoism has no absolute sway in this life, for it destroys itself when it tries to preserve itself through its arrogant assertion, and that perfect peace is only attained when I recognize myself in you and you in me. Let us all be enlightened as to these things, and our ignorance and egoism are forever departed; the wall that divides is destroyed, and there is nothing which prevents us from loving Our enemies; and the source of divine love is open in our hearts, the eternal current of sympathy has now found its unobstructed path. This is the reason why Buddhism is called the religion of enlightenment.

Now that we stand on this eminence of religious sanctity, we know what Buddhist practical faith is. It is threefold: W to cease from wrong-doing, (2) to promote goodness, and (3) to enlighten the ignorant. Buddhist ethics is the simplest thing to Practise in the world. It has nothing mysterious, nothing superstitious, nothing idolatrous, nothing supernatural. Stop doing anything wrong, which is against the reason of things; do whatever is good, which advances the course of reason in this life; and finally help those who are still behind and weary of life to realize enlightenment: and here is Buddhism in a nutshell. It has nothing to do with prayer and worship and singing and what not. Our simple everyday life of love and sympathy is all that is needed to be a good Buddhist. I was once asked whether there was such a thing as religious life particularly. To which my answer was simple enough: "Attend to Your daily business, do all you can for the promotion of goodness in this world, and out of fullness of heart help your fellow-beings to gain the path of enlightenment. Outside of this there cannot be anything to be specially called a religious life."

In the latter part of the T'ang Dynasty in China, there was a famous poet-statesman who is known in Japanese as Hak-Rak-Ten. He learned that there resided in his district a Buddhist monk greatly noted for his saintly life and scholarly learning. The governor went to see him, intending to discuss some deeply religious topics. As soon as he was ushered into the pretence of the monk, he inquired what was thought by the saint to be the most fundamental teaching of Buddhism. The monk immediately replied that it is the teaching of all enlightened ones to cease doing anything evil, to promote goodness, and to purify one's own heart.

Hak-Rak-Ten was nonplused to receive such a commonplace instruction from the mouth of such a scholarly personage professing the faith of Buddha; for he secretly expected to have something highly metaphysical and profoundly speculative, which would naturally lead them to further philosophizing and contentless abstraction. The poet-statesman therefore retorted: "This is what every child of three summers is familiar with. I desire on the other hand what is most abstruse, most essential, most vital in Buddhism." The monk, however, coldly replied: "Every child of three summers may know what I said now, but even a silvery-haired man of eighty winters finds it difficult to put the Buddhist instruction into the practice of everyday life."

And it is said that thereupon the Governor reverentially bowed and went home wiser.

What is philosophical in Buddhism is no more than a preliminary step toward what is practical in it. Every religion, if it deserves the name, must be essentially practical and conducive to the promotion of the general welfare and to the realization of Reason. Though intellectualism is one of the most characteristic features of Buddhism, making it so distinct from any other religious system, it never forgets the fact that our religious consciousness ever demands something concrete, that which is visible to our senses, that which is observable in our everyday life. Religion does not necessarily consist in talking on such subjects as the continuation after death of individual personality, original sin committed by some mythical personages, the last judgment to be given by an unknown quantity, a special historical revelation which takes place in a congested brain, and what not. At least, practical Buddhism does not trouble itself with solving these problems through speculation or imagination or sophistry. Let those theologians who delight in abstraction and supernaturalism discuss them to their hearts' content, for that is their profession. We, plain ordinary Buddhists, will keep on removing selfishness, seeking the light that is everywhere, practising lovingkindness that does not contradict or discriminate. Says an ancient sage, "The Way is near, and thou seekest it afar." Why, then, shall we ever attempt to walk away from the path which extends right in front of us, so wide and well paved?

THE LIFE OF THE BUDDHA

The Names of the Buddha

Accounts of the life of the Buddha, meaning "the enlightened one," contain historical and legendary materials, which are difficult to distinguish clearly. He was named at birth Siddhartha, meaning "he who will succeed," belonged to the Gautama clan, and was called Shakyamuni, "sage of the Shakya people."

Birth and Youth of the Siddhartha (563-547)

According to traditional accounts, Siddhartha was born in 563BC. His father was Shuddhodana, a leader of the Shakya peoples, who ruled from Kapilavastu, near the border between India and Nepal. At his conception, his mother, Maya, dreamt that a great white king elephant touched her with a lotus blossom. As the time of his birth neared, she set out for her native village of Devadaha, but when she reached a grove at Lumbini, she gave birth, Siddhartha appearing from her side. She died only seven days after his birth. The Mauryan Emperor Ashoka (r. 273-36] erected a pillar to mark the place, which was rediscovered in 1898.

The circumstances of his conception and manner of his birth made it evident that he was no ordinary child. This was confirmed when a sage named Asita came down from the Himalayas to see the child, and, after inspecting his features, declared that he would either be a world conqueror or become the enlightened one (Buddha).

To those who are lost in the desert tracks of Samsara, he shall proclaim a way which shall lead to liberations;...creatures scorched by the fire go greed fueled by sense objects, he will refresh with the rain of the Law (dharma).

Lamenting that he would not live to hear his teachings, he directed his disciple Nalaka to follow the new teacher.

The King, naturally pleased that his son might become a world-conqueror and equally alarmed at the prospect he might become a religious teacher, resolved that his son would know only the pleasures of the princely life and never encounter anything which might tempt him toward religion.

Prince Siddhartha accordingly grew up amid the luxury and pleasures of the palace, became adept at archery, and excelled in other princely accomplishments. A princely education included the Vedas, together with phonetics, ritual, grammar, etymology, metrics, and astronomy, which made it possible to better understand their meaning. Yet even though kept away from the sorrows of the world, the boy evinced an unusual sensitivity that presaged his future.

Once when his father was performing a ritual plowing ceremony, the boy, effortlessly and without any training, became absorbed in a deep meditative concentration, which would later be called the First Meditation (dhyana). On another occasion, he observed birds pulling worms from the earth, and reflected on how every living thing harms other things as a consequence merely of living.

Marriage, Awakening, and the Great Renunciation (547-533)

Despite these awakenings of his meditative nature, at 16 he married Yasodhara and continues to live a life of ease and luxury, having three palaces-one for the hot season, one for the cold, and one for the rainy season. Later he is said to have recalled: I was delicate, excessively delicate. In my father's house were three lotus ponds made expressly for me, one with blue lotuses, one with red and another with white. I used no sandalwood except that of Kashi and my turban, tunic, dress, and cloak were all from Kashi. A white umbrella was held over me night and day so that I would be untouched by heat or cold, dust, leaves or dew.

But when he ventured out of the palace, he encountered human misery. Four episodes are counted as his awakening. When he saw an old man, Prince Siddhartha reflected that though old age is unwelcomed it is inevitable. Later he saw a cripple and reflected that though people try to avoid contact with sick people, illness is unavoidable. And when he saw a corpse, he realized that though people hate death it is the inevitable end of all. Finally when he saw an ascetic, he reflected that it was possible to renounce worldly things and be free of the entanglements of things and he came to realize that the pleasures of the palace were a hindrance to his development.

A life in a household is cramped and confined, a den of dust, but the life of the homeless wanderer is as the open air of heaven! About this time his son was born and named Rahula because his father said "an impediment (rahu) has been born; a fetter has been created." Against his parents' wishes, and in the middle of the night on his birthday at 29, he awoke to see the dancing girls from the party sleeping:

Some with their bodies wet with trickling phlegm and spittle; some grinding their teeth, and muttering and talking in their sleep; some with their mouth agape; some with their clothing dishelved displaying their nakedness.

The scene awakened in the Prince an aversion to sensual pleasures, showing him such pleasures concealed loathsomeness of material things. So Siddhartha secretly left the palace on his favourite horse with his charioteer to seek the good (kusala). When he reached the Anoma river, he shaved his head, put on the robes of an ascetic, giving his charioteer his princely clothes to return to the palace. He then continued southward toward Rajagriha, the capital of Magadha.

The Intellectual Milieu

In India there was an ancient tradition of meditation and asceticism, dating to the Indus Valley civilization about 2500BC. A great body of literature, called the Upanishads, had developed which summarized the teachings of ascetics. There were two patterns of asceticism: that of the brahmans (priests) and that of the wandering ascetics, called sramanas, "those who strive." The Brahmans followed the Four Stages of life: studying under a teacher when young; returning home to marry and raise a family; turning over daily affairs to a son and taking up meditative practices; and, finally, leaving home to live in the forest, there to die.

The Sramanas take up the life of wandering as youths, discipline themselves through austerities, and practice a "discipline" or yoga. The goal of all their efforts was Liberation, which was defined differently by different thinkers. But a common thread was disdain for the gods and practices of the Vedas and a ferment of ideas, ranging from atheism to personal devotion to a personal god (bhakti). We know from Buddhist and Jain texts that more than twenty different sects, today mostly known only by name, flourished at that time.

The Six Teachers

- At the time Siddhartha began his life as a wandering ascetic, there were in northern India six famous ascetics who led groups of disciplines: Purana Kassapa who argued that the person is unaffected by the goodness or badness of his actions. Morality did not exist; murder and theft were acceptable as those acts did not harm those who performed them.

- Makkhali Gosala who contended that a person's success or failure was due to fate and that an individual's actions could not influence the course of his life. His followers were knows as the Ajivakas, which probably refers to their practice of extreme austerities, love of solitude, and disdain for any kind of comfort. So difficult a practice never had many followers, yet the school continued to exist until the 14th century AD.
- Ajita Keshakambala, who was materialist, held that everything was composed of four elements (earth, water, fire, and wind), and that moral acts were meaningless. This position was later maintained by the Lokayata or Charvaka tradition.
- Pakudha Kacchayana who held that there were seven elements, the four recognized by Ajita plus pain, pleasure, and life. The elements are unchanging and are the only reality. Thus if a person is stabbed with a knife, the knife does nothing but pass through the spaces between the elements, thus is of no consequence, even if the person dies. This position is later represented in the Vaisesika school.
- Sanjaya Bellatthiputta who refused to answer any question directly, being a skeptic because of doubts about the nature of knowledge and investigations of logic, and who, through his students, exercised a significant influence on Buddhism.
- Mahavira, one of the founding figures of Jainism. Mahavira belonged to the nirgrantha ascetics, those who freed themselves from all fetters through the practice of austerities until they conquered (jain) ignorance. Jainism belongs with Buddhism as one of the great heterodox schools of Indian thought.

The Wandering Ascetic (533-528)

Siddharta as Student of Meditation: When Siddhartha reached Magadha, an important kingdom in Central India, he studied first under Alara Kalama from whom he learned the technique of meditation that enabled the adept to attain a state of nothingness. But Siddhartha found this teaching lacking, so he left. On his way to another teacher, King Bimbisara offered to make him a minister, but Siddhartha declined. He then sent a retainer to persuade Siddhartha to abandon his meditation, but to no avail. Siddhartha then sought out Uddaka Ramaputta who taught the technique of meditation of neither perception nor non-perception, a meditation which removed the mind from all contact with the world of sensation. Though more profound than the meditation of nothingness, when the meditation was over, the problems of the world returned, thus quieting the mind was an inadequate technique for attaining true wisdom.

Siddharta as a Forest Ascetic

In the company of Kondanna, Bhaddiya, Vappa, Mahanama, and Assaji, Siddharta entered the forests to practice the greatest austerities of self-mortification in order to gain wisdom and freedom. He would clench his teeth and press his tongue against his palate continually, learning to ignore the pain. He once tried to stop all breathing, closing his nose and mouth, only to have his ears begin to breath which he stopped for a while only with the greatest effort.

He experienced pain as strong as if a "man were to bore one's skull with a sharp drill" or to "bind one's head tightly with a hard leather thong" or to "rip up the belly with a sharp butcher's knife" or to "seize a man by his arms and scorch and thoroughly burn him in a pit of charcoal." Finally he began a great fast, gradually reducing the amount of food he ate until he no longer required food. He became progressively more emaciated, his hair fell out, his skin hung loose in folds, the skin of his stomach clinging to his backbone, and his body was in constant pain.

To such a pitch of asceticism have I gone that naked was I, flouting life's decencies, licking my hands after meals....I have visited only one house a day ... or one every seven days, or only once a fortnight ... and there taken only one morsel of food. ...I have plucked out the hair of my head and the hair of my beard, ... have couched on thorns, have gone down to the water punctually thrice before night fall to wash away the evil within. In such a fashion have I lived to torment and torture my body, to such a length in asceticism have I gone.

In this state he discovered a fundamental truth about austerity and self-mortification: the pain such practices create produces in turn delusions, fears, and doubts magnified by deprivation and by clinging to life. It will not, cannot, lead to wisdom. He was closer to wisdom as a small child when he fell into the First Meditation. For six years he had practiced austerities and self-mortifications so extreme that they amazed his companions, but now he resolved to abandon them, to their disappointment and disgust at his apparent weakness. "The ascetic Gautama has fallen into luxurious ways and abandoned his spiritual efforts," they decided and abandoned him. Later legend says that he performed these austerities near Mount Dandaka in Gandhara.

The Attainment of Enlightenment (April/May 528)

Having rejected the luxury of the princely life with his "great renunciation" and now having abandoned its opposite, the way of austerity and self-mortification, Siddhartha returned to his first intuitions, meditation without austerity, but disciplined with the yoga he has learned from Alara Kalama and Uddaka Ramaputta. He took enough food to gain some strength, accepting rice and milk from Sujata, and sat under a ficus tree, later called the bodhi or enlightenment tree at Bodhgaya. What was needed was to move beyond all that could be experienced, until it came to an end, which did not reveal ultimate reality as was usually assumed, but was a state of non-cognition.

According to the Therevada tradition the enlightenment occurred on the night of the full moon, in the month of Visakha, corresponding to April/May of the Western calendar. Later legend explains that as Siddhartha sat under the tree, the demon Mara came terrorizing him with the fear of death, in the form of a huge army with soldiers holding every imaginable weapon, windstorms, whirlwinds, showers of hot rocks, sandstorms, but none could come close to the meditating Prince. Mara then tried darkness, but the light of his meditation defeated it. Clubs, spears, axes, arrows, and other weapons hurled at him turned into fragrant flowers that fell harmlessly at his feet. No one can escape the desire for life, and the food and sleep that sustain it, and the fear of death is the most difficult thing to over come. But Siddhartha overcame all the challenges of Mara, at the most desperate moment touching the earth for security. The earth responded with a deafening roar that scattered the frightened hosts of Mara. When Mara was vanquished, Siddhartha attained enlightenment and became the Buddha.

The legendary account of Mara's temptation is to seen as a parable of Siddhartha's struggles to understand what binds us to existence. Having returned to a disciplined meditation, Pali tradition says that in the first part of the crucial night he acquired a supernatural ability to remember all his previous lives and he began to reflect on his past and how his lives had been directed by certain factors. Then in the middle of the night, he saw how similar factors directed the lives of others, understanding how one's own actions contribute to the course of life and how things beyond one's total control also influence it. He saw that greed and hatred produced evil consequences which destroyed both the person who had them and what they exercised that greed and hatred on, that one's own dispositions and lusts urged on one courses of action which needed to be curbed, and that confusion, our inability to understand what our actions entail and how our lives are shaped, bedevils us longest. We must eliminate them, one by one, and as we do so our freedom and wisdom increase. At the end of the night, he discovered the Four Noble Truths, became the Buddha, and called himself the Tathagata, "he who has arrived," meaning he had attained the truth.

What, then, was the content of his insight and how did it occur? Was it only the Four Noble Truths, or these and the Chain of Dependent Origination, or another of his first teachings? Was it a matter of a disciplined control over our desires and dispositions or knowledge that overcame the ignorance which kept us from wisdom? Was it attained by series of progressively more profound insights into the nature of existence or of deeper meditative states? Was it a sudden leap of understanding that transfigures the mind and its grasp of the world? Did it consist in a discipline of meditation or action which could be mastered, or in a body of wisdom which could be taught, or in intuition which were beyond language and thought and could be attained but not directly taught? None of these questions can, or could be answered, and important differences among Buddhist philosophers hinge on the different answers to these questions. The meaning of the words which Siddhartha, now the Buddha, did use-moksa "freedom" or "release" (vimoksa, vimukti) and nirvana "cessation"-do not resolve any uncertainty.

The First Sermon

After he had attained Enlightment, the Buddha sat beneath the Bodhi tree for seven days in a deep meditation. When he emerged from it, he went and sat under a different tree to consider what he had come to understand and the bliss it produced.

According to Buddhist religious beliefs, others had reached the state of enlightment before Siddhartha, but had entered into nirvana without ever having taught. The Buddha, too, had doubts about teaching and was hesitant to do so, for reasons unknown but subject to much learned discussion. Legend says that the Buddha decided to teach only after the god Brahma encouraged him to do so. He first thought he should approach his former teachers Alara Kalama and Uddaka Ramaputta, but they had died.

His first sermon was delivered in the Deer Park outside Benares, represented in art as "the turning of the Wheel of the Law." There he proclaimed the Middle Way that abjured a life of self-indulgence as well as of self-mortification. A life of moderation and self-discipline which could be practiced by all. He told the five men who became his first disciples the Four Noble Truths and the Eight-Fold Way which are the core of his doctrine and are accepted by all who call themselves Buddhists. His second sermon enunciated the doctrine of "no-self" (anatta), which characterizes philosophical Buddhism. From Benares,

Buddha went to Uruvela where he converted a thousand people who worshiped fire, led by the Kassapa brothers, and delivered the Fire Sermon.

All things are on fire; the eye is on fire; the body is on fire; the perception of the eye is on fire; the impressions received by the eye are on fire; and what ever sensation originates from the impressions received by the eye are also on fire. And how are these things on fire? Lust, anger, and illusion-these are the fires that consume the eye and the other senses and the mind. This is why the wise man experiences disgust for the things of the senses, rids himself of desire for the things of the senses, and so removes from his heart the cause of suffering. When they heard this sermon, the Kassapa brothers and their followers all became followers of the Buddha.

The Missionary Effort and the Buddhist Order (523-483)

Within three months, the Buddha had converted sixty monks to his cause, from every class, brahmans to outcastes. He travelled between the capitals of the main states of north India--Magadha, the Licchavi Confederacy, Kosala, and Kashi. During the twenty years of travel when he never had a home, he converted many to his teachings. Buddha accepted people from every part of society, men and women, whoever sought enlightenment. At first his mendicant followers stayed in caves and forests, begging for food and dressing in rags, and were called bhikkhu or "beggars." To prevent excesses of indulgence or mortification, the Buddha developed a simple rule for the monks. They were permitted to live in monasteries, accept food and clothing from the faithful, and take medicines from physicians. At the urging of his step-mother who cut off her hair and wore the yellow robes of the Order, the Buddha accepted women into the Order, but provided special rules for nunneries. At the beginning Buddha himself accepted lay persons as monks with the simple proclamation: "Come, Oh Monk." Those accepted into the order shaved their heads, removed their moustaches, dressed in yellow robes, and studied under a teacher. Monks took their refuge in the Buddha, his teachings (the law or Dharma), and the Order (Sangha), the Three Jewels of Buddhism.

The monastic movement began to take shape after Buddha's conversion of King Bimbisara when Kalanda donated a bamboo grove and the King built a monastery, known as the Bodhimandala, for the Buddha and his thousand followers. Two disciples of the ascetic Sanjaya, Sariputta noted for his wisdom and Moggallana noted for his psychic powers, converted to Buddhism and became among his most important disciples. A third disciple of importance was Mahakassapa who was noted for his asceticism. The Buddha enjoined his disciples to convert others saying:

Go forth, O Monks, on your journey, for the profit of the many, for the bliss of the many, out of compassion for the world, for the welfare, the profit, the bliss of the gods and mankind. Go not any two together. Proclaim, O Monks, the Law (dharma), good in its beginning, in its middle, and in its ending. ...Make known the perfect, pure, and righteous life.

There are beings with but a little dust of passion on their eyes, who perish through not hearing the Law. There will be some who will understand. The converts to Buddhism were of two types, lay people who accepted the Three Jewels and the mendicant monks who instructed lay believers and were supported by them. They were expected to observe the Five Precepts:

1. Not to kill
2. Not to steal
3. Not to engage in sexual misconduct
4. Not to utter false statements
5. Not to drink intoxicants.

In addition, they were expected to abstain from eating after midday, attending music or dance performances, and using perfumes and garlands on six days each month. Observance was an injunction, but it was not compulsary and there was no penalty for violations. For monks and nuns the Rule was compulsary and there were penalties the most severe of which might involve suspension from the Order or, in extreme cases, expulsion. Expulsion might result from sexual misconduct, stealing, taking human life, or lying about spiritual attainments. Monks wandered for most of the year, but during the rainy season, they congregated at retreats where they undertook concentrated study of the Law and Rule.

The character of the Buddha's teaching is well illustrated by a Burmese account of two princes who were quarrelling about where to place a dam. They were about to fight over the matter when the Buddha suddenly appeared, asked about the conflict, was told the reasons, and then asked:

Tell me, O Kings, is earth of any intrinsic value?

"Of no value whatever," they replied.

"Is water of any intrinsic value?"

"Of no value whatever."

"And the blood of kings, is that of any intrinsic value?"

"Its value is priceless"

"Is it then reasonable," asked the Tathagata, "that what is priceless should be risked over what has no value whatever?"

The angry kings saw the wisdom of this reasoning and abandoned their dispute.

Return to Kapilavastu, 516BC

Seven years after he had left the palace, the Buddha returned to see his father, wife and child. During the visit, at the urging of his mother, Rahula asked to be made the next king, but the Buddha replied "What you want to inherit is impermanent and will make you suffer," and turning to his disciple Sariputta, said "receive him into the Order."

While staying there the Buddha converted his father, many members of his family, including Devadatta who would later oppose him, and many of the Shakya people. On his return, a wealthy merchant offered him land and buildings in Kosala which became the second important monastery, the Jetavanna Grove, where he spent the last twenty years of his life.

The Death or Parinirvana of Buddha 483 BC

After a lifetime of missionary efforts, called retreats, the Buddha saw dissent among his followers. His cousin Devadatta and Prince Ajatasatru, who had killed his father King Bimbisara, plotted to take control of the order and the kingdom of Magadha. Devadatta asked to lead the order, but the Buddha refused, saying that the monks follow his teachings not his person, leading Devadatta to attempt to kill him. First he released a mad elephant which charged the Buddha, thundering "like the black clouds at the end of the world," but was stopped by the Buddha raising his hand, evoking in the elephant a loving kindness and causing it to kneel down in homage. Devadatta then pushed a boulder which broke apart merely scratching the Buddha's foot and proposed new austerities for monks in the attracting new recruits. All his efforts failed. Prince Ajatasatru, now King, regretted the murder of his father and became a Buddhist. Devadatta created a schism, but the Buddha sent Moggallana and Sariputta to win them back, and they returned to the Order. Devadatta regretted his error and was received back into the Order as well.

The Buddha, now about 80, left for a visit to Vaisali where he converted the courtesan Amrapali who gave her garden to the Order. He continued his journey and was given some food by a blacksmith which poisoned him, causing violent diarrhea and hemorrhaging. Weakened by this, he continued on to Kusinagara where he died in a grove of sala trees.

He refused to name a successor, saying "What does the Order expect of me? I have preached without distinguishing between secret and public doctrines. In the teachings of the Buddha there is no closed fist in which the teacher hides things from his disciples." The Buddhist Order was to be a community held together by a common understanding of the truth which was not something secret which some might know and others not know. "If some other person thinks that he should lead the Order or that the Order depends on him, let that person lay down instructions concerning the Order. But the Thatagata has no such thought, so why should he leave instructions?" Then he urged his disciples not to think that his words died with him and that they no longer had a teacher, for the "teachings (dharma) and the rules (vinaya) I have set forth should be your teacher after I die." He reminded them that each monk should "Be a lamp unto yourselves. Be refuges unto yourselves. Let the Law be your lamp. Let that be your refuge." His last words were "All composite things must decay; be diligent in striving for freedom"

His body was cremated, as was the custom of the time, and his remains were divided among the peoples of northern India who constructed stupas to enshrine them. The account of the division (the Mahaparinibbana-sutta) of his relics gives us a detailed view of the extent of the Buddhist community, the number of adherents in particular places, and a synopsis of his teachings. In 1898, Peppe excavated an old stupa at Piprahwa and found an urn with an inscription from the time of King Asoka or before which stated that the contents were the remains of the Buddha. In 1958 another urn was discovered in Vaisali and, though without an inscription, has been identified as containing his remains on the basis of its similarity to the one found by Peppe.

The Conversion of Sariputta and Moggallana

Now at that time, Sanjaya, the wandering ascetic, was dwelling at Rajagriha in company with a large following of wandering ascetics, two hundred and fifty in number; and at that time Sariputta and Moggallana were leading the religious life under Sanjaya, the wandering ascetic. And they had made this compact: "That one of us who shall first attain to the deathless is to tell it to the other." Then the venerable Assaji, having put on his tunic in the morning and taken his bowl and his robes, entered Rajagriha for alms, winning the minds of men with his advancing and his retiring, with his looking and his gazing, with his drawing in his arms and his stretching out his arms, and having his eyes cast down, and perfect in his deportment. And Sariputta, the wandering ascetic, saw the venerable Assaji going the rounds of Rajagriha for alms, winning the minds of men with his advancing and his retiring, with his looking and his gazing, with his drawing in arms and his stretching out his arms, and having his eyes cast down, and perfect in his deportment. And when he had seen him, it occurred to him as follows:-

"This must be a monk who is either an arhat already, or has entered the path which conducts to becoming an arhat. What if now I draw near to this monk, and ask him, 'To follow whom, brother, did you retire from the world? Who is your teacher? and whose doctrine do you approve?'" Then it occurred to Sariputta, the wandering ascetic, as follows: "It is not a fit time to ask this monk questions while he is inside the city, and going the rounds for alms. What if now I follow in the wake of this monk in the manner approved of for those who have requests to prefer?"

Then the venerable Assaji, after he had gone the rounds of Rajagriha and obtained alms, issued from the city; and Sariputta, the wandering ascetic, drew near to where the venerable Assaji was; and having drawn near, he exchanged greetings with the venerable Assaji; and having passed with him the greetings of friendship and civility, he stood respectfully at one side. And standing respectfully at one side, Sariputta, the wandering ascetic, spoke to the venerable Assaji as follows: "Placid, brother, are all your organs of sense; clear and bright is the colour of your skin. To follow whom, brother, did you retire from the world? Who is your teacher? and whose doctrine do you approve?"

"Brother, there is a great Shakyaputta monk, one who has retired from the world out of the Shakya clan. To follow this Blessed One have I retired from the world, and this Blessed One is my teacher, and the Doctrine of this Blessed One do I approve."

"But what, venerable sir, is your teacher's doctrine? and what does he proclaim?"

"Brother, I am a novice and a new-comer, and the time is but short since I retired from the world under this Doctrine and Discipline. I am not able to expound to you the Doctrine at any great length, but I can tell you the substance of it in brief."

Then Sariputta, the wandering ascetic, spoke to the venerable Assaji as follows: "So be it, brother. Whether little or much, tell it me. Tell me only the substance; it is the substance I want. Why should you make a long matter of it?"

Then the venerable Assaji recited to Sariputta, the wandering ascetic, the following exposition of the Doctrine:-

The Tathagata has explained the causes

Of all things springing from a cause,

And also how things cease to be-

This the great Adept has proclaimed.

On hearing this exposition of the Doctrine, there arose in the mind of Sariputta, the wandering ascetic, a clear and distinct perception of the Doctrine that whatever is subject to origination is subject also to cessation. "If this is the Doctrine " said he, "then, indeed, have you reached the sorrowless state lost sight of and neglected for many myriads of world-cycles."

Then Sariputta, the wandering ascetic, drew near to where Moggallana, the wandering ascetic, was. And Moggallana, the wandering ascetic, saw Sariputta, the wandering ascetic, approaching from afar; and when he had seen him, he spoke to Sariputta, the wandering ascetic, as follows:-

"Placid, brother, are all your organs of sense; clear and bright is the colour of your skin. Brother, have you attained to the deathless?"

"Yes, brother, I have attained to the deathless."

"But how, brother, did you attain to the deathless?"

"Brother, just now I saw Assaji the monk going the rounds of Rajagriha for alms, winning the minds of men with his advancing and his retiring, with his looking and his gazing, with his drawing in his arms and his stretching out his arms, and having his eyes cast down, and perfect in his deportment; and when I had seen him, it occurred to me as follows:-

"This must be a monk who is either an arhat already, or has entered the path which conducts to becoming an arhat. What if now I were to draw near to this monk, and ask him,

'To follow whom, brother, did you retire from the world? Who is your teacher? and whose doctrine do you approve?' Then, brother, it occurred to me as follows: 'It is not a fit time to ask this monk questions while he is inside the city and going the round for alms. What if now I follow in the wake of this monk in the manner approved of for those who have requests to prefer?' Then, brother, Assaji the monk, after he had gone the rounds of Rajagriha and obtained alms, left the city; and I, brother, drew near to where Assaji the monk was; and having drawn near, I exchanged greetings with the venerable Assaji; and having passed with him the greetings of friendship and civility, I stood respectfully at one side. And standing respectfully at one side, I spoke, brother, to the venerable Assaji as follows: 'Placid, brother, are all your organs of sense; clear and bright is the colour of your skin.

To follow whom, brother, did you retire from the world? Who is your teacher? and whose doctrine do you approve?' 'Brother, there is a great Shakyaputta monk, one who has retired from the world out of the Shakya clan. To follow this Blessed One have I retired from the world, and this Blessed One is my teacher, and the Doctrine of this Blessed One do I approve.'

'But what, venerable sir, is your teacher's doctrine? and what does he proclaim?' 'Brother, I am a novice and a newcomer, and the time is but short since I retired from the world under the Doctrine and Discipline. I am not able to expound to you the Doctrine at any great length, but I can tell you the substance of it in brief.' 'So be it, brother. Whether little or much, tell it me. Tell me only the substance; it is the substance I want. Why should you make a long matter of it? ' Then, brother, Assail the monk recited to me the following exposition of the Doctrine:-

The Tathagata has explained the causes

Of all things springing from a cause,

And also how things cease to be-

This the great Adept has proclaimed."

On hearing this exposition of the Doctrine, there arose in the mind of Moggallana, the wandering ascetic, a clear and distinct perception of the Doctrine that whatever is subject to origination is subject also to cessation. "If this is the Doctrine," said he, "then, indeed, have you reached the sorrowless state, lost sight of and neglected for many myriads of world-cycles."

The Fire Sermon

Then The Blessed One, having dwelt in Uruvela as long as he wished, proceeded on his wanderings in the direction of Gaya Head, accompanied by a great congregation of priests, a thousand in number, who had all of them aforetime been monks with matted hair. And there in Gaya, on Gaya Head, the Blessed One dwelt, together with the thousand priests. And there The Blessed One addressed the priests:-

"All things, O priests, are on fire. And what, O priests, are all these things which are on fire?

"The eye, O priests, is on fire; forms are on fire; eye-consciousness is on fire; impressions received by the eye are on fire; and whatever sensation, pleasant, unpleasant, or indifferent, originates in dependence on impressions received by the eye, that also is on fire.

"And with what are these on fire?

"With the fire of passion, say I, with the fire of hatred, with the fire of infatuation; with birth, old age, death, sorrow, lamentation, misery, grief, and despair are they on fire.

"The ear is on fire; sounds are on fire;... the nose is on fire; odors are on fire;... the tongue is on fire; tastes are on fire;... the body is on fire; things tangible are on fire;... the mind is on fire; ideas are on fire;... mind-consciousness is on fire; impressions received by the mind are on fire; and whatever sensation, pleasant, unpleasant, or indifferent, originates in dependence on impressions received by the mind, that also is on fire.

"And with what are these on fire?

"With the fire of passion, say I, with the fire of hatred, with the fire of infatuation; with birth, old age, death, sorrow, lamentation, misery, grief, and despair are they on fire.

"Perceiving this, O priests, the learned and noble disciple conceives an aversion for the eye, conceives an aversion for forms, conceives an aversion for eye-consciousness, conceives an aversion for the impressions received by the eye; and whatever sensation, pleasant, unpleasant, or indifferent, originates in dependence on impressions received by the eye, for that also he conceives an aversion. Conceives an aversion for the ear, conceives an aversion for sounds,... conceives an aversion for the nose, conceives an aversion for odors,... conceives an aversion for the tongue, conceives an aversion for tastes,... conceives an aversion for the body, conceives an aversion for things tangible,... conceives an aversion for the mind, conceives an aversion for ideas, conceives an aversion for mind-consciousness, conceives an aversion for the impressions received by the mind; and whatever sensation, pleasant, unpleasant, or indifferent, originates in dependence on impressions received by the mind, for this also he conceives an aversion. And in conceiving this aversion, he becomes divested of passion, and by the absence of passion he becomes free, and when he is free he becomes aware that he is free; and he knows that rebirth is exhausted, that he has lived the holy life, that he has done what it behooved him to do, and that he is no more for this world."

Now while this exposition was being delivered, the minds of the thousand priests became free from attachment and delivered from the depravities.

The Synopsis of the Truth

Thus have I heard. Once when the Lord was staying at Benares in the Isipatana deer park, he addressed the monks as follows: It was here in this very deer park at Benares that the Truth-finder, Arhat, all-enlightened, set in motion the supreme Wheel of the Doctrine-which shall not be turned back from its onward course by ascetic or Brahmin, god or Mara or Brahma or by anyone in the universe,-the announcement of the Four Noble Truths, the teaching, declaration, and establishment of those Four Truths, with their unfolding, exposition, and manifestation.

What are these four?-The announcement, teaching... and manifestation of the Noble Truth of sufferings [dukkha]-of the origin of suffering-of the cessation of suffering-of the path that leads to the cessation of suffering.

Follow, monks, Sariputta and Moggallana and be guided by them; they are wise helpers unto their fellows in the higher life.... Sariputta is able to announce, teach... and manifest the Four Noble Truths in all their details.

Having thus spoken, the Blessed One arose and went into his own cell.

The Lord had not been gone long when the reverent Sariputta proceeded to the exposition of the Truth-finder's Four Noble Truths, as follows:

What, reverend sirs, is the Noble Truth of suffering?-Birth is a suffering; decay is a suffering; death is a suffering; grief and lamentation, pain, misery and tribulation are sufferings; it is a suffering not to get what is desired;-in brief all the factors of the fivefold grip on existence are suffering.

Birth is, for living creatures of each several class, the being born or produced, the issue, the arising or the re-arising, the appearance of the psychic constructions, the growth of faculties.

Decay, for living creatures of each several class, is the decay and decaying, loss of teeth, gray hair, wrinkles, a dwindling term of life, sere faculties.

Death, for living creatures of each several class, is the passage and passing hence, the dissolution, disappearance, dying, death, decease, the dissolution of the impressions, the discarding of the dead body.

Grief is the grief, grieving, and grievousness, the inward grief and inward anguish of anyone who suffers under some misfortune or is in the grip of some type of suffering.

Lamentation is the lament and lamentation, the wailing and the lamenting of anyone who suffers under some misfortune or is in the grip of some type of suffering. Pain is any bodily suffering or bodily evil, and suffering bred of bodily contact, any evil feeling. Misery is mental suffering and evil, any evil feeling of the mind. Tribulation is the tribulation of heart and mind, the state to which tribulation brings them, in anyone who suffers under some misfortune or is in the grip of some type of suffering. There remains not to get what is desired. In creatures subject to birth-or decay-or death-or grief and lamentation, pain, misery, and tribulation-the desire arises not to be subject thereto but to escape them. But escape is not to be won merely by desiring it; and failure to win it is another suffering.

What are in brief all the factors of the fivefold grip on existence which are sufferings?-They are: the factors of form, sensation, perception, psychic dispositions, and consciousness. The foregoing, sirs, constitutes the Noble Truth of suffering.

What now is the Noble Truth of the origin of suffering? It is any craving that makes for re-birth and is tied up with passion's delights and culls satisfaction now here now there-such as the craving for sensual pleasure, the craving for continuing existence, and the craving for annihilation

Next, what is the Noble Truth of the cessation of suffering?-It is the utter and passionless cessation of this same craving,-the abandonment and rejection of craving, deliverance from craving, and aversion from craving.

Lastly, what is the Noble Truth of the Path that leads to the cessation of suffering?-It is just the Noble Eightfold Path, consisting of right outlook, right resolves, right speech, right acts, right livelihood, right endeavour, right mindfulness and right rapture of concentration.

Right outlook is to know suffering, the origin of suffering, the cessation of suffering, and the path that leads to the cessation of suffering. Right resolve is the resolve to renounce the world and to do no hurt or harm.

Right speech is to abstain from lies and slander, from reviling, and from tattle. Right acts are to abstain from taking life, from stealing, and from lechery.

Right livelihood is that by which the disciple of the Noble One supports himself, to the exclusion of wrong modes of livelihood.

Right endeavour is when a monk brings his will to bear, puts forth endeavour and energy, struggles and strives with all his heart, to stop bad and wrong qualities which have not yet arisen from ever arising, to renounce those which have already arisen, to foster good qualities which have not yet arisen, and, finally, to establish, clarify, multiply, enlarge, develop, and perfect those good qualities which are there already.

Right mindfulness is when realizing what the body is-what feelings are-what the heart is-and what the mental states are-a monk dwells ardent, alert, and mindful, in freedom from the wants and discontents attendant on any of these things.

Right rapture of concentration is when, divested of lusts and divested of wrong dispositions, a monk develops, and dwells in the first ecstasy with all its zest and satisfaction, a state bred of aloofness and not divorced from observation and reflection. By laying to rest observation and reflection, he develops and dwells in inward serenity, in the focussing of heart, in the zest and satisfaction of the second ecstasy, which is divorced from observation and reflection and is bred of concentration-passing thence to the third and fourth ecstasies.

This, sirs, constitutes the Noble Truth of the Path that leads to the cessation of suffering....

QUESTIONS WHICH DO NOT LEAD TO EDIFICATION

Sermon I

Thus have I heard:

On a certain occasion the Blessed One was dwelling at Savatthi in Jetavana monastery in Anathapindika's Park. Now it happened to the venerable Malunkyaputta, being in seclusion and plunged in meditation, that a consideration presented itself to his mind, as follows:-

"These theories which the Blessed One has left unelucidated, has sat aside and rejected,-that the world is eternal, that the world is not eternal, that the world is finite, that the world is infinite, that the soul and the body are identical, that the soul is one thing and the body another, that the saint exists after death, that the saint does not exist after death, that the saint both exists and does not exist after death, that the saint neither exists nor does not exist after death,-these the Blessed One does not elucidate to me. And the fact that the Blessed One does not elucidate them to me does not please me nor suit me.

Therefore I will draw near to the Blessed One and inquire of him concerning this matter. If the Blessed One will elucidate to me, either that the world is eternal, or that the world is not eternal, or that the world is finite, or that the world is infinite, or that the soul and the body are identical, or that the soul is one thing and the body another, or that the saint exists after death, or that the saint does not exist after death, or that the saint both exists and does not exist after death, or that the saint neither exists nor does not exist after death, in that case will I lead the religious life under the Blessed One.

If the Blessed One will not elucidate to me, either that the world is eternal, or that the world is not eternal,... or that the saint neither exists nor does not exist after death, in that case will I abandon religious training and return to the lower life of a layman." Then the venerable Malunkyaputta arose at eventide from his seclusion, and drew near to where the Blessed One was, and having drawn near and greeted the Blessed One, he sat down respectfully at one side. And seated respectfully at one side, the venerable Malunlkyaputta spoke to the Blessed One as follows:-

"Reverend Sir, it happened to me, as I was just now in seclusion and plunged in meditation, that a consideration presented itself to my mind, as follows: 'These theories which the Blessed One has left unelucidated, has set aside and rejected,-that the world is eternal, that the world is not eternal,... that the saint neither exists nor does not exist after death,-these the Blessed One does not elucidate to me. And the fact that the Blessed One does not elucidate them to me does not please me nor suit me. I will draw near to the Blessed One and inquire of him concerning this matter. If the Blessed One will elucidate to me, either that the world is eternal, or that the world is not eternal,... or that the saint neither exists nor does not exist after death, in that case will I lead the religious life under the Blessed One. If the Blessed One will not elucidate to me, either that the world is eternal, or that the world is not eternal,... or that the saint neither exists nor does not exist after death, in that case will I abandon religious training and return to the lower life of a layman."

"If the Blessed One knows that the world is eternal, let the Blessed One elucidate to me that the world is eternal, if the Blessed One knows that the world is not eternal, let the Blessed One elucidate to me that the world is not eternal. If the Blessed One does not know either that the world is eternal or that the world is not eternal, the only upright thing for one who does not know, or who has not that insight, is to say, 'I do not know, I have not that insight.'

"If the Blessed One knows that the world is finite,..."

"If the Blessed One knows that the soul and the body are identical,..."

"If the Blessed One knows that the saint exists after death,..."

"If the Blessed One knows that the saint both exists and does not exist after death, let the Blessed One elucidate to me that the saint both exists and does not exist after death, if the Blessed One knows that the saint neither exists nor does not exist after death, let the Blessed One elucidate to me that the saint neither exists nor does not exist after death. If the Blessed One does not know either that the saint both exists and does not exist after death, or that the saint neither exists nor does not exist after death, the only upright thing for one who does not know, or who has not that insight, is to say, 'I do not know, I have not that insight."'

"Pray, Malunkyaputta, did I ever say to you, 'Come, Malunkyaputta, lead the religious life under me, and I will elucidate to you either that the world is eternal, or that the world is not eternal,... or that the saint neither exists nor does not exist after death?'"

"Nay, verily, Reverend Sir."

"Or did you ever say to me, 'Reverend Sir, I will lead the religious life under the Blessed One, on condition that the

Blessed One elucidate to me either that the world is eternal, or that the world is not eternal,... or that the saint neither exists nor does not exist after death?'"

"Nays verily, Reverend Sir."

"So you acknowledge, Malunkyaputta, that I have not said to you, Malunkyaputta, lead the religious life under me and I will elucidate to you either that the world is eternal, or that the world is not eternal,... or that the saint neither exists nor does not exist after death;' and again that you have not said to me, 'Reverend Sir, I will lead the religious life under the Blessed One, on condition that the Blessed One elucidate to me either that the world is eternal, or that the world is not eternal,... or that the saint neither exists nor does not exist after death.' That being the case, vain man, whom are you so angrily denouncing?

"Malunkyaputta, any one who should say, 'I will not lead the religious life under the Blessed One until the Blessed One shall elucidate to me either that the world is eternal, or that the world is not eternal,... or that the saint neither exists nor does not exist after death;'-that person would die, Malunkyaputta, before the Tathagata had ever elucidated this to him. "It is as if, Malunkyaputta, a man had been wounded by an arrow thickly smeared with poison, and his friends and companions, his relatives and kinsfolk, were to procure for him a physician or surgeon; and the sick man were to say, 'I will not have this arrow taken out until I have learnt whether the man who wounded me belonged to the warrior caste, or to the Brahman caste, or to the agricultural caste, or to the menial caste.'

"Or again he were to say, 'I will not have this arrow taken out until I have learnt the name of the man who wounded me, and to what clan he belongs.'

"Or again he were to say, 'I will not have this arrow taken out until I have learnt whether the man who wounded me was tall, or short, or of the middle height.'

"Or again he were to say, 'I will not have this arrow taken out until I have learnt whether the man who wounded me was black, or dusky, or of a yellow skin.' "Or again he were to say, 'I will not have this arrow taken out until I have learnt whether the man who wounded me was from this or that village, or town, or city.'

"Or again he were to say, 'I will not have this arrow taken out until I have learnt whether the bow which wounded me was a capa, or a kodanda.'

"Or again he were to say, 'I will not have this arrow taken out until I have learnt whether the bow-string which wounded me was made from swallow-wort, or bamboo, or sinew, or maruva, or from milk-weed.'

"Or again he were to say, 'I will not have this arrow taken out until I have learnt whether the shaft which wounded me was a kaccha or a ropima.'

"Or again he were to say, 'I will not have this arrow taken out until I have learnt whether the shaft which wounded me was feathered from the wings of a vulture, or of a heron, or of a falcon, or of a peacock, or of a sithilahanu.'

"Or again he were to say, 'I will not have this arrow taken out until I have learnt whether the shaft which wounded me was wound round with the sinews of an ox, or of a buffalo, or of a ruru deer, or of a monkey.' "Or again he were to say, 'I will not have this arrow taken out until I have learnt whether the arrow which wounded me was an ordinary arrow, or a claw-headed arrow, or a vekanda, or an iron arrow, or a calf-tooth arrow, or a karavirapatta.' That man would die, Malunkyaputta, without ever having learnt this.

"In exactly the same way, Malunkyaputta, any one who should say, 'I will not lead the religious life under the Blessed One until the Blessed One shall elucidate to me either that the world is eternal, or that the world is not eternal,... or that the saint neither exists nor does not exist after death"-that person would die, Malunkyaputta, before the Tathagata had ever elucidated this to him."

"The religious life, Malunkyaputta, does not depend on the dogma that the world is eternal; nor does the religious life, Malunkyaputta, depend on the dogma that the world is not eternal. Whether the dogma obtain, Malunkyaputta, that the world is eternal, or that the world is not eternal, there still remain birth, old age, death, sorrow, lamentation, misery, grief, and despair, for the extinction of which in the present life I am prescribing.

"The religious life, Malunkyaputta, does not depend on the dogma that the world is finite;...

"The religious life, Malunkyaputta, does not depend on the dogma that the soul and the body are identical;...

"The religious life, Malunkyaputta, does not depend on the dogma that the saint exists after death;...

" The religious life, Malunkyaputta, does not depend on the dogma that the saint both exists and does not exist after death; nor does the religious life, Malunkyaputta, depend on the dogma that the saint neither exists nor does not exist after death. Whether the dogma obtain, Malunkyaputta, that the saint both exists and does not exist after death, or that the saint neither exists nor does not exist after death, there still remain birth, old age, death, sorrow, lamentation, misery, grief, and despair, for the extinction of which in the present life I am prescribing.

"Accordingly, Malunkyaputta, bear always in mind what it is that I have not elucidated, and what it is that I have elucidated. And what, Malunkyaputta, have I not elucidated? I have not elucidated, Malunkyaputta, that the world is eternal; I have not elucidated that the world is not eternal; I have not elucidated that the world is finite; I have not elucidated that the world is infinite; I have not elucidated that the soul and the body are identical; I have not elucidated that the soul is one thing and the body another; I have not elucidated that the saint exists after death; I have not elucidated that the saint does not exist after death; I have not elucidated that the saint both exists and does not exist after death; I have not elucidated that the saint neither exists nor does not exist after death. And why, Malunkyaputta, have I not elucidated this? Because, Malunkyaputta, this profits not, nor has to do with the fundamentals of religion, nor tends to aversion, absence of passion, cessation, quiescence, the supernatural faculties, supreme wisdom, and Nirvana; therefore have I not elucidated it.

"And what, Malunkyaputta, have I elucidated? Misery (dukkha), Malunkyaputta, have I elucidated; the origin of misery have I elucidated; the cessation of misery have I elucidated; and the path leading to the cessation of misery have I elucidated. And why, Malunkyaputta, have I elucidated this? Because, Malunkyaputta, this does profit, has to do with the fundamentals of religion, and tends to aversion, absence of passion, cessation, quiescence, knowledge, supreme wisdom, and Nirvana; therefore have I elucidated it. Accordingly, Malunkyaputta, bear always in mind what it is that I have not elucidated, and what it is that I have elucidated."

Thus spake the Blessed One; and, delighted, the venerable Malunkyaputta applauded the speech of the Blessed One.

Sermon II

Thus have I heard:

On a certain occasion the Blessed One was dwelling at Savatthi in Jetavana monastery in Anathapindika's Park. Then drew near Vaccha, the wandering ascetic, to where the Blessed One was; and having drawn near, he greeted the Blessed One; and having passed the compliments of friendship and civility, he sat down respectfully at one side. And seated respectfully at one side, Vaccha, the wandering ascetic, spoke to the Blessed One as follows:-

"How is it, Gautama? Does Gautama hold that the world is eternal, and that this view alone is true, and every other false?"

"Nay, Vaccha. I do not hold that the world is eternal, and that this view alone is true, and every other false."

"But how is it, Gautama? Does Gautama hold that the world is not eternal, and that this view alone is true, and every other false?"

"Nay, Vaccha. I do not hold that the World is not eternal, and that this view alone is true, and every other false."

"How is it, Gautama? Does Gautama hold that the world is finite,..."

"How is it, Gautama? Does Gautama hold that the soul and the body are identical,..."

"How is it, Gautama? Does Gautama hold that the saint exists after death,..." "How is it, Gautama? Does Gautama hold that the saint both exists and does not exist after death, and that this view alone is true, and every other false?"

"Nay, Vaccha. I do not hold that the saint both exists and does not exist after death, and that this view alone is true, and every other false."

"But how is it, Gautama? Does Gautama hold that the saint neither exists nor does not exist after death, and that this view alone is true, and every other false?"

Nay, Vaccha. I do not hold that the saint neither exists nor does not exist after death, and that this view alone is true, and every other false."

"How is it, Gautama, that when you are asked, 'Does the monk Gautama hold that the world is eternal, and that this view alone is true, and every other false?' you reply, 'Nay, Vaccha. I do not hold that the world is eternal, and that this view alone is true, and every other false?'

"But how is it, Gautama, that when you are asked, 'Does the monk Gautama hold that the world is not eternal, and that this view alone is true, and every other false?' you reply, 'Nay, Vaccha. I do not hold that the world is not eternal, and that this view alone is true, and every other false?'

"How is it, Gautama, that when you are asked, 'Does Gautama hold that the world is finite,...?'

"How is it, Gautama, that when you are asked, 'Does Gautama hold that the soul and the body are identical,...?'

"How is it, Gautama, that when you are asked, Does Gautama hold that the saint exists after death,...?'

"How is it, Gautama, that when you are asked, 'Does the monk Gautama hold that the saint both exists and does not exist after death, and that this view alone is true, and every other false?' you reply, 'Nay, Vaccha. I do not hold that the saint both exists and does not exist after death, and that this view alone is true, and every other false?'

"But how is it, Gautama, that when you are asked, 'Does the monk Gautama hold that the saint neither exists nor does not exist after death, and that this view alone is true, and every other false?' you reply, ' Nay, Vaccha. I do not hold that the saint neither exists nor does not exist after death, and that this view alone is true, and every other false?' What objection does Gautama perceive to these theories that he has not adopted any one of them?"

"Vaccha, the theory that the world is eternal, is a jungle, a wilderness, a puppet-show, a writhing, and a fetter, and is coupled with misery, ruin, despair, and agony, and does not tend to aversion, absence of passion, cessation, quiescence, knowledge, supreme wisdom, and Nirvana.

[The intervening paragraphs which make the same reply to each of the assertions Vaccha mentions are omitted.]

"Vaccha, the theory that the saint neither exists nor does not exist after death, is a jungle, a wilderness, a puppet-show, a writhing, and a fetter, and is coupled with misery, ruin, despair, and agony, and does not tend to aversion, absence of passion, cessation, quiescence, knowledge, supreme wisdom, and Nirvana.

"This is the objection I perceive to these theories, so that I have not adopted any one of them."

"But has Gautama any theory of his own?"

"The Tathagata, O Vaccha, is free from all theories; but this, Vaccha, does the Tathagata know,-the nature of form, and how form arises, and how form perishes; the nature of sensation, and how sensation arises, and how sensation perishes; the nature of perception, and how perception arises, and how perception perishes; the nature of the psychic constructions, and how the psychic constructions arise, and how the psychic constructions perish; the nature of consciousness, and how consciousness arises, and how consciousness perishes. Therefore say I that the Tathagata has attained deliverance and is free from attachment, inasmuch as all imaginings, or agitations, or proud thoughts concerning a self or anything pertaining to a self, have perished, have faded away, have ceased, have been given up and relinquished."

"But, Gautama, where is the monk reborn who has attained to this deliverance for his mind?"

"Vaccha, to say that he is reborn would not fit the case."

"Then, Gautama, he is not reborn."

"Vaccha, to say that he is not reborn would not fit the case."

"Then, Gautama, he is both reborn and is not reborn."

"Vaccha, to say that he is both reborn and not reborn would not fit the case."

"Then, Gautama, he is neither reborn nor not reborn."

"Vaccha, to say that he is neither reborn nor not reborn would not fit the case."

"When I say to you, 'But, Gautama, where is the monk reborn who has attained to this deliverance for his mind?' you reply, 'Vaccha, to say that he is reborn would not fit the case.' And when I say to you, 'Then, Gautama, he is not reborn,' you reply, 'Vaccha, to say that he is not reborn would not fit the case.' And when I say to you, 'Then, Gautama, he is both reborn and not reborn,' you reply, 'Vaccha, to say that he is both reborn and not reborn would not fit the case.' And when I say to you, 'Then, Gautama, he is neither reborn nor not reborn,' you reply, ' Vaccha, to say that he is neither reborn nor not reborn would not fit the case.' Gautama, I am at a loss what to think in this matter, and I have become greatly confused, and the faith in Gautama inspired by a former conversation has now disappeared."

"Enough, O Vaccha! Be not at a loss what to think in this matter, and be not greatly confused. Profound, O Vaccha, is this doctrine, recondite, and difficult of comprehension, good, excellent, and not to be reached by mere reasoning, subtile, and intelligible only to the wise; and it is a hard doctrine for you to learn, who belong to another sect, to another faith, to another persuasion, to another discipline, and sit at the feet of another teacher. Therefore, Vaccha, I will now question you, and do you make answer as may seem to you good. What think you, Vaccha? Suppose a fire were to burn in front of you, would you be aware that the fire was burning in front of you?"

"Gautama, if a fire were to burn in front of me, I should be aware that a fire was burning in front of me."

"But suppose, Vaccha, some one were to ask you, 'On what does this fire that is burning in front of you depend ?' what would you answer, Vaccha?"

"Gautama, if some one were to ask me, 'On what does this fire that is burning in front of you depend?' I would answer, Gautama, 'It is on fuel of grass and wood that this fire that is burning in front of me depends.'"

""But, Vaccha, if the fire in front of you were to become extinct, would you be aware that the fire in front of you had become extinct?"

"Gautama, if the fire in front of me were to become extinct, I should be aware that the fire in front of me had become extinct."

"But, Vaccha, if some one were to ask you, 'In which direction has that fire gone,-east, or west, or north, or south?' what would you say, O Vaccha?"

"The question would not fit the case, Gautama. For the fire which depended on fuel of grass and wood, when that fuel has all gone, and it can get no other, being thus without nutriment, is said to be extinct."

"In exactly the same way, Vaccha, all form by which one could predicate the existence of the saint, all that form has been abandoned, uprooted, pulled out of the ground like a palmyra-tree, and become non-existent and not liable to spring up again in the future. The saint, O Vaccha, who has been released from what is styled form, is deep, immeasurable, unfathomable, like the mighty ocean. To say that he is reborn would not fit the case. To say that he is not reborn would not fit the case. To say that he is both reborn and not reborn would not fit the case. To say that he is neither reborn nor not reborn would not fit the case."

"All sensation...

"All perception...

"All the psychic constructions...

"All consciousness by which one could predicate the existence of the saint, all that consciousness has been abandoned, uprooted, pulled out of the ground like a palmyra-tree, and become non-existent and not liable to spring up again in the future.

The saint, O Vaccha, who has been released from what is styled consciousness, is deep, immeasurable, unfathomable, like the mighty ocean. To say that he is reborn would not fit the case. To say that he is not reborn would not fit the case. To say that he is both reborn and not reborn would not fit the case. To say that he is neither reborn nor not reborn would not fit the case."

When the Blessed One had thus spoken, Vaccha, the wandering ascetic, spoke to him as follows:

"It is as if, O Gautama, there were a mighty sala-tree near to some village or town, and it were to lose ill dead branches and twigs, and its loose shreds of bark, and its unsound wood, so that afterwards, free from those branches and twigs, and the loose shreds of bark, and the unsound wood, it were to stand neat and clean in its strength.

In exactly the same way doth the word of Gautama, free from branches and twigs, and from loose shreds of bark, and from unsound wood, stand neat and clean in its strength. O wonderful is it, Gautama! O wonderful is it, Gautama! It is as if, O Gautama, one were to set up that which was overturned; or were to disclose that which was hidden; or were to point out the way to a lost traveller; or were to carry a lamp into a dark place, that they who had eyes might see forms. Even so has Gautama expounded the Doctrine in many different ways. I betake myself to Gautama for refuge, to the Doctrine, and to the Congregation of the monks. Let Gautama receive me who have betaken myself to him for refuge, and accept me as a disciple from this day forth as long as life shall last."

DEATH AND LAST INSTRUCTIONS OF THE BUDDHA

...Then the Blessed One addressed the monks.-

" Where, O monks, is Ananda? "

"Reverend Sir, the venerable Ananda has entered the monastery, and leaning against the bolt of the door, he weeps, saying, 'Behold, I am but a learner, and not yet perfect, and my Teacher is on the point of passing into Nirvana, he who was so compassionate to me.'"

Then the Blessed One addressed a certain monk, saying,-

"Go, O monk, and say to the venerable Ananda from me, 'The Teacher calls you, brother Ananda.'"

...Ananda ... drew near to where The Blessed One was; and having drawn near and greeted The Blessed One, he sat down respectfully at one side. And the venerable Ananda being seated respectfully at one side, The Blessed One spoke to him as follows:-

"Enough, Ananda, do not grieve, nor weep. Have I not already told you, Ananda, that it is in the very nature of all things near and dear unto us that we must divide ourselves from them, leave them, sever ourselves from them? How is it possible, Ananda, that whatever has been born, has come into being, is organized and perishable, should not perish? That condition is not possible.

For a long time, Ananda, have you waited on the Tathagata with a kind, devoted, cheerful, single-hearted, unstinted service of body, with a kind, devoted, cheerful, single-hearted, unstinted service of voice, with a kind, devoted, cheerful, single-hearted, unstinted service of mind. You have acquired much merit, Ananda; exert yourself, and soon will you be free from all depravity."

'Go thou, Ananda, and enter the city Kusinara, and announce to the Kusinara-Mallas:-

"Tonight, O you Vasetthas, in the last watch, the Tathagata will pass into Nirvana. Be favourable, be favorable, O you Vasetthas, and suffer not that afterwards you feel remorse, saying, 'The Tathagata passed into Nirvana while in our borders, but we did not avail ourselves of the opportunity of being present at the last moments of the Tathagata.'"

...The Mallas, on hearing the speech of the venerable Ananda, and their children and their daughters-in-law and their wives were grieved and sorrowful and overwhelmed with anguish of mind, and some let fly their hair and cried aloud, and stretched out their arms and cried aloud, and fell headlong to the ground and rolled to and fro, saying, "All too soon will The Blessed One pass into Nirvana; all too soon will The Happy One pass into Nirvana; all too soon will The Light of the World vanish from sight." Then the Mallas and their children and their daughters-in-law and their wives, being grieved and sorrowful and overwhelmed with anguish of mind, drew near to the sala-tree grove Upavattana of the Mallas, and to where the venerable Ananda was.

Now at that time Subhadda, a wandering ascetic, was dwelling at Kusinara. And Subhadda, the wandering ascetic, heard the report:-

"Tonight, in the last watch, the monk Gautama will pass into Nirvana."

Then it occurred to Subhadda, the wandering ascetic, as follows:-

"I have heard wandering ascetics, that were old men, advanced in years, teaches, and teachers' teachers, declare, 'But seldom, and on rare occasions, does a Tathagata, a saint, and Supreme Buddha arise in the world.' And tonight, in the last watch, the monk Gautama will pass into Nirvana. And a certain question has arisen in my mind, and I am persuaded of the monk Gautama that he can so teach me the Doctrine that I shall be relieved of this my doubt."

Then Subhadda, the wandering ascetic, drew near to the sala-tree grove Upavattana of the Dallas, and to where the venerable Ananda was, and having drawn near, he spoke to the venerable Ananda as follows:- "Ananda, I have heard wandering ascetics, that were old men, advanced in years, teaches, and teachers' teachers, declare, 'But seldom, and on rare occasions, does a Tathagata, a saint, and Supreme Buddha arise in the world.' And tonight, in the last watch, the monk Gautama will pass into Nirvana. And a certain doubt has arisen in my mind, and I am persuaded of the monk Gautama that he can so teach me the Doctrine that I shall be relieved of this my doubt. Let me, then, Ananda, have an opportunity of seeing the monk Gautama."

When Subhadda, the wandering ascetic, had so spoken, the venerable Ananda spoke to him as follows:-

"Enough of that, brother Subhadda; trouble not the Tathagata. The Blessed One is weary."

[Subhadda persisted a second and a third time, and was refused by Ananda each time.] ... Now the Blessed One chanced to hear the conversation between the venerable Ananda and the wandering ascetic Subhadda. And The Blessed One called to the venerable Ananda:-

" Enough, Ananda; hinder not Subhadda. Let Subhadda, Ananda, have an opportunity of beholding the Tathagata. Whatever Subhadda shall ask of me, he will ask for the sake of information, and not for the sake of troubling me, and he will quickly understand my answers to his questions."

Then the venerable Ananda spoke to Subhadda, the wandering ascetic, as follows:-

"You may come, brother Subhadda; The Blessed One grants you an audience."

Then Subhadda, the wandering ascetic, drew near to where The Blessed One was; and having drawn near, he exchanged greetings with The Blessed One; and having passed with him the greetings of friendship and civility, he sat down respectfully at one side. And seated respectfully at one side, Subhadda, the wandering ascetic, spoke to The Blessed One as follows:-

"Gautama, all those monks and Brahmans who possess a large following and crowds of hearers and disciples, and who are distinguished, renowned leaders of sects, and highly esteemed by the multitudes,-to writ, Purana Kassapa, Makkhali Gosala, Ajita Kesakambali, Pakudha Kaccayana, Sanjaya Belatthiputta, Nigantha Nathaputta,-have they all done as they maintain, discovered the truth, or have they not? or have some of them done so, and others not? "

"Enough, O Subhadda! let us leave the question, 'Have they all done as they maintain, discovered the truth, or have they not? or have some of them done so, and others not?' The Doctrine will I teach you, Subhadda. Listen to me, and pay strict attention, and I will speak."

" Yes, Reverend Sir," said Subhadda, the wandering ascetic, to The Blessed One in assent. And The Blessed One spoke as follows:-

"Subhadda, in whatever doctrine and discipline the noble eightfold path is not found, therein also is not found the monk of the first degree, nor the monk of the second degree, nor the monk of the third degree, nor the monk of the fourth degree; and in whatever doctrine and discipline, O Subhadda, the noble eightfold path is found, therein also are found the monk of the first degree, and the monk of the second degree, and the monk of the third degree, and the monk of the fourth degree.

Now in this Doctrine and Discipline, O Subhadda, the noble eightfold path is found: and therein alone, O Subhadda, are found the monk of the first degree, and the monk of the second degree, and the monk of the third degree, and the monk of the fourth degree.

Destitute of true monks are all other creeds. But let these my monks, O Subhadda, live rightly, and the world will not be destitute of saints.

What time my age was twenty-nine,

Subhadda, I left the world to seek the highest good.

Now fifty years and more have passed, Subhadda,

Since I renounced the world and lived ascetic

Within the Doctrine's pale, that rule of conduct

Outside of which no genuine monk exists, nor the monk of the second degree, nor the monk of the third degree, nor the monk of the fourth degree. Destitute of monks are all other creeds. But let these my monks, O Subhadda, live rightly, and the world will not be destitute of saints."

When The Blessed One had thus spoken, Subhadda, the wandering ascetic, spoke to him as follows:-

"O wonderful is it, Reverend Sir! O wonderful is it, Reverend Sir! It is as if, Reverend Sir, one were to set up that which was overturned, or were to disclose that which was hidden, or were to point out the way to a lost traveller, or were to carry a lamp into a dark place that they who had eyes might see forms. Even so has The Blessed One expounded the Doctrine in many different ways. Reverend Sir, I betake myself to The Blessed One for refuge, to the Doctrine, and to the Congregation of the monks. Suffer me to retire from the world under The Blessed One; suffer me to receive ordination."

"Subhadda, any one who aforetime has been an adherent of another sect and afterwards desires to retire from the world and receive ordination under this Doctrine and Discipline, must first spend four months on probation; and after the lapse of four months, strenuous-minded monks receive him into the Order and confer on him the monkly ordination. Nevertheless, in this matter of probation I recognize a difference in persons."

"Reverend Sir, if all they who aforetime have been adherents of other sects and afterwards desire to retire from the world and receive ordination under this Doctrine and Discipline, must first spend four months on probation, and after the lapse of four months strenuous-minded monks receive them into the Order, and confer on them the monkly ordination, then am I ready to spend four years on probation, and after the lapse of four years, let strenuous-minded monks receive me into the Order and confer on me the monkly ordination."

Then The Blessed One said to the venerable Ananda,

"Well, then, Ananda, receive Subhadda into the Order."

Then The Blessed One addressed the venerable Ananda:-

"It may be, Ananda, that some of you will think, 'The word of The Teacher is a thing of the past; we have now no Teacher.' But that, Ananda, is not the correct view. The Doctrine and Discipline, Ananda, which I have taught and enjoined upon you is to be your teacher when I am gone. But whereas now, Ananda, all the monks address each other with the title of 'brother,' not so must they address each other after I am gone. A senior monk, Ananda, is to address a junior monk either by his given name, or by his family name, or by the title of 'brother;' a junior monk is to address a senior monk with the title 'reverend sir,' or 'venerable.' If the Order, Ananda, wish to do so, after I am gone they may abrogate all the lesser and minor precepts. On Channa, Ananda, after I am gone, the higher penalty is to be inflictod."

"Reverend Sir, what is this higher penalty?"

"Let Channa, Ananda, say what he likes, he is not to be spoken to nor admonished nor instructed by the monks."

Then The Blessed One addressed the monks:-

"It may be, O monks, that some monk has a doubt or perplexity respecting either The Buddha or the Doctrine or the Order or the Path or the course of conduct. Ask any questions, O monks, and suffer not that afterwards you feel remorse, saying, 'Our Teacher was present with us, but we failed to ask him all our questions.'"

When he had so spoken, the monks remained silent.

And a second time The Blessed One, and a third time The Blessed One addressed the monks:-...

And a third time the monks remained silent.

Then The Blessed One addressed the monks:-

"It may be, O monks, that it is out of respect to The Teacher that you ask no questions. Then let each one speak to his friend."

And when he had thus spoken, the monks remained silent.

Then the venerable Ananda spoke to The Blessed One as follows:-

"It is wonderful, Reverend Sir! It is marvelous, Reverend Sir! Reverend Sir, I have faith to believe that in this congregation of monks not a single monk has a doubt or perplexity respecting either The Buddha or the Doctrine or the Order or the Path or the course of conduct."

"With you, Ananda, it is a matter of faith, when you say that; but with the Tathagata, Ananda, it is a matter of knowledge that in this congregation of monks not a single monk has a doubt or perplexity respecting either The Buddha or the Doctrine or the Order or the Path or the course of conduct. For of all these five hundred monks, Ananda, the most backward one has become converted, and is not liable to pass into a lower state of existence, but is destined necessarily to attain supreme wisdom."

Then The Blessed One addressed the monks:-

"And now, O monks, I take my leave of you; all composite things are transitory; strive onward diligently."

And this was the last word of the Tathagata.

Thereupon The Blessed One entered the first stage of meditation, and rising from the first stage of meditation, he entered the second stage of meditation; and rising from the second stage of meditation, he entered the third stage of meditation; and rising from the third stage of meditation, he entered the fourth stage of meditation, and rising from the fourth stage of meditation, he entered the realm of the infinity of space; and rising from the realm of the infinity of space, he entered the realm of the infinity of consciousness; and rising from the realm of the infinity of consciousness, he entered the realm of nothingness; and rising from the realm of nothingness, he entered the realm of neither perception nor yet non-perception; and rising from the realm of neither perception nor yet non-perception, he arrived at the cessation of perception and sensation.

Thereupon the venerable Ananda spoke to the venerable Anuruddha as follows:-

"Reverend Anuruddha, The Blessed One has passed into Nirvana."

"Nay, brother Ananda, The Blessed One has not passed into Nirvana; he has arrived at the cessation of perception and sensation."

Thereupon The Blessed One rising from the cessation of his perception and sensation, entered the realm of neither perception nor yet non-perception; and rising from the realm of neither perception nor yet non-perception, he entered the realm of nothingness; and rising from the realm of nothingness, he entered the realm of the infinity of consciousness; and rising from the realm of the infinity of consciousness, he entered the realm of the infinity of space; and rising from the realm of the infinity of space, he entered the fourth stage of meditation; and rising from the fourth stage of meditation, he entered the third stage of meditation; and rising from the third stage of meditation, he entered the second stage of meditation; and rising from the second stage of meditation, he entered the first stage of meditation; and rising from the first stage of meditation, he entered the second stage of meditation; and rising from the second stage of meditation, he entered the third stage of meditation; and rising from the third stage of meditation, he entered the fourth stage of meditation; and rising from the fourth stage of meditation, immediately The Blessed One passed into Nirvana.

2

TEACHINGS OF BUDDHA

TEACHINGS AND WORLD FAITH

These are the basic teachings and concepts in Buddhism.

Karma: Actions have consequences; so our lives are conditioned by our past actions.

Rebirth: Consciousness continues after death, and finds expression in a future life.

Liberation from Karma: By following the Buddha's path one escapes the cycle of craving and suffering.

The Four Noble Truths: These are the essentials of Buddhism.

Enlightenment: The highest goal of life is to reach Enlightenment; a state of being that goes beyond suffering.

Dharma: The teachings and hence the way to nirvana.

The Core of Buddhist Teaching: At the heart of the Buddha's teaching lie The Four Noble Truths and The Eightfold Path which lead the Buddhist towards the path of Enlightenment.

Facing the Truth: The Buddha taught that the human tendency is to avoid the difficult truths of life and this in turn leads to suffering.

By enabling the mind to be at peace through meditation a human being can confront reality and overcome hatred and craving.

Buddhism and Slavery

Slavery would seem to be incompatible with a fundamental idea of Buddhism; that of freeing oneself of attachments:

Thus the ideal community of the selfless arahants form an ideal, or a standard on which ethical and moral judgement of lay societies are based.

Thus such violations of human rights as slavery, torture, etc. could only be a movement in the opposite direction to the ideal, for these violations all result from strong attachment to the self of the violators of human rights.

Wayne R. Husted, Damien V. Keown, Charles S. Prebish, Buddhism and Human Rights, 1998

Buddhist teachings don't explicitly forbid slavery, but the eightfold path says that engaging in trade in living beings is not a right form of livelihood. This appears to ban Buddhists from engaging in the slave trade.

...a lay follower should not engage in five types of business. Which five? Business in weapons, business in living beings, business in meat, business in intoxicants, and business in poison. Eightfold path

Other texts seem incompatible with many aspects of slavery itself.

For example, this quotation requires Buddhists to ensure that their workers and servants are properly treated:

In five ways should a master minister to his servants and employees:

by assigning them work according to their ability,

by supplying them with food and with wages,

by tending them in sickness,

by sharing with them any delicacies,

by granting them leave at times.

Sigalovada Sutta

Despite these texts there's no doubt that slavery was part of some Buddhist cultures, although many of these slaves were servants, rather than slaves of the sort traded across the Atlantic.

Richard Gombrich has argued that the Buddha did not intend to do away with slavery: Though it could well be argued that the Buddha made life in the world more worth living, that surely was an unintended consequence of his teaching. To present him as a sort of socialist is a serious anachronism.

He never preached against social inequality, only declared its irrelevance to salvation. He neither tried to abolish the caste system nor to do away with slavery.

While a famous sermon, the Sumanna-phala Sutta, stresses the practical benefits for a slave in leaving his servitude and joining the Order, in fact runaway slaves were not allowed to join the Order. Moreover, though in ancient India there was no caste or other form of social ranking within the Order itself, the Order soon came to own (lay) slaves.

Richard F. Gombrich, Theravada Buddhism: A Social History from Ancient Benares to Modern Colombo, 1988

In fact the restrictions placed on monks required them to have some form of servant in monastic communities. So for example if monks were to obey the rule barring the cooking and storing of food, they would need somebody to do it for them. Some Buddhist commentaries warn that slaves are not allowed, unless they are called "called monastery servants (aramika) or legalisers (kappiya-karaka)".

Gombrich also notes that:

> *at one point the Vinaya commentary says in so many words that kings gave slaves to monasteries, and that they could not be ordained unless they had first been freed. Inscriptions record that people gave money for the specific purpose of maintaining monastic slaves-and offered the resulting merit to all living beings. Richard F. Gombrich, Theravada Buddhism: A Social History from Ancient Benares to Modern Colombo, 1988*

If granting endowments to maintain slaves at monasteries was considered meritorious, freeing them from slavery was considered even more meritorious. Thus the device of offering slaves to monasteries provided a two-fold way for the acquisition of merits. Rahula, Walpola (1956), History of Buddhism in Ceylon: the Anuradhapura Period, Colombo. Quoted in Gombrich

Some kings in Ceylon offered themselves to the monastic community "as slaves and then redeemed themselves, thus combining a symbolic gesture of total humility with extreme munificence".

In 9th century China Buddhist institutions are reputed to have employed 150,000 slaves, who were taken over by the Taoist Emperor Wu-tsung in 845 as part of his action against the Buddhist community.

In some parts of South East Asia Buddhist locations were a sanctuary for those fleeing more oppressive forms of slavery:

Where Buddhist monastic orders had claimed political retreats from state military power, their estates and temple complexes became sanctuaries where peasants sought the exemption from state conscription and corvee that 'slavery' to a privileged individual or institution provided. Gwyn Campbell, The Structure of Slavery in Indian Ocean Africa and Asia, 2004

Pagoda Slaves

In some Buddhist cultures a male slave would become free if their owner allowed them to become a Buddhist monk.

In Kampuchea a person could be made a 'Pagoda Slave' if they were found guilty of certain crimes-as could members of their family up to seven degrees removed. Pagoda slaves did domestic and maintenance work on temple sites. While pagoda slaves might have a relatively easy life for a slave they ranked very low on the social ladder and had an extra disadvantage:

Pagoda slaves, who were supposed to belong only to Buddha, could not be redeemed. Gwyn Campbell, The Structure of Slavery in Indian Ocean Africa and Asia, 2004. Because pagoda slaves could not be redeemed their children inherited slave status. Pagoda slaves were found mostly in what are now Burma and Thailand. Pagoda slaves weren't only 'criminals' or the descendants of slaves; people could be given to monasteries for slave use.

Among Buddhist reformers of slavery was King Thibaw of Burma, a former monk. He paid 40,000 rupees in 1883 to buy the freedom of many slaves; 1,000 of those he freed are said to have become Buddhist monks and novices.

Slavery and Karma

Some writers think that slavery is justified by the doctrine of karma. They argue that people are born into slavery or become slaves because of their bad actions in a previous life. The way for a slave to progress towards salvation was to obey his or her owner, and do so willingly and without any bad feelings.

PURE LAND BUDDHISM

Pure Land Buddhism: Pure Land Buddhism offers a way to enlightenment for people who can't handle the subtleties of meditation, endure long rituals, or just live especially good lives. The essential practice in Pure Land Buddhism is the chanting of the name of Amitabha Buddha with total concentration, trusting that one will be reborn in the Pure Land, a place where it is much easier for a being to work towards enlightenment. Pure Land Buddhism adds mystical elements to the basic Buddhist teachings which make those teachings easier (and more comforting) to work with.

These elements include faith and trust and a personal relationship with Amitabha Buddha, who is regarded by Pure Land Buddhists as a sort of saviour; and belief in the Pure Land, a place which provides a stepping stone towards enlightenment and liberation. Pure Land Buddhism is particularly popular in China and Japan.

History: Pure Land Buddhism as a school of Buddhist thinking began in India around the 2nd century BCE.

It spread to China where there was a strong cult of Amitabha by the 2nd century CE, and then spread to Japan around the 6th century CE. Pure Land Buddhism received a major boost to its popularity in the 12th century with the simplifications made by Honen.

A century later Shinran (1173-1262), a disciple of Honen, brought a new understanding of the Pure Land ideas, and this became the foundation of the Shin (true) sect. Pure Land Buddhism took off in Japan when the monk Honen (1133-1212) simplified the teachings and practices of the sect so that anyone could cope with them. He eliminated the intellectual difficulties and complex meditation practices used by other schools of Buddhism. Honen taught that rebirth in the Pure Land was certain for anyone who recited the name with complete trust and sincerity. Honen said that all that was needed was...

saying "Namu Amida Butsu" with a conviction that by saying it one will certainly attain birth in the Pure Land.

The result was a form of Buddhism accessible to anyone, even if they were illiterate or stupid.

Honen didn't simplify Buddhism through a patronising attitude to inferior people. He believed that most people, and he included himself, could not achieve liberation through any of their own activities. The only way to achieve Buddhahood was through the help of Amitabha.

The Shin Sect

A century after Honan, one of his disciples, Shinran (1173-1262) brought a new understanding of the Pure Land ideas. Shinran taught that what truly mattered was not the chanting of the name but faith. Chanting on its own had no value at all. Those who follow the Shin school say that liberation is the consequence of a person achieving genuine faith in Amitabha Buddha and his vow to save all beings who trusted in him.

AMITABHA

Amitabha in context: The Pure Land sect emphasises the important role played in liberation by Amitabha (which means Immeasurable Light) who is also called Amitayus (which means Immeasurable Life). People who sincerely call on Amitabha for help will be reborn in Sukhavati-The Pure Land or The Western

Paradise-where there are no distractions and where they can continue to work towards liberation under the most favourable conditions.

The nature of Amitabha is not entirely clear. Encyclopedia Britannica describes him as "the great saviour deity worshiped principally by members of the Pure Land sect in Japan." Another writer says "Amitabha is neither a God who punishes and rewards, gives mercy or imposes tests, nor a divinity that we can petition or beg for special favours". The mystical view of Amitabha regards him as an eternal Buddha, and believes that he manifested himself in human history as Gautama, or "The Buddha". Amitabha translates as "Amito-fo" in Chinese and "Amida" in Japanese.

The Story of Amitabha

Once there was a king who was so deeply moved by the suffering of beings in the world that he gave up his throne and became a monk named Dharmakara. Dharmakara was heavily influenced by the 81st Buddha and vowed to become a Buddha himself, with the aim of creating a Buddha-land that would be free of all limitations.

He meditated at length on other Buddha-lands and set down what he learned in 48 vows. Eventually he achieved enlightenment and became Amitabha Buddha and established his Buddha-land of Sukhavati.

His most important vow was the 18th, which said: "If I were to become a Buddha, and people, hearing my Name, have faith and joy and recite it for even ten times, but are not born into my Pure Land, may I not gain enlightenment." Since he did gain enlightenment, it follows that those who do have faith and joy and who recite his name will be born into the Pure Land.

PURE LAND ESSENTIALS

Nembutsu: This means concentration on Buddha and his virtues, or recitation of the Buddha's name. No special way of reciting the name is laid down. It can be done silently or aloud, alone or in a group and with or without musical accompaniment.

The important thing is to chant the name single-mindedly, while sincerely wishing to be reborn in the Pure Land.

Scripture: The Pure Land scriptures include The Infinite Life Sutra, The Contemplation Sutra and The Amitabha Sutra.

Chanting: Chanting the name of Amitabha Buddha does not do anything at all to help the person to the Pure Land. Chanting is nothing more than an expression of gratitude to Amitabha Buddha and an expression of the chanter's faith. But it's not possible to do away with the chanting: Shinran wrote "the True Faith is necessarily accompanied by the utterance of the Name".

Faith: Shin Buddhists say that faith in Amitabha Buddha is not something that the believer should take the credit for since it's not something that the believer does for themselves. Their faith is a gift from Amitabha Buddha. And in keeping with this style of humility, Shin Buddhists don't accept the idea that beings can earn merit for themselves by their own acts; neither good deeds, nor performing rituals help. This has huge moral implications in that it implies (and Shinran quite explicitly said) that a sinner with faith will be made welcome in the Pure Land-even more welcome than a good man who has faith and pride.

Popularity: The sect's teachings brought it huge popularity in Japan, since here was a form of Buddhism that didn't require a person to be clever, or a monk, and that was open to the outcasts of society. It remains a popular group in Buddhism-and the reasons that made it popular 700 years ago are exactly the same ones that make it popular today.

UNDERSTANDING PURE LAND

Is this a new understanding of Buddhism? On the surface Pure Land Buddhism seems to have moved a very long way from the basic Buddhist ideas, and it's important to see how it might actually fit in. The way to do this is to tackle each issue and see what's really going on.

Amitabha Buddha is treated as if he were God: On the surface, yes. But perhaps chanting Amitabha Buddha's name is not praying to an external deity, but really a way of calling out one's own essential Buddha nature. However some of Shinran's writings do speak of Amitabha Buddha in language that a westerner would regard as describing God.

The Pure Land appears to be a supernatural place: On the surface, yes. But perhaps the Pure Land is really a poetic metaphor for a higher state of consciousness. Chanting the name can then be seen as a meditative practice that enables the follower to alter their state of mind.

(This argument is quite hard to sustain in the face of the importance given to chanting the name in faith at the moment of death-when some supernatural event is clearly expected by most followers. And the chanting is not regarded solely as a meditative practice by most followers. However gaps between populist and sophisticated understanding of religious concepts are common in all faiths.) There is no reliance on the self to achieve enlightenment.

On the surface, yes. But in fact this is just a further move in the direction that Mahayana Buddhism has already taken to allow assistance in the journey to liberation. And the being still has much work to do when they arrive in the Pure Land. (Shinran however taught that arriving in the Pure Land was actually the final liberation-the Pure Land was nirvana.)

TIBETAN BUDDHISM

Tibetan Buddhism is a religion in exile, forced from its homeland when Tibet was conquered by the Chinese. At one time it was thought that 1 in 6 Tibetan men were Buddhist monks. The best known face of Tibetan Buddhism is the Dalai Lama, who has lived in exile in India since he fled Chinese occupation of his country in 1959.

Tibetan Buddhism combines the essential teachings of Mahayana Buddhism with Tantric and Shamanic, and material from an ancient Tibetan religion called Bon. Although Tibetan Buddhism is often thought to be identical with Vajrayana Buddhism, they are not identical-Vajrayana is taught in Tibetan Buddhism together with the other vehicles.

History: Buddhism became a major presence in Tibet towards the end of the 8th century CE. It was brought from India at the invitation of the Tibetan king, Trisong Detsen, who invited two Buddhist masters to Tibet and had important Buddhist texts translated into Tibetan. First to come was Shantarakshita, abbot of Nalanda in India, who built the first monastery in Tibet. He was followed by Padmasambhava, who came to use his wisdom and power to overcome "spiritual" forces that were stopping work on the new monastery.

Groups within Tibetan Buddhism

- Nyingmapa: Founded by Padmasambhava, this is oldest sect, noted in the West for the teachings of the Tibetan Book of the Dead.
- Kagyupa: Founded by Tilopa [988-1069), the Kagyupa tradition is headed by the Karmapa Lama. Important Kagyupa teachers include Naropa, Marpa, and Milarepa.
- Sakyapa: Created by Gonchok Gyelpo (1034-1102) and his son Gunga Nyingpo (1092-1158).
- Gelugpa: (The Virtuous School) Founded by Tsong Khapa Lobsang Drakpa (also called Je Rinpoche) (1357-1419), this tradition is headed by the Dalai Lama.

Special Features of Tibetan Buddhism

- the status of the teacher or "Lama"
- preoccupation with the relationship between life and death
- important role of rituals and initiations
- rich visual symbolism
- elements of earlier Tibetan faiths
- mantras and meditation practice

Tibetan Buddhist practice features a number of rituals, and spiritual practices such as the use of mantras and yogic techniques.

Supernatural beings are prominent in Tibetan Buddhism. Buddhas and bodhisattvas abound, gods and spirits taken from earlier Tibetan religions continue to be taken seriously. Bodhisattvas are portrayed as both benevolent godlike figures and wrathful deities. This metaphysical context has allowed Tibetan Buddhism to develop a strong artistic tradition, and paintings and other graphics are used as aids to understanding at all levels of society.

Visual aids to understanding are very common in Tibetan Buddhism-pictures, structures of various sorts and public prayer wheels and flags provide an ever-present reminder of the spiritual domain in the physical world. Tibetan Buddhism is strong in both monastic communities and among lay people.

The lay version has a strong emphasis on outwardly religious activities rather than the inner spiritual life: there is much ritual practice at temples, pilgrimage is popular-often including many prostrations, and prayers are repeated over and over-with the use of personal or public prayer wheels and flags. There are many festivals, and funerals are very important ceremonies. Lay people provide physical support to the monasteries as well as relying on the monks to organise the rituals.

ASPECTS OF FAITH

Lamas

A lama is a teacher. They are often a senior member of a monastic community-a monk or a nun-but lay people and married people can also be lamas. They are very often reincarnations of previous lamas. As well as being learned in Buddhist texts and philosophy, lamas often have particular skills in ritual.

The Dalai Lama

Dalai is a Mongol word meaning ocean, and refers to the depth of the Dalai Lama's wisdom. The first Dalai Lama to bear the title was the 3rd Dalai Lama, Sonam Gyatso. (The two previous incarnations were named "Dalai Lama" after their deaths.) The current Dalai Lama (2002), Tenzin Gyatso, was born in Amdo, Tibet in 1935 and is the fourteenth Dalai Lama.

The Karmapa Lama

Karmapa means "one who performs the activity of a Buddha". The current incarnation (2002) is the 17th Karmapa. Two individuals have been declared the 17th Karmapa; Orgyen Trinley Dorje is generally and officially recognised as the official 17th Karmapa, however a rival Buddhist group give their allegiance to Trinlay Thaye Dorje.

Tantra: Tibetan Buddhism was much influenced by Tantra, and this has brought in a wealth of complex rituals and symbols and techniques. Tantra originated in India and appears in both the Hindu and Buddhist traditions.

It brings Tibetan Buddhism a magical element and a rich portfolio of heavenly beings. It also brings a wide variety of spiritual techniques such as mantras, mandalas, ceremonies, and many varieties of yoga.

Rituals: Rituals and simple spiritual practices such as mantras are popular with lay Tibetan Buddhists. They include prostrations, making offerings to statues of Buddhas or bodhisattvas, attending public teachings and ceremonies. Tibetan temple ceremonies are often noisy and visually striking, with brass instruments, cymbals and gongs, and musical and impressive chanting by formally dressed monks. It takes place in strikingly designed temples and monasteries.

Advanced Practices: Tibetan Buddhism also involves many advanced rituals. These are only possible for those who have reached a sophisticated understanding of spiritual practice. There are also advanced spiritual techniques. These include elaborate visualisations and demanding meditations. It's said that senior Tibetan yoga adepts can achieve much greater control over the body than other human beings, and are able to control their body temperature, heart rate and other normally automatic functions.

Living and Dying: Tibetan Buddhism emphasises awareness of death and impermanence. Everything is always dying-the cells of our bodies are dying even while we live, reminding us of our own impermanence. And all the living things around us are dying, too.

This awareness should not produce sadness or despair, nor should it cause a Buddhist to start a frantic pursuit of the impermanent pleasures of life. Instead, it should lead the Buddhist to see the value of every moment of existence, and be diligent in their meditation and other religious practice.

Awareness of death, combined with the understanding of the impermanence of everything, leads the Buddhist to realise that only spiritual things have any lasting value.

Preparing for Death: Tibetan Buddhists use visualisation meditations and other exercises to imagine death and prepare for the bardo. They work towards a holistic understanding and acceptance of death as an inevitable part of their journey.

Another way of preparing for death is to take part in helping those who have died through their experience in the bardo. This not only aids the dead, but enables the living practitioner to gain a real experience of the bardo, before they themselves enter it.

Even those who cannot gain the spiritual awareness to have a consciousness of the bardo are helped by achieving a greater experience of the impermanence of everything.

Tibetan Book of the Dead: This is one of the great texts of Tibetan Buddhism, and a big seller in the west. The English title is not a translation of the Tibetan title-the book's true name is Great Liberation through hearing during the intermediate state, commonly known in Tibet as Liberation through hearing. The book deals with the experiences of a person as they pass between death and rebirth.

Bardo

Bardo is the state between death and rebirth. The different schools of Tibetan Buddhism have different understandings of this state which is regarded as lasting for 49 days.

The experience of a person during bardo depends on their spiritual training during life. An untrained person is thought to be confused as to where they are, and may not realise that they have died. People are often unwilling to give up attachment to their previous life-and their negative emotions-may cause their rebirth to be less good than it would otherwise have been.

In traditional Tibetan Buddhism, the dead person is helped through bardo by a lama who reads prayers and performs rituals from the Book of the Dead, advising the deceased to break free from attachment to their past life and their dead body. In some schools of Tibetan Buddhism, the lama will actively help the dead person to transfer their consciousness from their body, in preparation for rebirth.

Many Tibetan Buddhists believe that it is possible for those left behind to assist the dead person on their journey by doing spiritual work that increases the merits of the deceased and thus helps them to a better rebirth. During the 49 day period the dead can see clearly into the minds of those left behind, which allows the living to help the dead by thinking good thoughts, meditating on Buddha and other virtuous beings, and engaging in spiritual practices.

3

Schools of Buddhistic Teachings

The Consciousness-Only School

The starting point of the Consciousness-Only School is that everything is created from the mind as is "consciousness-only". Everything, from birth and death to the cause of attaining nirvana, is based upon the coming into being and the ceasing to be of consciousness, that is, of distinctions in the mind. Consciousness-Only doctrine is characterized by its extensive and sophisticated inquiry into the characteristics of dharmas. For if we can distinguish what is real from what is unreal, if we can distinguish what is distinction-making consciousness and not mistake it for the originally clear, pure, bright enlightened mind, then we can quickly leave the former and dwell in the latter. Ch'an Master Han-shan (AD 1546-1623) has said, "When Consciousness- Only was made known to them (i.e., those of the Hinayana vehicles), they knew that [all dharmas] had no existence independent from their own minds.

If one does not see the mind with the mind, then no characteristic can be got at. Therefore, in developing the spiritual skill necessary for meditative inquiry, people are taught to look into what is apart from heart, mind, and consciousness and to seek for what is apart from the states of unreal (polluted) thinking." The founder of the Consciousness-Only School was the Bodhisattva Maitreya, who transmitted its teaching to the Venerable Asanga. He and his brother Vasubandhu were responsible for its early spread in India. The school was influential in Jung-Gwo (i.e., China) primarily because of the efforts of Tripitaka Master Hsuan-Tsang.

Asanga (Bodhisattva)

Together with his teacher the Bodhisattva Maitreya, Asanga was the founder of the Yogacara, or Consciousness-Only, School of Mahayana Buddhism. The oldest of three sons, all called Vasubandhu, born in Purusapura (Peshwar) who were members of the Kausika family of Indian brahmins. All three became Buddhist Bhikshus. Asanga's youngest brother was known as Virincivatsa, while the middle brother was known merely as Vasubandhu.

Asanga was a man who was endowed with the innate character of a Bodhisattva. He became a Bhikshu of the Sarvastivada School, but afterwards he practiced meditation and became free from desire. Though he investigated the doctrine of emptiness, he could not understand it. He was about to commit suicide. Pindola, an Arhat, who was then in Eastern Purvavideha, having perceived this, came to him from that region and expounded the doctrine of emptiness peculiar to the Hinayana. He arranged his thoughts according to what he was taught and at once comprehended it. Though he had attained the doctrine of emptiness peculiar to the Hinayana, he, nevertheless, did not find comfort in it. Thinking that it would not be right to drop the matter altogether, he went up to the Tusita Heaven using the supernatural power peculiar to the Hinayana and inquired of Maitreya, the Bodhisattva, who expounded for him the doctrine of emptiness belonging to the Mahayana. When he returned to Jambudvipa, he investi-gated according to the methods explained to him and soon became enlightened. While he was engaged in investigation, the earth began to quake (of its own accord) in six ways. Since he understood the doctrine of emptiness, he called himself "Asanga", which means "without attachment". He afterwards often went up to the Tusita Heaven in order to ask Maitreya about the doctrines of the Mahayana sutras.

The Bodhisattva explained them extensively for him. Whenever he acquired any new understanding, he would come back to Jambudvipa and teach it to others. Most of those hearing him did not believe him. Asanga, Teacher of the Dharma, then prayed, saying, "I now intend to bring all beings to believe fully in the doctrine of the Mahayana. I only pray that you, O Great Master, come down to Jambudvipa to expound the Mahayana so that all beings may become fully convinced of its truth." Maitreya, thereupon, in accordance with his prayer, came down to Jambudvipa at night, flooding it with great rays of light, had a large assembly of those connected with the Dharma called in a lecture hall, and began to recite the Saptadasabhumi-sutra.

After having recited a passage, he would explain its purport. The seventeen bhumis were finished during the nights of four months. Although all were together in one and the same hall listening to the discourse, it was, neverthe-less, only Asanga, Teacher of the Dharma,, who had access to the Bodhisattva Maitreya, while the others could merely hear him from afar. At night, all together heard the religious discourse by Maitreya, while in the daytime Asanga, Teacher of the Dharma, commented once again, for the sake of others, upon what had been taught by the Bodhisattva. In this way all the people could hear and believe in the doctrine of the Mahayana. Maitreya, the Bodhisattva, taught Asanga, Teacher of the Dharma, to learn the "sunlight" samadhi. As he learned according to what he had been taught, he subsequently attained entry into that samadhi. After he attained entry into that samadhi, what he formerly could not understand all became intelligible.

Whatever he heard or saw was never forgotten, his memory having become retentive, whereas he formerly could not fully understand the sutras of the Mahayana, such as the Avatamsaka, previously taught by the Buddha. Maitreya explained for him all these in the Tusita heaven; thus the Teacher of the Dharma became well-versed in them and remembered them all. Afterwards in Jambudvipa he composed several upadesa on the sutras of the Mahayana, in which he expounded all the teachings of the Mahayana taught by the Buddha. (Paramartha, "The Life of Vasubandhu", J. Takakusu, tr. [with some editing], pp. 273-275)

Vasubandhu (Bodhisattva) (fl. 4th cent. AD)

The second of three sons, born in Purusapura (Peshwar), India, into the Kausika family of Indian Brahmins. All three sons were called Vasubandhu and all three became Buddhist Bhikshus. His older brother was known as Asanga and his younger brother as Virincivatsa. He is known simply as Vasubandhu. In his youth he adhered to the Hinayana teachings of the Sautrantika School and wrote the Abhidharmakosa, perhaps the most well-known of all treatises on the Abhidharma. He was converted to the Mahayana by his older brother the Bodhisattva Asanga. After his conversion, he wrote many celebrated works on the Consciousness-Only School of the Mahayana, including the Twenty Verses on Consciousness-Only and the Thirty Verses on Consciousness-Only.

Vasubandhu's Conversion

"Asanga, teacher of the Law [Dharma], saw that his younger brother was endowed with an intelligence surpassing that of others, his knowledge being deep and wide, and himself well-versed in esoteric and exoteric doctrines. He was afraid that the latter might compose a sastra and crush the Mahayana. He was living then in the land of the Hero (Purusa-pura) and sent a messenger to Vasubandhu in Ayodhya with the following message: "I am seriously ill at present. You had better attend to me quickly." Vasubandhu followed the messenger to his native land, saw his brother and inquired what was the cause of his illness. He answered: "I have now a serious disease of the heart, which arose on account of you." Vasubandhu again asked: "Why do you say on account of me?" He answered: "You dot no believe in the Mahayana and are always attacking and discrediting it. For this wickedness you will be sure to sink forever in a miserable Life. I am now grieved and troubled for your sake to such an extent that my life will no long survive. On hearing this Vasubandhu was surprised and alarmed and asked his brother to expound the Mahayana for him. He then gave him a concise explanation of the essential principles of the Mahayana. Thereupon the Teacher of the Law (Vasubandhu), who was possessed of clear intelligence and especially of deep insight, became at once convinced that the truth of the Mahayana excelled even that of the Hinayana.

"He then fully investigated, under his brother, the principles of the Mahayana. Soon after he became as thoroughly acquainted with the whole as his brother was. When its meaning was already clear to him, he would meditate on it. From the beginning to the end everything was perfectly in accordance with the truth, there being nothing contradictory to it. For the first time he realized that the Hinayana was wrong and the Mahayana right. If there were no Mahayana, then (he thought) there would be no path (marga) and no fruition (phala) of the Tri-yana [Three Vehicles]. Since he formerly did harm by speaking ill of the Mahayana, in which he then had no faith, he was now afraid that he might fall into a miserable life on account of that wickedness. He deeply reproached himself and earnestly repented of his previous fault. He approached his brother and confessed his error, saying: 'I now desire to make a confession. I do not know by what means I can be pardoned for my former slander.' He said (further): 'I formerly did harm speaking ill (of the truth) by means of my tongue. I will now cut out my tongue in order to atone for my crime.' His brother answered: 'Even if you cut out your tongue a thousand times, you cannot wipe out your crime. If you really want to wipe out your crime, you must find some other means.' Thereupon he asked his brother to explain the means of wiping out the offence. The latter said: 'Your tongue was able to speak very skillfully and effectively against the Mahayana, and thus discredit it. If you want to wipe out your offence, you must now propound the Mahayana equally skillfully and effectively.'" (The Life of Vasubandhu, J. Takakusu, tr., pp. 290-292)

A eulogy says:

It is difficult to practice two teachings at once.

He brought forth the secret meanings of the Compassionate Sage.

In awesome Shastras like piled up clouds,
Explaining the untransmitted doctrine,
Revealing the Consciousness-Only,
complete in both the Nature and Appearance Schools.
An eternal Dharma lamp,
He lights a million generations.
(Vajra Bodhi Sea #20, p. 2)

Hsuan-Tsang (Tripitaka Master) (596-664)

Great enlightened master, translator, and founder of the Consciousness-Only School in China.

"This Bhikshu's contributions to Buddhism have been exceptionally great. It can be said that from ancient times to the present, there has never been anyone who can compare to this Dharma Master in his achievements. His worldly name was Ch'a. His father was an official, but a poor one. Why did he end up a poor official? It was because he didn't take bribes. He wasn't after the citizens' money nor that of the government. He wasn't like people today who hold office and always feel they are earning too little money so that on top of their government salary they force the citizens to give them their hard-earned money as well. Dharma Master Hsuan-Tsang's father didn't want money. He remained a poor official all his life. Even though he was poor, he had a virtuous nature and because of that he had two sons who left the home-life, lectured Sutras, and were adept cultivators of the Way.

"Dharma Master Hsuan-Tsang left the home-life at the age of thirteen and commenced his study of the Buddhadharma. During those early years of study, if there was a Dharma Master lecturing a Buddhist text, no matter who the Dharma Master was or how far away the lecture was being held, he was sure to go to listen, whether it was a Sutra lecture, a Shastra lecture or a Vinaya lecture. He went to listen to them all. Wind and rain couldn't keep him away from lectures on the Tripitaka, to the point that he even forgot to be hungry. He just ate the Dharma, taking the Buddhadharma as his food and drink. He did this for five years and then took the Complete Precepts.

"However, the principles lectured by the Dharma Masters he heard were all different. They all explained the same Sutras in very different ways--each with his own interpretation. And there was a big difference between the lectures of those with wisdom and those without wisdom. But Dharma Master Hsuan-Tsang had not yet really become enlightened, and he didn't have the Selective Dharma Eye, and so how could he know whose lectures to rely on? At that time he vowed to go to India, saying, The Buddhadharma has been transmitted from India, and so there is certainly true and genuine Buddhadharma to be found in India.

Thereupon, he wrote a request for permission to go to India to seek the Dharma and presented it to the emperor. Emperor Tai Dzung of the Tang Dynasty did not grant his wish, but Dharma Master Hsuan-Tsang, who had already vowed to go, said, 'I would prefer to disobey the son of Heaven and have my head cut off than not to go and seek the Dharma.' And so he returned to the monastery and began to practice mountain-climbing. He piled chairs, tables, and benches together to simulate a mountain and practiced jumping from one piece of furniture to the next. This was his method of practicing mountain-climbing. From morning till night he leaped from table to chair. Probably there weren't any big mountains--where he lived, and so he had to practice in the temple. All the young, old, and older novices wondered what he was up to, jumping on furniture all day long instead of reciting Sutras or cultivating. He didn't tell anyone that he was training to climb the Himalayas, and so most people thought he was goofing off. Eventually he trained his body so that it was very strong, and then when he was physically able, he started his trip through Siberia.

"On the day of his departure, when Emperor Tai-Dzung learned he intended to go even without imperial consent, the emperor asked him, 'I haven't given you permission and you still insist on going. When will you be back?'

"Dharma Master Hsuan-Tsang replied, 'Look at this pine tree. The needles are pointing toward the west. Wait until those needles turn around and face east. That is the time when

I will return.' He didn't say how many years that would be. And so he set out. At that time there were no airplanes, steamboats, buses, or trains. There were boats, but they were made of wood and not too sturdy. Besides, since he didn't have imperial permission, he probably could not have gotten the use of a boat anyway. And so he travelled by land through many countries, from the Siberian area of the Russian border to India. He was gone for more than a decade. When he reached India, he didn't know the language at all. But bit-by-bit he studied Sanskrit and listened to many Dharma Masters lecture the Buddhadharma. Some people say this took him fourteen years. Others say it took nineteen. In general he went through a great deal of suffering and difficulty to study the Buddhadharma and then when he'd completed his studies, he returned to China.

"When his return was imminent, the needles on the pine tree turned to the east. As soon as the emperor saw that the pine needles were indeed pointing east, he knew that Dharma Master Hsuan-Tsang was coming back and he sent out a party of officials to the western gate to welcome him and escort him back. When they reached the gate, there indeed, was Dharma Master Hsuan-Tsang returning.

"Dharma Master Hsuan-Tsang then concentrated on translating the Sutras and other works that he had brought back with him. He translated from Sanskrit into Chinese. At the time when he was translating the Mahaprajnaparamita-sutra, within one single year, the peach trees blossomed six times. That was a sign of the auspiciousness of the Mahaprajnaparamita-sutra and its importance to all of us. The fact that it was being translated moved even the wood and plants to display their delight.

"Dharma Master Hsuan-Tsang translated a great many sutras. While in India, he bowed to the Buddha's sarira and bones. He saw where the Buddha in a previous life had given up his eyes, and went to the place where the Buddha in a previous life had practiced the conduct of patience, and went to the place where the Buddha in a previous life had given up his life for the sake of a tiger. He also went to see the Bodhi tree under which the Buddha realized the Way. He went to all of those places celebrated in Buddhism. These pilgrimages are another indication of the extent of his true sincerity. While in India, whenever he met Dharma Masters, he never looked down on them, no matter how little they may have cultivated. He was extremely respectful. He wasn't the least bit arrogant or haughty. When he finished his studies, many Small vehicle Dharma Masters and masters of externalist ways came to debate with him, but none was able to defeat him.

Dharma Master Hsuan-Tsang is known as a Tripitaka Master (Tripitaka='Three Treasuries', 'Three Baskets'). The Tripitaka includes the Sutra Treasury, the Shastra Treasury, and the Vinaya Treasury. He was honoured with this title because he understood all three Treasuries without obstruction....

"As to his name, Sywan means 'esoteric and wonderful.' He was esoteric in the sense that none could really understand him. Dzang means 'awe-inspiring.' He was awe-inspiring in that he could do what others could not do. He was an outstanding person among his peers...." (HD 15-17)

The Master's name has also been transliterated as follows: Xuanzang, Sywan-Dzang, Yuan Chwang, etc.

TRANSFORMATION OF CONSCIOUSNESS INTO WISDOM

In the Chinese Consciousness-Only School of Buddhism, Buddhahood, characterized by the perfectly enlightened mind of True Suchness (bhutatathata) is understood as the final realization of a systematic and gradual path. Buddhahood is not a goal which is attained through the acquisition of a special conceptual understanding. Rather it is the end product of a fundamental internal transformation of all mental activity. In the language of Consciousness-Only, that process is referred to as the transformation of "consciousness" that has attachment to distinctions as its basic nature, into "wisdom" that is by its very nature totally free from attachment. "Wisdom", therefore, indicates a radically, qualitatively and totally different type of mental functioning. The purpose of this paper is twofold: 1) to delineate briefly the stages of transformation, and 2) after transformation is complete and Buddhahood has been realized, to indicate how the immanent aspect of Buddhahood utilizes wisdom tofunction in the world. Below we shall try to give a sketch of the prescriptions given by the School to rid oneself of the basic obstacles on the pathway to Buddhahood and to indicate briefly the manner in which one functions in the world after those obstacles have been removed.

The System of the Eight Consciousnesses

The Consciousness-Only School describes the mind as a system of seven active consciousnesses (vijnana) which all develop out of the eighth, or storehouse, consciousness. The latter is passive and contains the potentials, or "seeds" (bija) for the development and activity of the first seven consciousnesses. The seventh consciousness contains the sense of self or of ego individuality with which it defiles the first six consciousnesses. The sixth consciousness is a perceptual and cognitive processing centre, while the first five consciousnesses are the perceptual awarenesses of eyes, ears, nose, tongue and body.

Although with the emanation of these consciousnesses out of the eighth formal division is made among them, the distinction is totally based upon mental distinction. The eight are still basically "one." To use a simple analogy, let us think of a room with seven light-bulbs. You flick the light switch and seven distinct lights shine. Turn the switch off and the lights disappear. Yet there is just one electric current, and its source is comparable to the storehouse consciousness, or, as it is understood in the transformation of consciousness, to the enlightened mind. The system of eight consciousnesses, and the mental dharmas (caittas) which arise out of them and are dependent upon them, was developed as an important part of a pragmatic psychology of mind. The system can be used to describe in a manner which is accurate and practical both mental functioning and the specific techniques employed on the Path to the enlightenment of Buddhahood.

It provides a way to account for mental processes without recourse to the notions of a real, permanent self (atman) or of real, permanent external (and internal) objects (dharma). All actual and potential realms of experience are shown to be contained within the transformations of consciousness and appear as manifestations of the distinction-making mind. Nevertheless, because of our attachment to and belief in the reality of self and the reality of the "objects" (dharmas) which we perceive and understand to be the external world, the true nature of ourselves and the world is obscured so that we are unaware of it.

The Types of Attachment

The basic obstacles which arise from the distinction-making character of consciousness are the division of the world into 1) subject, or one who grasps onto distinctions (the grasper), and 2) object, those distinctions which are grasped (the grasped). This distinction occurs on various levels and is reflected in each of the eight consciousnesses. The grasper corresponds to attachment to self and the grasped to attachment to dharmas. The former is often referred to as the obstacle of the afflictions and the latter as the obstacle of the knowable. These obstacles or attachments are of two types: 1) innate, and 2) distinguished or learned. The innate attachments are quite subtle and have existed from beginningless time as part of the human (or more generally, the sentient) condition.

The distinguished attachments, on the other hand, are coarser and arise from the distinction-making of our cognitive and perceptual processes. These attachments, the innate and distinguished attachments to self and the innate and distinguished attachments to dharmas, are the only obstacles to the realization of Buddhahood.

The Attachment to Self

The innate attachment to self is twofold. By taking the eighth consciousness, more specifically its "perceived portion," as its object, the seventh consciousness generates a continuous image of the eighth or storehouse consciousness as a real permanent self. Secondly, by taking the manifestation of the five aggregates (form, feeling, cognition, formation, and consciousness) as object, the sixth consciousness generates various non-continuous concepts of self. The distinguished attachment to self belongs solely to the realm of the sixth consciousness and is much coarser in nature than the innate attachment of the seventh consciousness. The sixth consciousness either takes various aspects of the aggregates as object and conceives them to be the real self or independently generates self-concepts and takes them to be the real self. Such wrong conceptualization is often the result of misinformed religious or philosophical teaching.

The Attachment to Dharmas

The innate attachment to dharmas is also twofold. As the seventh consciousness takes the eighth consciousness as its object, it can also use it, more specifically its "perceived portion," to generate a continuous mental image of the eighth consciousness as dharmas. Likewise, the sixth consciousness can take aspects of the aggregates and the perceptual faculties and their objects to be real dharmas; however, in contrast to the seventh consciousness, the functioning of the sixth consciousness in this manner is discontinuous. The distinguished attachment to dharmas is exclusively an aspect of functioning of the sixth consciousness and is relatively coarse in its nature. The sixth consciousness can either take concepts of the Hinayana Buddhist dharmas to be real or take the various objective categories or elements of non-Buddhist schools to be real. In other words, it mistakes its own concepts of an external reality for a real external reality.

The Five-stage Path of the Bodhisattva

Now that we have briefly outlined the nature of the obstacles to the realization of Buddhahood, we are in a position to discuss the Consciousness-Only School's prescriptions for their elimination. This is the gradual five-stage process known as the Path of the Bodhisattva. It begins with the birth of the intention to become fully enlightened (bodhicittotpada), which marks the entrance into the first stage, that of gathering provisions or Resources. It is followed by the stages of Application, Vision, Meditational Development, and culminates in the final stage which is Perfection, the perfect enlightenment of Buddhahood, the full realization of True Suchness.

The Stage of Resources

In the stage of developing his Resources, the Bodhisattva develops his deep faith in and understanding of the teachings of Consciousness-Only. During this period the Bodhisattva is merely able to subdue the rise in consciousness of the coarse, learned aspects of the grasper and the grasped, that is, of attachment to self and dharmas. In other words, he learns to see through and replace with dharmic analysis the learned conceptual analysis of perceiving and thinking about the world in terms of a real self and real objects. He does this by learning to prevent such concepts from arising and then snowballing into verbal and physical activities (the creation of karma). Thus he is able to utilizc effectively the Consciousness-Only School's doctrinal framework in his everyday thinking and functioning in the world.

The Stage of Application

In the following stage, that of Application, concentration and insight are developed through preliminary meditational practices called the Four Aids to Penetration: Heat, Summit, Patience, and Highest Worldly Dharma. The Heat, Summit, and first two portions of the Patience Aid are practiced in meditations in which one enters into the first three dhyanas. The remainder of Patience and Highest Worldly Dharma Aids can only be practiced by entering into the fourth dhyana. During this gradual process not only is manifestation of the coarse, learned aspect of grasper and grasped subdued so that it no longer arises in consciousness, but the seeds of its manifestation, which are stored in the eighth consciousness, are completely destroyed. Since the seeds have been destroyed, they cannot sprout in dharmas; therefore, this coarse aspect of the attachment to self and dharmas can never again appear. It is the completion of this process that allows entrance into the third stage.

The Stage of the Path of Vision

Entrance onto the Path of Vision provides the first realexperience of True Suchness. It marks leaving the worldly flow and entering the flow of the Holy Ones. It corresponds to entrance onto the first of the "grounds" (bhumi) of the Path of the Bodhisattva, the Ground of Extreme Joy. It is at this point that the gradual transformation of consciousness into wisdom begins. This pure wisdom is the activity or functioning of True Suchness. The process of transformation is a gradual one and takes place as the Bodhisattva passes through the Ten Grounds of the Bodhisattva.

The Stage of the Path of Meditational Development

On the Path of Meditational Development (from dwelling on the first ground of the Bodhisattva through the final, tenth, ground) the wisdom, which first appeared on the Path of Vision, gradually eliminates the manifestations and the seeds of the manifestations of the innate attachments of grasper and grasped. In passing through the first seven grounds, the Bodhisattva eliminates all the seeds of the subtle, innate attachment to self of both sixth and seventh consciousnesses (obstacle of the afflictions; the grasper). The single exception is the very subtle seeds of what is known as the spontaneous aspect of the obstacle afflictions. The Bodhisattva must preserve those seeds all the way up to the moment of realizing Buddhahood because they are the primary cause of the Bodhisattva's continued rebirth and, therefore, necessary for continued progress on the Path of the Bodhisattva. The subtle, innate attachment to dharmas, (the obstacle of the knowable); the grasped) is also eliminated in gradual stages as the Bodhisattva proceeds through the ten grounds. On the final, tenth ground, the last, extremely subtle attachments to all known dharmas and their seeds,together with the above-mentioned seeds of the spontaneous aspect of the affliction obstacle necessary for rebirth, are completely eliminated. Then there can no longer ever be any kind of attachment, coarse or subtle, to self or dharmas, grasper or grasped. The obstacle of the afflictions and the obstacle of the knowable are completely eliminated.

The Stage of Perfection

Having outlined briefly the Path to Buddhahood and the stages in which the various obstacles to that enlightenment are eliminated, we are now in a position to discuss in greater detail the types of wisdom in terms of how they are used on the Path. As we have already seen, the distinguished or learned aspects of attachment to self and dharmas, grasper and grasped, are destroyed at the moment of entrance onto the Path of Vision. Their elimination clears the way for the appearance of a pure wisdom that has two components. It is characterized as pure because of its complete lack of outflows (asraya), that is, the outward flowing of the mind and its attachment to various aspects of the conditioned world. Previous to this, the wisdom used as a guiding force in the meditational process was an impure, preliminary "applied" wisdom (prayogajnana) characterized by outflow. The first of the two components of the non-outflowing wisdom is called fundamental wisdom (mulajnana). It is characterized as non-distinction-making (nirvikalpa). In the process of its initial appearance, it naturally destroys the seeds of the distinguished attachment to self and dharmas. The destruction of the seeds and the appearance of the fundamental wisdom is a simultaneous and instantaneous process.

The second component of the non-outflowing wisdom is based on the first and for that reason is called subsequently attained wisdom (prsthalabdajnana). It is an expedient wisdom which operates in the world of distinctions. It analyzes the characteristics of dharmas, yet does not become attached to those characteristics as is the case with the preliminary "applied" wisdom, which has outflows. The subsequently attained wisdom reflects on the seeming characteristics of True Suchness and in this way is used to eliminate the seeds of learned attachment to self and dharmas. However, the mode of its functioning is gradual. It is employed in various meditational techniques to destroy the many separate aspects of the learned seeds.

The Functioning of Wisdom

Generally, wisdom functions in two ways. It acts to subdue the phenomenal activity of the mind (dharmas), and then, on a more fundamental level, it eliminates the seeds (bija), which are the source of that activity. Wisdom and distinction-making consciousness are like ice and water. As the water freezes, the ice appears; as the ice melts, the water appears. On the level of the phenomenal activity of the mind, the greater the attachment to distinctions, the weaker the functioning of wisdom; the stronger the functioning of wisdom, the less attachment to distinctions. For attachment to distinctions to be permanently eliminated, wisdom must operate with sufficient basis and power to supercede not only the manifestation of the distinctions but also their seeds, which are their basic cause. Another image often used to describe the process is that of light superceding darkness. If the light can not only fill the darkness but also fully and permanently penetrate the barriers to the light, then the darkness is permanently eliminated.

At the beginning of the Path, the power of wisdom is weak and the power of distinction-making consciousness is strong. In the first two stages of the path, those of Resources and Application, there is no manifestation of pure wisdom, wisdom characterized by complete lack of outflows. In order to clear the mind so that the seeds of pure wisdom can grow and finally become actualized, the Bodhisattva temporarily employs preliminary "applied" wisdom, which is characterized by outflows. That is, it tends to seek out the characteristics of mental objects, and by nature depends upon them for support. By treating True Suchness as a perceived characteristic of the mind, this provisional wisdom utilizes its own characterization of True Suchness as a support for meditation on the emptiness of the grasper and the grasped. In this way, the coarse aspects of the distinguished obstacles are eliminated and the other aspects of the distinguished and innate obstacles are subdued, that is, they are partially or fully prevented from rising into active awareness.

As an aid to this type of meditation, the Bodhisattva gradually decreases the extent of phenomenal activity produced by the seeds of the two obstacles by the use of resolution (adhimaksa), a special mental state, and of remorse (hri) and shame (apatrapa), both wholesome mental states. Resolution, remorse, and shame are all technical "dharmas," which are included in the One Hundred Dharmas of the Consciousness-Only School. Resolution is explained as that mental state which examines dharmas and comes to a decision about their natures. Employing resolution helps the Bodhisattva to see the conditioned, empty nature of all dharmas so that he will not become attached to them. Remorse and shame are the inner and outer recognition of one's own improper behavior and of a desire to change it.

With the successful completion of the first two stages, the balance shifts. The turning point is the entrance onto the Path of Vision. At that point wisdom no longer functions totally in dependence upon distinction-making consciousness. For the first time its non-outflow potential actually becomes operative as the basis for further progress on the Path. As we have already noted, the entrance onto the Path of Vision marks the initial experience of the nature of True Suchness. It is then fully realized as the Ten Grounds are passed through. With each step in the progressive elimination of the obstacles to Buddhahood, there is a corresponding step in the development of wisdom. On the Path of Vision, fundamental wisdom instantaneously destroys the seeds of the distinguished attachment to grasper and grasped, while subsequently attained wisdom is used to eliminate gradually the various distinguished characteristics which are an obstruction to True Suchness. During this stage the preliminary "applied" wisdom does not operate.

On the first seven grounds of the Path of Meditational Development all three types of wisdom operate. The preliminary, "applied" wisdom, though characterized by outflows, functions because outflowing attachments are still present and practice is still intentional. That is, it involves an act of will, signifying a tension be-tween two competing aspects of mind. The subsequently attained wisdom is utilized in meditations with characteristics, whereas fundamental wisdom is employed in the meditations without characteristics.

Starting with the Eighth Ground and continuing to the realization of Buddhahood, outflows and the innate attachment to self are totally ended (except for that extremely subtle, spontaneous attachment necessary for rebirth). Because there is no longer any self, cultivation proceeds completely spontaneously. Since there is no longer any personal effort, the preliminary "applied" wisdom no longer functions (though its seeds are not totally eliminated until Buddhahood). All meditation is without characteristics and utilizes fundamental wisdom, while all actionsproceed spontaneously from the functioning of subsequently attained wisdom.

Development of the Four Types of Enlightened Wisdom

Fundamental wisdom and subsequently attained wisdom are classifications of wisdom, that is, the activity or functioning of True Suchness in terms of whether or not they act to distinguish the characteristics of dharmas. The Four Types of wisdom is another classification of the activity of True Suchness, in this instance, in terms of the functions which they inherit from the eight consciousnesses of which they are transformations.

'The first five perceptual consciousnesses are transformed into the Wisdom of Successful Performance; the sixth consciousness, the perceptual and cognitive processing centre, is transformed into the Wisdom of Wonderful Contemplation; the seventh consciousness, which ordinarily de-files the first six consciousnesses with self and self-related afflictions, is transformed into the Wisdom of Equality; and the eighth, the storehouse consciousness, is transformed into the Great Mirror Wisdom.

Both the Wisdom of Equality and the Wisdom of Wonderful Contemplation first begin to function on the Path of Vision. As attachment to the distinctions of the sixth and seventh consciousnesses diminishes, the power of these two types of wisdom increases. The functioning of the Wisdom of Equality is occasionally interrupted up through the Seventh Ground of the Bodhisattva when there are outflows (innate attachments) in the sixth consciousness that evoke the outflowing functioning of the seventh consciousness as support. This occurs because the seventh consciousness's attachment to grasper and grasped has not yet been fully eliminated. The Wisdom of Wonderful Contemplation has two aspects, corresponding to understanding of the emptiness of self and of the emptiness of dharmas. They both function as long as there is no outflowing functioning of the sixth consciousness, which would naturally interfere. This type of wisdom is not active during the course of meditation without characteristics. (Meditation without characteristics becomes predominant on the Sixth Ground and is the exclusive type of meditation from the Seventh Ground on.)

On the first seven grounds, the progress which takes place has to do with the transformation of the sixth and seventh consciousnesses into their respective wisdoms. During this period, meditations with characteristics, which emplcy the sixth consciousness, are gradually phased out and replaced by meditations without characteristics. At the entrance onto the Eighth Ground, all outflowing activity of the seventh and sixth consciousnesses is permanently ended and the functioning of the Wisdoms of Equality and of Wonderful Contemplation proceeds spontaneously and without effort.

Both the Great Mirror Wisdom and the Wisdom of Successful Performance begin to function only at the moment of the realization of Buddhahood. The eighth consciousness must continue to exist upto that point as a receptacle of the wholesome outflowing seeds which allow the Bodhisattva to be reborn and to continue progress on the Path from the Eighth Ground to entry into Buddhahood.

By the moment of entry, the eighth consciousness has become so pure that it can no longer serve as support for the seeds of outflowing dharmas, no matter how fine. Although from the Eighth Ground, the eighth consciousness continues to act as the supporting basis for the extremely subtle spontaneous affliction that the Bodhisattva purposely preserves as the vehicle of his continued rebirth in the world, in every other sense the eighth consciousness is undefiled and no longer the cause of rebirth. From the latter point of view, the Eighth Ground marks the beginning of the laying of the groundwork for the Great Mirror Wisdom.

The activity of the Wisdom of Successful Performance must await the appearance of the Buddha's pure non-outflowing perceptual faculties, because the faculties of a Bodhisattva, even after the Eighth Ground, are based on a body which is the result of the subtle seeds of affliction and, therefore, could not provide the proper support.

This kind of wisdom is active only when attention is directed to the perceptual faculties. The groundwork for it is laid when the awareness of the faculty of pure form, an aspect of the perceiver portion of the eighth consciousness, no longer associates itself with the characteristics of perceived objects, that is, the dharmas arising from the perceived portion of the eighth consciousness. (This also marks the initial emergence of subsequently attained wisdom.)

The Four Types of Wisdom and Buddhahood

Having discussed when on the Path the Four Types of Wisdom arise, we can now describe their functioning after the full realization of True Suchness at Buddhahood. All seeds and all dharmas, the entire universe both potential and actual, are reflected without distortion in the Great Mirror Wisdom.

Its awareness of True Suchness is the functioning of the fundamental component of this type of wisdom, while its awareness of the activity of seeds and dharmas (as an aspect of True Suchness) is the functioning of its subsequently attained component. The Great Mirror Wisdom is equated with that aspect of the functioning of the reward-body (svasambhogakaya) and pure land of the Buddha which has no purpose beyond what it is in itself.

The Wisdom of Equality understands the nature of the equality of self and other and of all beings. It appears as images of the Buddhas which are limitless. It is equated with that aspect of the reward-body (parasambhogakaya) of the Buddha that functions for the sake of others. More specifically, it is the mode of wisdom which the Buddha uses to teach the great Bodhisattvas.

It is also called the great transformation body (nisyandakaya). As is the case with the Great Mirror Wisdom, both components of wisdom function here to include both True Suchness and "worldly" aspects in their understanding. The

Wisdom of Wonderful Contemplation understands withoutdistortion the individual and universal characteristics of all dharmas in both their True Suchness and worldly aspects. According to Master Kuiji, it "examines the merits and abilities of all beings and rains the great rain of Dharma to destroy the great net of doubts and to benefit all sentient beings. " (59:32b)

The Wisdom of Successful Performance operates as the countless transformation bodies of the Buddhas and as the lands both with and without outflows in which they teach living beings. It is exclusively concerned with those dharmas that are the dharmas of perception, that is, the transformation bodies of the Buddha and the phenomena which the faculties of those bodies perceive. Therefore, only the subsequently attained component of wisdom functions in relation to it.

In other words, the Buddha employs the Wisdom of Successful Performance to appear in his ordinary earthly body (and other transformation bodies) and to function perceptually within that body. He sees, hears, smells, tastes, and touches without any obstruction or distortion of feeling not only in the ordinary range of perception but in an unlimited manner, universally in time and space.

With the Wisdom of Wonderful Contemplation he knows clearly, without distortion or obstruction, all dharmas which are the objects of his perception and all other dharmas which are exclusively the objects of cognitive processes. In this way he knows the mental and physical condition of all beings and speaks and acts accordingly in all the various ways necessary to teach them most effectively.

SUMMARY

The Consciousness-Only School teaches that our true nature and the true nature of the world is Consciousness-Only, which is ultimately understood to be True Suchness. True Suchness is covered over by the distinction-making consciousnesses' attachments to grasper and grasped, self and dharmas. These attachments are systematically overcome on the Bodhisattva Path by the use of wisdom. One component of wisdom, fundamental wisdom, knows True Suchness as the real, underlying nature of distinction-making consciousness. As such, it eliminates confusion about principle (deviant views, their accompanying afflictions, and the seeds of both), radically undermining it.

The other component, subsequently attained wisdom, works on the level of the distinctions themselves to eliminate attachment to them. Based on fundamental wisdom, it acts to eliminate confusion about phenomena, particularly the dharmas of greed and other primary afflictions. Upon the total realization of True Suchness at Buddhahood, the subsequently attained component, previously used as a tool for progress on the Bodhisattva Path, is the modality through which the Buddha operates in the world of distinctions made by sentient beings and through which he teaches them the Buddhadharma, a Path for the transformation of distinction-making consciousness into True Suchness and its Four Types of Wisdom.

4

THE BUDDHISTIC PATH OF DHARMA

THE PATH OF DHAMMA

The Pairs Heedfulness

1. Mind precedes all mental states. Mind is their chief; they are all mind-wrought. If with an impure mind a person speaks or acts suffering follows him like the wheel that follows the foot of the ox.
2. Mind precedes all mental states. Mind is their chief; they are all mind-wrought. If with a pure mind a person speaks or acts happiness follows him like his never-departing shadow.
3. "He abused me, he struck me, he overpowered me, he robbed me." Those who harbor such thoughts do not still their hatred.
4. "He abused me, he struck me, he overpowered me, he robbed me." Those who do not harbor such thoughts still their hatred.
5. Hatred is never appeased by hatred in this world. By non-hatred alone is hatred appeased. This is a law eternal.
6. There are those who do not realize that one day we all must die. But those who do realize this settle their quarrels.
7. Just as a storm throws down a weak tree, so does Mara overpower the man who lives for the pursuit of pleasures,

who is uncontrolled in his senses, immoderate in eating, indolent, and dissipated.

8. Just as a storm cannot prevail against a rocky mountain, so Mara can never overpower the man who lives meditating on the impurities, who is controlled in his senses, moderate in eating, and filled with faith and earnest effort.
9. Whoever being depraved, devoid of self-control and truthfulness, should don the monk's yellow robe, he surely is not worthy of the robe.
10. But whoever is purged of depravity, well-established in virtues and filled with self-control and truthfulness, he indeed is worthy of the yellow robe.
11. Those who mistake the unessential to be essential and the essential to be unessential, dwelling in wrong thoughts, never arrive at the essential.
12. Those who know the essential to be essential and the unessential to be unessential, dwelling in right thoughts, do arrive at the essential.
13. Just as rain breaks through an ill-thatched house, so passion penetrates an undeveloped mind.
14. Just as rain does not break through a well-thatched house, so passion never penetrates a well-developed mind.
15. The evil-doer grieves here and hereafter; he grieves in both the worlds. He laments and is afflicted, recollecting his own impure deeds.
16. The doer of good rejoices here and hereafter; he rejoices in both the worlds. He rejoices and exults, recollecting his own pure deeds.
17. The evil-doer suffers here and hereafter; he suffers in both the worlds. The thought, "Evil have I done," torments him, and he suffers even more when gone to realms of woe.
18. The doer of good delights here and hereafter; he delights in both the worlds. The thought, "Good have I done,"

delights him, and he delights even more when gone to realms of bliss.

19. Much though he recites the sacred texts, but acts not accordingly, that heedless man is like a cowherd who only counts the cows of others-he does not partake of the blessings of the holy life.
20. Little though he recites the sacred texts, but puts the Teaching into practice, forsaking lust, hatred, and delusion, with true wisdom and emancipated mind, clinging to nothing of this or any other world-he indeed partakes of the blessings of a holy life.
21. Heedfulness is the path to the Deathless. Heedlessness is the path to death. The heedful die not. The heedless are as if dead already.
22. Clearly understanding this excellence of heedfulness, the wise exult therein and enjoy the resort of the Noble Ones.
23. The wise ones, ever meditative and steadfastly persevering, alone experience Nibbana, the incomparable freedom from bondage.
24. Ever grows the glory of him who is energetic, mindful and pure in conduct, discerning and self-controlled, righteous and heedful.
25. By effort and heedfulness, discipline and self-mastery, let the wise one make for himself an island which no flood can overwhelm.
26. The foolish and ignorant indulge in heedlessness, but the wise one keeps his heedfulness as his best treasure.
27. Do not give way to heedlessness. Do not indulge in sensual pleasures. Only the heedful and meditative attain great happiness.
28. Just as one upon the summit of a mountain beholds the groundlings, even so when the wise man casts away heedlessness by heedfulness and ascends the high tower of wisdom, this sorrowless sage beholds the sorrowing and foolish multitude.

29. Heedful among the heedless, wide-awake among the sleepy, the wise man advances like a swift horse leaving behind a weak jade.
30. By Heedfulness did Indra become the overlord of the gods. Heedfulness is ever praised, and heedlessness ever despised.
31. The monk who delights in heedfulness and looks with fear at heedlessness advances like fire, burning all fetters, small and large.
32. The monk who delights in heedfulness and looks with fear at heedlessness will not fall. He is close to Nibbana.
33. Just as a fletcher straightens an arrow shaft, even so the discerning man straightens his mind-so fickle and unsteady, so difficult to guard.
34. As a fish when pulled out of water and cast on land throbs and quivers, even so is this mind agitated. Hence should one abandon the realm of Mara.
35. Wonderful, indeed, it is to subdue the mind, so difficult to subdue, ever swift, and seizing whatever it desires. A tamed mind brings happiness.
36. Let the discerning man guard the mind, so difficult to detect and extremely subtle, seizing whatever it desires. A guarded mind brings happiness.
37. Dwelling in the cave (of the heart), the mind, without form, wanders far and alone. Those who subdue this mind are liberated from the bonds of Mara.
38. Wisdom never becomes perfect in one whose mind is not steadfast, who knows not the Good Teaching and whose faith wavers.
39. There is no fear for an awakened one, whose mind is not sodden (by lust) nor afflicted (by hate), and who has gone beyond both merit and demerit.
40. Realizing that this body is as fragile as a clay pot, and fortifying this mind like a well-fortified city, fight out Mara with the sword of wisdom. Then, guarding the conquest, remain unattached.

41. Ere long, alas! this body will lie upon the earth, unheeded and lifeless, like a useless log.
42. Whatever harm an enemy may do to an enemy, or a hater to a hater, an ill-directed mind inflicts on oneself a greater harm.
43. Neither mother, father, nor any other relative can do one greater good than one's own well-directed mind.
44. Who shall overcome this earth, this realm of Yama and this sphere of men and gods? Who shall bring to perfection the well-taught path of wisdom as an expert garland-maker would his floral design?
45. A striver-on-the path shall overcome this earth, this realm of Yama and this sphere of men and gods. The striver-on-the-path shall bring to perfection the well-taught path of wisdom, as an expert garland-maker would his floral design.
46. Realizing that this body is like froth, penetrating its mirage-like nature, and plucking out Mara's flower-tipped arrows of sensuality, go beyond sight of the King of Death!
47. As a mighty flood sweeps away the sleeping village, so death carries away the person of distracted mind who only plucks the flowers (of pleasure).
48. The Destroyer brings under his sway the person of distracted mind who, insatiate in sense desires, only plucks the flowers (of pleasure).
49. As a bee gathers honey from the flower without injuring its colour or fragrance, even so the sage goes on his alms-round in the village.
50. Let none find fault with others; let none see the omissions and commissions of others. But let one see one's own acts, done and undone.
51. Like a beautiful flower full of colour but without fragrance, even so, fruitless are the fair words of one who does not practice them.

52. Like a beautiful flower full of colour and also fragrant, even so, fruitful are the fair words of one who practices them.

53. As from a great heap of flowers many garlands can be made, even so should many good deeds be done by one born a mortal.

54. Not the sweet smell of flowers, not even the fragrance of sandal, tagara, or jasmine blows against the wind. But the fragrance of the virtuous blows against the wind. Truly the virtuous man pervades all directions with the fragrance of his virtue.

55. Of all the fragrances-sandal, tagara, blue lotus and jasmine-the fragrance of virtue is the sweetest.

56. Faint is the fragrance of tagara and sandal, but excellent is the fragrance of the virtuous, wafting even amongst the gods.

57. Mara never finds the path of the truly virtuous, who abide in heedfulness and are freed by perfect knowledge.

58. Upon a heap of rubbish in the road-side ditch blooms a lotus, fragrant and pleasing.

59. Even so, on the rubbish heap of blinded mortals the disciple of the Supremely Enlightened One shines resplendent in wisdom.

60. Long is the night to the sleepless; long is the league to the weary. Long is worldly existence to fools who know not the Sublime Truth.

61. Should a seeker not find a companion who is better or equal, let him resolutely pursue a solitary course; there is no fellowship with the fool.

62. The fool worries, thinking, "I have sons, I have wealth." Indeed, when he himself is not his own, whence are sons, whence is wealth?

63. A fool who knows his foolishness is wise at least to that extent, but a fool who thinks himself wise is a fool indeed.

64. Though all his life a fool associates with a wise man, he no more comprehends the Truth than a spoon tastes the flavour of the soup.
65. Though only for a moment a discerning person associates with a wise man, quickly he comprehends the Truth, just as the tongue tastes the flavour of the soup.
66. Fools of little wit are enemies unto themselves as they move about doing evil deeds, the fruits of which are bitter.
67. Ill done is that action of doing which one repents later, and the fruit of which one, weeping, reaps with tears.
68. Well done is that action of doing which one repents not later, and the fruit of which one, reaps with delight and happiness.
69. So long as an evil deed has not ripened, the fool thinks it as sweet as honey. But when the evil deed ripens, the fool comes to grief.
70. Month after month a fool may eat his food with the tip of a blade of grass, but he still is not worth a sixteenth part of the those who have comprehended the Truth.
71. Truly, an evil deed committed does not immediately bear fruit, like milk that does not turn sour all at once. But smoldering, it follows the fool like fire covered by ashes.
72. To his own ruin the fool gains knowledge, for it cleaves his head and destroys his innate goodness.
73. The fool seeks undeserved reputation, precedence among monks, authority over monasteries, and honour among householders.
74. "Let both laymen and monks think that it was done by me. In every work, great and small, let them follow me"- such is the ambition of the fool; thus his desire and pride increase.
75. One is the quest for worldly gain, and quite another is the path to Nibbana. Clearly understanding this, let not the monk, the disciple of the Buddha, be carried away by worldly acclaim, but develop detachment instead.

76. Should one find a man who points out faults and who reproves, let him follow such a wise and sagacious person as one would a guide to hidden treasure. It is always better, and never worse, to cultivate such an association.

77. Let him admonish, instruct and shield one from wrong; he, indeed, is dear to the good and detestable to the evil.

78. Do not associate with evil companions; do not seek the fellowship of the vile. Associate with the good friends; seek the fellowship of noble men.

79. He who drinks deep the Dhamma lives happily with a tranquil mind. The wise man ever delights in the Dhamma made known by the Noble One (the Buddha).

80. Irrigators regulate the rivers; fletchers straighten the arrow shaft; carpenters shape the wood; the wise control themselves.

81. Just as a solid rock is not shaken by the storm, even so the wise are not affected by praise or blame.

82. On hearing the Teachings, the wise become perfectly purified, like a lake deep, clear and still.

83. The good renounce (attachment for) everything. The virtuous do not prattle with a yearning for pleasures. The wise show no elation or depression when touched by happiness or sorrow.

84. He is indeed virtuous, wise, and righteous who neither for his own sake nor for the sake of another (does any wrong), who does not crave for sons, wealth, or kingdom, and does not desire success by unjust means.

85. Few among men are those who cross to the farther shore. The rest, the bulk of men, only run up and down the hither bank.

86. But those who act according to the perfectly taught Dhamma will cross the realm of Death, so difficult to cross.

87-88. Abandoning the dark way, let the wise man cultivate the bright path. Having gone from home to homelessness, let him yearn for that delight in detachment, so difficult to enjoy. Giving up sensual pleasures, with no attachment, let the wise man cleanse himself of defilements of the mind.

89. Those whose minds have reached full excellence in the factors of enlightenment, who, having renounced acquisitiveness, rejoice in not clinging to things-rid of cankers, glowing with wisdom, they have attained Nibbana in this very life.

90. The fever of passion exists not for him who has completed the journey, who is sorrowless and wholly set free, and has broken all ties.

91. The mindful ones exert themselves. They are not attached to any home; like swans that abandon the lake, they leave home after home behind.

92. Those who do not accumulate and are wise regarding food, whose object is the Void, the Unconditioned Freedom-their track cannot be traced, like that of birds in the air.

93. He whose cankers are destroyed and who is not attached to food, whose object is the Void, the Unconditioned Freedom-his path cannot be traced, like that of birds in the air.

94. Even the gods hold dear the wise one, whose senses are subdued like horses well trained by a charioteer, whose pride is destroyed and who is free from the cankers.

95. There is no more worldly existence for the wise one who, like the earth, resents nothing, who is firm as a high pillar and as pure as a deep pool free from mud.

96. Calm is his thought, calm his speech, and calm his deed, who, truly knowing, is wholly freed, perfectly tranquil and wise.

97. The man who is without blind faith, who knows the Uncreated, who has severed all links, destroyed all causes (for karma, good and evil), and thrown out all desires-he, truly, is the most excellent of men. 11

98. Inspiring, indeed, is that place where Arahants dwell, be it a village, a forest, a vale, or a hill.

99. Inspiring are the forests in which worldlings find no pleasure. There the passionless will rejoice, for they seek no sensual pleasures.

100. Better than a thousand useless words is one useful word, hearing which one attains peace.

101. Better than a thousand useless verses is one useful verse, hearing which one attains peace.

102. Better than reciting a hundred meaningless verses is the reciting of one verse of Dhamma, hearing which one attains peace.

103. Though one may conquer a thousand times a thousand men in battle, yet he indeed is the noblest victor who conquers himself.

104-105. Self-conquest is far better then the conquest of others. Not even a god, an angel, Mara or Brahma can turn into defeat the victory of a person who is self-subdued and ever restrained in conduct.

106. Though month after month for a hundred years one should offer sacrifices by the thousands, yet if only for a moment one should worship those of perfected minds that honour is indeed better than a century of sacrifice.

107. Though for a hundred years one should tend the sacrificial fire in the forest, yet if only for a moment one should worship those of perfected minds, that worship is indeed better than a century of sacrifice.

108. Whatever gifts and oblations one seeking merit might offer in this world for a whole year, all that is not worth one fourth of the merit gained by revering the Upright Ones, which is truly excellent.

109. To one ever eager to revere and serve the elders, these four blessing accrue: long life and beauty, happiness and power.

110. Better it is to live one day virtuous and meditative than to live a hundred years immoral and uncontrolled.

111. Better it is to live one day wise and meditative than to live a hundred years foolish and uncontrolled.

112. Better it is to live one day strenuous and resolute than to live a hundred years sluggish and dissipated.
113. Better it is to live one day seeing the rise and fall of things than to live as hundred years without ever seeing the rise and fall of things.
114. Better it is to live one day seeing the Deathless than to live a hundred years without ever seeing the Deathless.
115. Better it is to live one day seeing the Supreme Truth than to live a hundred years without ever seeing the Supreme Truth.
116. Hasten to do good; restrain your mind from evil. He who is slow in doing good, his mind delights in evil.
117. Should a person commit evil, let him not do it again and again. Let him not find pleasure therein, for painful is the accumulation of evil.
118. Should a person do good, let him do it again and again. Let him find pleasure therein, for blissful is the accumulation of good.
119. It may be well with the evil-doer as long as the evil ripens not. But when it does ripen, then the evil-doer sees (the painful results of) his evil deeds.
120. It may be ill with the doer of good as long as the good ripens not. But when it does ripen, then the doer of good sees (the pleasant results of) his good deeds.
121. Think not lightly of evil, saying, "It will not come to me." Drop by drop is the water pot filled. Likewise, the fool, gathering it little by little, fills himself with evil.
122. Think not lightly of good, saying, "It will not come to me." Drop by drop is the water pot filled. Likewise, the wise man, gathering it little by little, fills himself with good.
123. Just as a trader with a small escort and great wealth would avoid a perilous route, or just as one desiring to live avoids poison, even so should one shun evil.

124. If on the hand there is no wound, one may carry even poison in it. Poison does not affect one who is free from wounds. For him who does no evil, there is no ill.

125. Like fine dust thrown against the wind, evil falls back upon that fool who offends an inoffensive, pure and guiltless man.

126. Some are born in the womb; the wicked are born in hell; the devout go to heaven; the stainless pass into Nibbana.

127. Neither in the sky nor in mid-ocean, nor by entering into mountain clefts, nowhere in the world is there a place where one may escape from the results of evil deeds.

128. Neither in the sky nor in mid-ocean, nor by entering into mountain clefts, nowhere in the world is there a place where one will not be overcome by death.

129. All tremble at violence; all fear death. Putting oneself in the place of another, one should not kill nor cause another to kill.

130. All tremble at violence; life is dear to all. Putting oneself in the place of another, one should not kill nor cause another to kill.

131. One who, while himself seeking happiness, oppresses with violence other beings who also desire happiness, will not attain happiness hereafter.

132. One who, while himself seeking happiness, does not oppress with violence other beings who also desire happiness, will find happiness hereafter.

133. Speak not harshly to anyone, for those thus spoken to might retort. Indeed, angry speech hurts, and retaliation may overtake you.

134. If, like a broken gong, you silence yourself, you have approached Nibbana, for vindictiveness is no longer in you.

135. Just as a cowherd drives the cattle to pasture with a staff, so do old age and death drive the life force of beings (from existence to existence).

136. When the fool commits evil deeds, he does not realize (their evil nature). The witless man is tormented by his own deeds, like one burnt by fire.

137. He who inflicts violence on those who are unarmed, and offends those who are inoffensive, will soon come upon one of these ten states:

138-140. Sharp pain, or disaster, bodily injury, serious illness, or derangement of mind, trouble from the government, or grave charges, loss of relatives, or loss of wealth, or houses destroyed by ravaging fire; upon dissolution of the body that ignorant man is born in hell.

141. Neither going about naked, nor matted locks, nor filth, nor fasting, nor lying on the ground, nor smearing oneself with ashes and dust, nor sitting on the heels (in penance) can purify a mortal who has not overcome doubt.

142. Even though he be well-attired, yet if he is posed, calm, controlled and established in the holy life, having set aside violence towards all beings-he, truly, is a holy man, a renunciate, a monk.

143. Only rarely is there a man in this world who, restrained by modesty, avoids reproach, as a thoroughbred horse avoids the whip.

144. Like a thoroughbred horse touched by the whip, be strenuous, be filled with spiritual yearning. By faith and moral purity, by effort and meditation, by investigation of the truth, by being rich in knowledge and virtue, and by being mindful, destroy this unlimited suffering.

145. Irrigators regulate the waters, fletchers straighten arrow shafts, carpenters shape wood, and the good control themselves.

146. When this world is ever ablaze, why this laughter, why this jubilation? Shrouded in darkness, will you not see the light?

147. Behold this body-a painted image, a mass of heaped up sores, infirm, full of hankering-of which nothing is lasting or stable!

148. Fully worn out is this body, a nest of disease, and fragile. This foul mass breaks up, for death is the end of life.

149. These dove-colored bones are like gourds that lie scattered about in autumn. Having seen them, how can one seek delight?

150. This city (body) is built of bones, plastered with flesh and blood; within are decay and death, pride and jealousy.

151. Even gorgeous royal chariots wear out, and indeed this body too wears out. But the Dhamma of the Good does not age; thus the Good make it known to the good.

152. The man of little learning grows old like a bull. He grows only in bulk, but, his wisdom does not grow.

153. Through many a birth in samsara have I wandered in vain, seeking in the builder of this house (of life). Repeated birth is indeed suffering!

154. O house-builder, you are seen! You will not build this house again. For your rafters are broken and your ridgepole shattered. My mind has reached the Unconditioned; I have attained the destruction of craving.

155. Those who in youth have not led the holy life, or have failed to acquire wealth, languish like old cranes in the pond without fish.

156. Those who in youth have not lead the holy life, or have failed to acquire wealth, lie sighing over the past, like worn out arrows (shot from) a bow.

157. If one holds oneself dear, one should diligently watch oneself. Let the wise man keep vigil during any of the three watches of the night.

158. One should first establish oneself in what is proper; then only should one instruct others. Thus the wise man will not be reproached.

159. One should do what one teaches others to do; if one would train others, one should be well controlled oneself. Difficult, indeed, is self-control.

160. One truly is the protector of oneself; who else could the protector be? With oneself fully controlled, one gains a mastery that is hard to gain.

161. The evil a witless man does by himself, born of himself and produced by himself, grinds him as a diamond grinds a hard gem.

162. Just as a single creeper strangles the tree on which it grows, even so, a man who is exceedingly depraved harms himself as only an enemy might wish.

163. Easy to do are things that are bad and harmful to oneself. But exceedingly difficult to do are things that are good and beneficial.

164. Whoever, on account of perverted views, scorns the Teaching of the Perfected Ones, the Noble and Righteous Ones-that fool, like the bamboo, produces fruits only for self destruction.

165. By oneself is evil done; by oneself is one defiled. By oneself is evil left undone; by oneself is one made pure. Purity and impurity depended on oneself; no one can purify another.

166. Let one not neglect one's own welfare for the sake of another, however great. Clearly understanding one's own welfare, let one be intent upon the good.

167. Follow not the vulgar way; live not in heedlessness; hold not false views; linger not long in worldly existence.

168. Arise! Do not be heedless! Lead a righteous life. The righteous live happily both in this world and the next.

169. Lead a righteous life; lead not a base life. The righteous live happily both in this world and the next.

170. One who looks upon the world as a bubble and a mirage, him the King of Death sees not.

171. Come! Behold this world, which is like a decorated royal chariot. Here fools flounder, but the wise have no attachment to it.

172. He who having been heedless is heedless no more, illuminates this world like the moon freed from clouds.

173. He, who by good deeds covers the evil he has done, illuminates this world like the moon freed from clouds.

174. Blind is the world; here only a few possess insight. Only a few, like birds escaping from the net, go to realms of bliss.

175. Swans fly on the path of the sun; men pass through the air by psychic powers; the wise are led away from the world after vanquishing Mara and his host.

176. For a liar who has violated the one law (of truthfulness) who holds in scorn the hereafter, there is no evil that he cannot do.

177. Truly, misers fare not to heavenly realms; nor, indeed, do fools praise generosity. But the wise man rejoices in giving, and by that alone does he become happy hereafter.

178. Better than sole sovereignty over the earth, better than going to heaven, better even than lordship over all the worlds is the supramundane Fruition of Stream Entrance.

179. By what track can you trace that trackless Buddha of limitless range, whose victory nothing can undo, whom none of the vanquished defilements can ever pursue?

180. By what track can you trace that trackless Buddha of limitless range, in whom exists no longer, the entangling and embroiling craving that perpetuates becoming?

181. Those wise ones who are devoted to meditation and who delight in the calm of renunciation-such mindful ones, Supreme Buddhas, even the gods hold dear.

182. Hard is it to be born a man; hard is the life of mortals. Hard is it to gain the opportunity of hearing the Sublime Truth, and hard to encounter is the arising of the Buddhas.

183. To avoid all evil, to cultivate good, and to cleanse one's mind-this is the teaching of the Buddhas.

184. Enduring patience is the highest austerity. "Nibbana is supreme," say the Buddhas. He is not a true monk who harms another, nor a true renunciate who oppresses

others.

185. Not despising, not harming, restraint according to the code of monastic discipline, moderation in food, dwelling in solitude, devotion to meditation-this is the teaching of the Buddhas.

186-187. There is no satisfying sensual desires, even with the rain of gold coins. For sensual pleasures give little satisfaction and much pain. Having understood this, the wise man finds no delight even in heavenly pleasures. The disciple of the Supreme Buddha delights in the destruction of craving.

188. Driven only by fear, do men go for refuge to many places-to hills, woods, groves, trees and shrines.

189. Such, indeed, is no safe refuge; such is not the refuge supreme. Not by resorting to such a refuge is one released from all suffering.

190-191. He who has gone for refuge to the Buddha, the Teaching and his Order, penetrates with transcendental wisdom the Four Noble Truths-suffering, the cause of suffering, the cessation of suffering, and the Noble Eightfold Path leading to the cessation of suffering.

192. This indeed is the safe refuge, this the refuge supreme. Having gone to such a refuge, one is released from all suffering.

193. Hard to find is the thoroughbred man (the Buddha); he is not born everywhere. Where such a wise man is born, that clan thrives happily.

194. Blessed is the birth of the Buddhas; blessed is the enunciation of the sacred Teaching; blessed is the harmony in the Order, and blessed is the spiritual pursuit of the united truth-seeker.

195-196. He who reveres those worthy of reverence, the Buddhas and their disciples, who have transcended all obstacles and passed beyond the reach of sorrow and lamentation-he who reveres such peaceful and fearless ones, his merit none can compute by any measure.

197. Happy indeed we live, friendly amidst the hostile. Amidst

hostile men we dwell free from hatred.

198. Happy indeed we live, friendly amidst the afflicted (by craving). Amidst afflicted men we dwell free from affliction.

199. Happy indeed we live, free from avarice amidst the avaricious. Amidst the avaricious men we dwell free from avarice.

200. Happy indeed we live, we who possess nothing. Feeders on joy we shall be, like the Radiant Gods.

201. Victory begets enmity; the defeated dwell in pain. Happily the peaceful live, discarding both victory and defeat.

202. There is no fire like lust and no crime like hatred. There is no ill like the aggregates (of existence) and no bliss higher than the peace (of Nibbana).

203. Hunger is the worst disease, conditioned things the worst suffering. Knowing this as it really is, the wise realize Nibbana, the highest bliss.

204. Health is the most precious gain and contentment the greatest wealth. A trustworthy person is the best kinsman, Nibbana the highest bliss.

205. Having savored the taste of solitude and peace (of Nibbana), pain-free and stainless he becomes, drinking deep the taste of the bliss of the Truth.

206. Good is it to see the Noble Ones; to live with them is ever blissful. One will always be happy by not encountering fools.

207. Indeed, he who moves in the company of fools grieves for longing. Association with fools is ever painful, like partnership with an enemy. But association with the wise is happy, like meeting one's own kinsmen.

208. Therefore, follow the Noble One, who is steadfast, wise, learned, dutiful and devout. One should follow only such a man, who is truly good and discerning, even as the moon follows the path of the stars.

209. Giving himself to things to be shunned and not exerting where exertion is needed, a seeker after pleasures, having given up his true welfare, envies those intent upon theirs.

210. Seek no intimacy with the beloved and also not with the unloved, for not to see the beloved and to see the unloved, both are painful.

211. Therefore hold nothing dear, for separation from the dear is painful. There are no bonds for those who have nothing beloved or unloved.

212. From endearment springs grief, from endearment springs fear. From him who is wholly free from endearment there is no grief, whence then fear?

213. From affection springs grief, from affection springs fear. From him who is wholly free from affection there is no grief, whence then fear?

214. From attachment springs grief, from attachment springs fear. From him who is wholly free from attachment there is no grief, whence then fear?

215. From lust springs grief, from lust springs fear. From him who is wholly free from craving there is no grief; whence then fear?

216. From craving springs grief, from craving springs fear. From him who is wholly free from craving there is no grief; whence then fear?

217. People hold dear him who embodies virtue and insight, who is principled, has realized the truth, and who himself does what he ought to be doing.

218. One who is intent upon the Ineffable (Nibbana), dwells with mind inspired (by supramundane wisdom), and is no more bound by sense pleasures-such a man is called "One Bound Upstream."

219. When, after a long absence, a man safely returns from afar, his relatives, friends and well-wishers welcome him home on arrival.

220. As kinsmen welcome a dear one on arrival, even so his own good deeds will welcome the doer of good who has gone from this world to the next.

221. One should give up anger, renounce pride, and overcome all fetters. Suffering never befalls him who clings not to mind and body and is detached.

222. He who checks rising anger as a charioteer checks a rolling chariot, him I call a true charioteer. Others only hold the reins.

223. Overcome the angry by non-anger; overcome the wicked by goodness; overcome the miser by generosity; overcome the liar by truth.

224. Speak the truth; yield not to anger; when asked, give even if you only have a little. By these three means can one reach the presence of the gods.

225. Those sages who are inoffensive and ever restrained in body, go to the Deathless State, where, having gone, they grieve no more.

226. Those who are ever vigilant, who discipline themselves day and night, and are ever intent upon Nibbana-their defilements fade away.

227. O Atula! Indeed, this is an ancient practice, not one only of today: they blame those who remain silent, they blame those who speak much, they blame those who speak in moderation. There is none in the world who is not blamed.

228. There never was, there never will be, nor is there now, a person who is wholly blamed or wholly praised.

229. But the man whom the wise praise, after observing him day after day, is one of flawless character, wise, and endowed with knowledge and virtue.

230. Who can blame such a one, as worthy as a coin of refined gold? Even the gods praise him; by Brahma, too, is he praised.

231. Let a man guard himself against irritability in bodily action; let him be controlled in deed. Abandoning bodily misconduct, let him practice good conduct in deed.

232. Let a man guard himself against irritability in speech; let him be controlled in speech. Abandoning verbal misconduct, let him practice good conduct in speech.

233. Let a man guard himself against irritability in thought; let him be controlled in mind. Abandoning mental misconduct, let him practice good conduct in thought.

234. The wise are controlled in bodily action, controlled in speech and controlled in thought. They are truly well-controlled.

235. Like a withered leaf are you now; death's messengers await you. You stand on the eve of your departure, yet you have made no provision for your journey!

236. Make an island for yourself! Strive hard and become wise! Rid of impurities and cleansed of stain, you shall enter the celestial abode of the Noble Ones.

237. Your life has come to an end now; You are setting forth into the presence of Yama, the king of death. No resting place is there for you on the way, yet you have made no provision for the journey!

238. Make an island unto yourself! Strive hard and become wise! Rid of impurities and cleansed of stain, you shall not come again to birth and decay.

239. One by one, little by little, moment by moment, a wise man should remove his own impurities, as a smith removes his dross from silver.

240. Just as rust arising from iron eats away the base from which it arises, even so, their own deeds lead transgressors to states of woe.

241. Non-repetition is the bane of scriptures; neglect is the bane of a home; slovenliness is the bane of personal appearance, and heedlessness is the bane of a guard.

242. Unchastity is the taint in a woman; niggardliness is the taint in a giver. Taints, indeed, are all evil things, both in this world and the next.

243. A worse taint than these is ignorance, the worst of all taints. Destroy this one taint and become taintless, O monks!

244. Easy is life for the shameless one who is impudent as a crow, is backbiting and forward, arrogant and corrupt.

245. Difficult is life for the modest one who always seeks purity, is detached and unassuming, clean in life, and discerning.

246-247. One who destroys life, utters lies, takes what is not given, goes to another man's wife, and is addicted to intoxicating drinks-such a man digs up his own root even in this world.

248. Know this, O good man: evil things are difficult to control. Let not greed and wickedness drag you to protracted misery.

249. People give according to their faith or regard. If one becomes discontented with the food and drink given by others, one does not attain meditative absorption, either by day or by night.

250. But he in who this (discontent) is fully destroyed, uprooted and extinct, he attains absorption, both by day and by night.

251. There is no fire like lust; there is no grip like hatred; there is no net like delusion; there is no river like craving.

252. Easily seen is the fault of others, but one's own fault is difficult to see. Like chaff one winnows another's faults, but hides one's own, even as a crafty fowler hides behind sham branches.

253. He who seeks another's faults, who is ever censorious-his cankers grow. He is far from destruction of the cankers.

254. There is no track in the sky, and no recluse outside (the Buddha's dispensation). Mankind delights in worldliness, but the Buddhas are free from worldliness.

255. There is not track in the sky, and no recluse outside (the Buddha's dispensation). There are no conditioned things that are eternal, and no instability in the Buddhas.

256. Not by passing arbitrary judgments does a man become just; a wise man is he who investigates both right and wrong.
257. He who does not judge others arbitrarily, but passes judgment impartially according to the truth, that sagacious man is a guardian of law and is called just.
258. One is not wise because one speaks much. He who is peaceable, friendly and fearless is called wise.
259. A man is not versed in Dhamma because he speaks much. He who, after hearing a little Dhamma, realizes its truth directly and is not heedless of it, is truly versed in the Dhamma.
260. A monk is not Elder because his head is gray. He is but ripe in age, and he is called one grown old in vain.
261. One in whom there is truthfulness, virtue, inoffensiveness, restraint and self-mastery, who is free from defilements and is wise-he is truly called an Elder.
262. Not by mere eloquence nor by beauty of form does a man become accomplished, if he is jealous, selfish and deceitful.
263. But he in whom these are wholly destroyed, uprooted and extinct, and who has cast out hatred-that wise man is truly accomplished.
264. Not by shaven head does a man who is indisciplined and untruthful become a monk. How can he who is full of desire and greed be a monk?
265. He who wholly subdues evil both small and great is called a monk, because he has overcome all evil.
266. He is not a monk just because he lives on others' alms. Not by adopting outward form does one become a true monk.
267. Whoever here (in the Dispensation) lives a holy life, transcending both merit and demerit, and walks with understanding in this world-he is truly called a monk.
268. Not by observing silence does one become a sage, if he be foolish and ignorant. But that man is wise who, as if holding a balance-scale accepts only the good.

269. The sage (thus) rejecting the evil, is truly a sage. Since he comprehends both (present and future) worlds, he is called a sage.

270. He is not noble who injures living beings. He is called noble because he is harmless towards all living beings.

271-272. Not by rules and observances, not even by much learning, nor by gain of absorption, nor by a life of seclusion, nor by thinking, "I enjoy the bliss of renunciation, which is not experienced by the worldling" should you, O monks, rest content, until the utter destruction of cankers (Arahantship) is reached.

273. Of all the paths the Eightfold Path is the best; of all the truths the Four Noble Truths are the best; of all things passionlessness is the best: of men the Seeing One (the Buddha) is the best.

274. This is the only path; there is none other for the purification of insight. Tread this path, and you will bewilder Mara.

275. Walking upon this path you will make an end of suffering. Having discovered how to pull out the thorn of lust, I make known the path.

276. You yourselves must strive; the Buddhas only point the way. Those meditative ones who tread the path are released from the bonds of Mara.

277. "All conditioned things are impermanent"-when one sees this with wisdom, one turns away from suffering. This is the path to purification.

278. "All conditioned things are unsatisfactory"-when one sees this with wisdom, one turns away from suffering. This is the path to purification.

279. "All things are not-self"-when one sees this with wisdom, one turns away from suffering. This is the path to purification.

280. The idler who does not exert himself when he should, who though young and strong is full of sloth, with a mind full of vain thoughts-such an indolent man does not find the path to wisdom.

281. Let a man be watchful of speech, well controlled in mind, and not commit evil in bodily action. Let him purify these three courses of action, and win the path made known by the Great Sage.

282. Wisdom springs from meditation; without meditation wisdom wanes. Having known these two paths of progress and decline, let a man so conduct himself that his wisdom may increase.

283. Cut down the forest (lust), but not the tree; from the forest springs fear. Having cut down the forest and the underbrush (desire), be passionless, O monks!

284. For so long as the underbrush of desire, even the most subtle, of a man towards a woman is not cut down, his mind is in bondage, like the sucking calf to its mother.

285. Cut off your affection in the manner of a man plucks with his hand an autumn lotus. Cultivate only the path to peace, Nibbana, as made known by the Exalted One.

286. "Here shall I live during the rains, here in winter and summer"-thus thinks the fool. He does not realize the danger (that death might intervene).

287. As a great flood carries away a sleeping village, so death seizes and carries away the man with a clinging mind, doting on his children and cattle.

288. For him who is assailed by death there is no protection by kinsmen. None there are to save him-no sons, nor father, nor relatives.

289. Realizing this fact, let the wise man, restrained by morality, hasten to clear the path leading to Nibbana.

290. If by renouncing a lesser happiness one may realize a greater happiness, let the wise man renounce the lesser, having regard for the greater.

291. Entangled by the bonds of hate, he who seeks his own happiness by inflicting pain on others, is never delivered from hatred.

292. The cankers only increase for those who are arrogant and heedless, who leave undone what should be done and do what should not be done.

293. The cankers cease for those mindful and clearly comprehending ones who always earnestly practice mindfulness of the body, who do not resort to what should not be done, and steadfastly pursue what should be done.

294. Having slain mother (craving), father (self-conceit), two warrior-kings (eternalism and nihilism), and destroyed a country (sense organs and sense objects) together with its treasurer (attachment and lust), ungrieving goes the holy man.

295. Having slain mother, father, two brahman kings (two extreme views), and a tiger as the fifth (the five mental hindrances), ungrieving goes the holy man.

296. Those disciples of Gotama ever awaken happily who day and night constantly practice the Recollection of the Qualities of the Buddha.

297. Those disciples of Gotama ever awaken happily who day and night constantly practice the Recollection of the Qualities of the Dhamma.

298. Those disciples of Gotama ever awaken happily who day and night constantly practice the Recollection of the Qualities of the Sangha.

299. Those disciples of Gotama ever awaken happily who day and night constantly practice Mindfulness of the Body.

300. Those disciples of Gotama ever awaken happily whose minds by day and night delight in the practice of non-violence.

301. Those disciples of Gotama ever awaken happily whose minds by day and night delight in the practice of meditation.

302. Difficult is life as a monk; difficult is it to delight therein. Also difficult and sorrowful is the household life. Suffering comes from association with unequals; suffering comes from wandering in samsara. Therefore, be not an aimless wanderer, be not a pursuer of suffering.

303. He who is full of faith and virtue, and possesses good repute and wealth-he is respected everywhere, in whatever land he travels.

304. The good shine from afar, like the Himalaya mountains. But the wicked are unseen, like arrows shot in the night.

305. He who sits alone, sleeps alone, and walks alone, who is strenuous and subdues himself alone, will find delight in the solitude of the forest.

306. The liar goes to the state of woe; also he who, having done (wrong), says, "I did not do it." Men of base actions both, on departing they share the same destiny in the other world.

307. There are many evil characters and uncontrolled men wearing the saffron robe. These wicked men will be born in states of woe because of their evil deeds.

308. It would be better to swallow a red-hot iron ball, blazing like fire, than as an immoral and uncontrolled monk to eat the alms of the people.

309. Four misfortunes befall the reckless man who consorts with another's wife: acquisition of demerit, disturbed sleep, ill-repute, and (rebirth in) states of woe.

310. Such a man acquires demerit and an unhappy birth in the future. Brief is the pleasure of the frightened man and woman, and the king imposes heavy punishment. Hence, let no man consort with another's wife.

311. Just as kusa grass wrongly handled cuts the hand, even so, a recluse's life wrongly lived drags one to states of woe.

312. Any loose act, any corrupt observance, any life of questionable celibacy-none of these bear much fruit.

313. If anything is to be done, let one do it with sustained vigour. A lax monastic life stirs up the dust of passions all the more.

314. An evil deed is better left undone, for such a deed torments one afterwards. But a good deed is better done, doing which one repents not later.

315. Just as a border city is closely guarded both within and without, even so, guard yourself. Do not let slip this opportunity (for spiritual growth). For those who let slip this opportunity grieve indeed when consigned to hell.

316. Those who are ashamed of what they should not be ashamed of, and are not ashamed of what they should be ashamed of-upholding false views, they go to states of woe.

317. Those who see something to fear where there is nothing to fear, and see nothing to fear where there is something to fear-upholding false views, they go to states of woe.

318. Those who imagine evil where there is none, and do not see evil where it is-upholding false views, they go to states of woe.

319. Those who discern the wrong as wrong and the right as right-upholding right views, they go to realms of bliss.

320. As an elephant in the battlefield withstands arrows shot from bows all around, even so shall I endure abuse. There are many, indeed, who lack virtue.

321. A tamed elephant is led into a crowd, and the king mounts a tamed elephant. Best among men is the subdued one who endures abuse.

322. Excellent are well-trained mules, thoroughbred Sindhu horses and noble tusker elephants. But better still is the man who has subdued himself.

323. Not by these mounts, however, would one go to the Untrodden Land (Nibbana), as one who is self-tamed goes by his own tamed and well-controlled mind.

324. Musty during rut, the tusker named Dhanapalaka is uncontrollable. Held in captivity, the tusker does not touch a morsel, but only longingly calls to mind the elephant forest.

325. When a man is sluggish and gluttonous, sleeping and rolling around in bed like a fat domestic pig, that sluggard undergoes rebirth again and again.

326. Formerly this mind wandered about as it liked, where it wished and according to its pleasure, but now I shall thoroughly master it with wisdom as a mahout controls with his ankus an elephant in rut.

327. Delight in heedfulness! Guard well your thoughts! Draw yourself out of this bog of evil, even as an elephant draws himself out of the mud.

328. If for company you find a wise and prudent friend who leads a good life, you should, overcoming all impediments, keep his company joyously and mindfully.

329. If for company you cannot find a wise and prudent friend who leads a good life, then, like a king who leaves behind a conquered kingdom, or like a lone elephant in the elephant forest, you should go your way alone.

330. Better it is to live alone; there is no fellowship with a fool. Live alone and do no evil; be carefree like an elephant in the elephant forest.

331. Good are friends when need arises; good is contentment with just what one has; good is merit when life is at an end, and good is the abandoning of all suffering (through Arahantship).

332. In this world, good it is to serve one's mother, good it is to serve one's father, good it is to serve the monks, and good it is to serve the holy men.

333. Good is virtue until life's end, good is faith that is steadfast, good is the acquisition of wisdom, and good is the avoidance of evil.

334. The craving of one given to heedless living grows like a creeper. Like the monkey seeking fruits in the forest, he leaps from life to life (tasting the fruit of his kamma).

335. Whoever is overcome by this wretched and sticky craving, his sorrows grow like grass after the rains.

336. But whoever overcomes this wretched craving, so difficult to overcome, from him sorrows fall away like water from a lotus leaf.

337. This I say to you: Good luck to all assembled here! Dig up the root of craving, like one in search of the fragrant

root of the birana grass. Let not Mara crush you again and again, as a flood crushes a reed.

338. Just as a tree, though cut down, sprouts up again if its roots remain uncut and firm, even so, until the craving that lies dormant is rooted out, suffering springs up again and again.

339. The misguided man in whom the thirty-six currents of craving strongly rush toward pleasurable objects, is swept away by the flood of his passionate thoughts.

340. Everywhere these currents flow, and the creeper (of craving) sprouts and grows. Seeing that the creeper has sprung up, cut off its root with wisdom.

341. Flowing in (from all objects) and watered by craving, feelings of pleasure arise in beings. Bent on pleasures and seeking enjoyment, these men fall prey to birth and decay.

342. Beset by craving, people run about like an entrapped hare. Held fast by mental fetters, they come to suffering again and again for a long time.

343. Beset by craving, people run about like an entrapped hare. Therefore, one who yearns to be passion-free should destroy his own craving.

344. There is one who, turning away from desire (for household life) takes to the life of the forest (i.e., of a monk). But after being freed from the household, he runs back to it. Behold that man! Though freed, he runs back to that very bondage!

345-346. That is not a strong fetter, the wise say, which is made of iron, wood or hemp. But the infatuation and longing for jewels and ornaments, children and wives-that, they say, is a far stronger fetter, which pulls one downward and, though seemingly loose, is hard to remove. This, too, the wise cut off. Giving up sensual pleasure, and without any longing, they renounce the world.

347. Those who are lust-infatuated fall back into the swirling current (of samsara) like a spider on its self-spun web.

This, too, the wise cut off. Without any longing, they abandon all suffering and renounce the world.

348. Let go of the past, let go of the future, let go of the present, and cross over to the farther shore of existence. With mind wholly liberated, you shall come no more to birth and death.

349. For a person tormented by evil thoughts, who is passion-dominated and given to the pursuit of pleasure, his craving steadily grows. He makes the fetter strong, indeed.

350. He who delights in subduing evil thoughts, who meditates on the impurities and is ever mindful-it is he who will make an end of craving and rend asunder Mara's fetter.

351. He who has reached the goal, is fearless, free from craving, passionless, and has plucked out the thorns of existence-for him this is the last body.

352. He who is free from craving and attachment, is perfect in uncovering the true meaning of the Teaching, and knows the arrangement of the sacred texts in correct sequence-he, indeed, is the bearer of his final body. He is truly called the profoundly wise one, the great man.

353. A victor am I over all, all have I known. Yet unattached am I to all that is conquered and known. Abandoning all, I am freed through the destruction of craving. Having thus directly comprehended all by myself, whom shall I call my teacher?

354. The gift of Dhamma excels all gifts; the taste of the Dhamma excels all tastes; the delight in Dhamma excels all delights. The Craving-Freed vanquishes all suffering.

355. Riches ruin only the foolish, not those in quest of the Beyond. By craving for riches the witless man ruins himself as well as others.

356. Weeds are the bane of fields, lust is the bane of mankind. Therefore, what is offered to those free of lust yields abundant fruit.

357. Weeds are the bane of fields, hatred is the bane of mankind. Therefore, what is offered to those free of hatred yields abundant fruit.

358. Weeds are the bane of fields, delusion is the bane of mankind. Therefore, what is offered to those free of delusion yields abundant fruit.

359. Weeds are the bane of fields, desire is the bane of mankind. Therefore, what is offered to those free of desire yields abundant fruit.

360. Good is restraint over the eye; good is restraint over the ear; good is restraint over the nose; good is restraint over the tongue.

361. Good is restraint in the body; good is restraint in speech; good is restraint in thought. Restraint everywhere is good. The monk restrained in every way is freed from all suffering.

362. He who has control over his hands, feet and tongue; who is fully controlled, delights in inward development, is absorbed in meditation, keeps to himself and is contented-him do people call a monk.

363. That monk who has control over his tongue, is moderate in speech, unassuming and who explains the Teaching in both letter and spirit-whatever he says is pleasing.

364. The monk who abides in the Dhamma, delights in the Dhamma, meditates on the Dhamma, and bears the Dhamma well in mind-he does not fall away from the sublime Dhamma.

365. One should not despise what one has received, nor envy the gains of others. The monk who envies the gains of others does not attain to meditative absorption.

366. A monk who does not despise what he has received, even though it be little, who is pure in livelihood and unremitting in effort-him even the gods praise.

367. He who has no attachment whatsoever for the mind and body, who does not grieve for what he has not-he is truly called a monk.

368. The monk who abides in universal love and is deeply devoted to the Teaching of the Buddha attains the peace of Nibbana, the bliss of the cessation of all conditioned things.

369. Empty this boat, O monk! Emptied, it will sail lightly. Rid of lust and hatred, you shall reach Nibbana.

370. Cut off the five, abandon the five, and cultivate the five. The monk who has overcome the five bonds is called one who has crossed the flood.

371. Meditate, O monk! Do not be heedless. Let not your mind whirl on sensual pleasures. Heedless, do not swallow a red-hot iron ball, lest you cry when burning, "O this is painful!"

372. There is no meditative concentration for him who lacks insight, and no insight for him who lacks meditative concentration. He in whom are found both meditative concentration and insight, indeed, is close to Nibbana.

373. The monk who has retired to a solitary abode and calmed his mind, who comprehends the Dhamma with insight, in him there arises a delight that transcends all human delights.

374. Whenever he sees with insight the rise and fall of the aggregates, he is full of joy and happiness. To the discerning one this reflects the Deathless.

375. Control of the senses, contentment, restraint according to the code of monastic discipline-these form the basis of holy life here for the wise monk.

376. Let him associate with friends who are noble, energetic, and pure in life, let him be cordial and refined in conduct. Thus, full of joy, he will make an end of suffering.

377. Just as the jasmine creeper sheds its withered flowers, even so, O monks, should you totally shed lust and hatred!

378. The monk who is calm in body, calm in speech, calm in thought, well-composed and who has spewn out worldliness-he, truly, is called serene.

379. By oneself one must censure oneself and scrutinize oneself. The self-guarded and mindful monk will always live in happiness.

380. One is one's own protector, one is one's own refuge. Therefore, one should control oneself, even as a trader controls a noble steed.

381. Full of joy, full of faith in the Teaching of the Buddha, the monk attains the Peaceful State, the bliss of cessation of conditioned things.

382. That monk who while young devotes himself to the Teaching of the Buddha illumines this world like the moon freed from clouds.

383. Exert yourself, O holy man! Cut off the stream (of craving), and discard sense desires. Knowing the destruction of all the conditioned things, become, O holy man, the knower of the Uncreated (Nibbana)!

384. When a holy man has reached the summit of two paths (meditative concentration and insight), he knows the truth and all his fetters fall away.

385. He for whom there is neither this shore nor the other shore, nor yet both, he who is free of cares and is unfettered-him do I call a holy man.

386. He who is meditative, stainless and settled, whose work is done and who is free from cankers, having reached the highest goal-him do I call a holy man.

387. The sun shines by day, the moon shines by night. The warrior shines in armor, the holy man shines in meditation. But the Buddha shines resplendent all day and all night.

388. Because he has discarded evil, he is called a holy man. Because he is serene in conduct, he is called a recluse. And because he has renounced his impurities, he is called a renunciate.

389. One should not strike a holy man, nor should a holy man, when struck, give way to anger. Shame on him who strikes a holy man, and more shame on him who gives way to anger.

390. Nothing is better for a holy man than when he holds his mind back from what is endearing. To the extent the intent to harm wears away, to that extent does suffering subside.

391. He who does no evil in deed, word and thought, who is restrained in these three ways-him do I call a holy man.

392. Just as a brahman priest reveres his sacrificial fire, even so should one devoutly revere the person from whom one has learned the Dhamma taught by the Buddha.

393. Not by matted hair, nor by lineage, nor by birth does one become a holy man. But he in whom truth and righteousness exist-he is pure, he is a holy man.

394. What is the use of your matted hair, O witless man? What of your garment of antelope's hide? Within you is the tangle (of passion); only outwardly do you cleanse yourself.

395. The person who wears a robe made of rags, who is lean, with veins showing all over the body, and who meditates alone in the forest-him do I call a holy man.

396. I do not call him a holy man because of his lineage or high-born mother. If he is full of impeding attachments, he is just a supercilious man. But who is free from impediments and clinging-him do I call a holy man.

397. He who, having cut off all fetters, trembles no more, who has overcome all attachments and is emancipated-him do I call a holy man.

398. He who has cut off the thong (of hatred), the band (of craving), and the rope (of false views), together with the appurtenances (latent evil tendencies), he who has removed the crossbar (of ignorance) and is enlightened-him do I call a holy man.

399. He who without resentment endures abuse, beating and punishment; whose power, real might, is patience-him do I call a holy man.

400. He who is free from anger, is devout, virtuous, without craving, self-subdued and bears his final body-him do I call a holy man.

401. Like water on a lotus leaf, or a mustard seed on the point of a needle, he who does not cling to sensual pleasures-him do I call a holy man.

402. He who in this very life realizes for himself the end of suffering, who has laid aside the burden and become emancipated-him do I call a holy man.

403. He who has profound knowledge, who is wise, skilled in discerning the right or wrong path, and has reached the highest goal-him do I call a holy man.

404. He who holds aloof from householders and ascetics alike, and wanders about with no fixed abode and but few wants-him do I call a holy man.

405. He who has renounced violence towards all living beings, weak or strong, who neither kills nor causes others to kill him do I call a holy man.

406. He who is friendly amidst the hostile, peaceful amidst the violent, and unattached amidst the attached-him do I call a holy man.

407. He whose lust and hatred, pride and hypocrisy have fallen off like a mustard seed from the point of a needle-him do I call a holy man.

408. He who utters gentle, instructive and truthful words, who imprecates none-him do I call a holy man.

409. He who in this world takes nothing that is not given to him, be it long or short, small or big, good or bad-him do I call a holy man.

410. He who wants nothing of either this world or the next, who is desire-free and emancipated-him do I call a holy man.

411. He who has no attachment, who through perfect knowledge is free from doubts and has plunged into the Deathless-him do I call a holy man.

412. He who in this world has transcended the ties of both merit and demerit, who is sorrowless, stainless and pure-him do I call a holy man.
413. He, who, like the moon, is spotless and pure, serene and clear, who has destroyed the delight in existence-him do I call a holy man.
414. He who, having traversed this miry, perilous and delusive round of existence, has crossed over and reached the other shore; who is meditative, calm, free from doubt, and, clinging to nothing, has attained to Nibbana-him do I call a holy man.
415. He who, having abandoned sensual pleasures, has renounced the household life and become a homeless one; has destroyed both sensual desire and continued existence-him do I call a holy man.
416. He who, having abandoned craving, has renounced the household life and become a homeless one, has destroyed both craving and continued existence-him do I call a holy man.
417. He who, casting off human bonds and transcending heavenly ties, is wholly delivered of all bondages-him do I call a holy man.
418. He who, having cast off likes and dislikes, has become tranquil, is rid of the substrata of existence and like a hero has conquered all the worlds-him do I call a holy man.
419. He who in every way knows the death and rebirth of all beings, and is totally detached, blessed and enlightened-him do I call a holy man.
420. He whose track no gods, no angels, no humans trace, the arahant who has destroyed all cankers-him do I call a holy man.
421. He who clings to nothing of the past, present and future, who has no attachment and holds on to nothing-him do I call a holy man.
422. He, the Noble, the Excellent, the Heroic, the Great Sage, the Conqueror, the Passionless, the Pure, the Enlightened one-him do I call a holy man.

423. He who knows his former births, who sees heaven and hell, who has reached the end of births and attained to the perfection of insight, the sage who has reached the summit of spiritual excellence-him do I call a holy man.

INSPIRATION FROM ENLIGHTENED NUNS

In this booklet we will be exploring poems composed by the arahant bhikkhunis or enlightened Buddhist nuns of old, looking at these poems as springs of inspiration for contemporary Buddhists. Most of the poems we will consider come from the Therigatha, a small section of the vast Pali canon. The Therigatha has been published twice in English translation by the Pali Text Society, London: first in 1909 (reprinted in 1980) by C. A. R. Rhys Davids in verse under the title Psalms of the Early Buddhists: The Sisters; and second in 1971 by K. R. Norman in prose under the title The Elders' Verses, II. We have used quotations from both translations here, referring to Psalms of the Early Buddhists by page number and to The Elders' Verses by verse number. Mrs. Rhys Davids' translations have sometimes been slightly modified. Our discussion will also draw upon the verses of bhikkhunis from the Samyutta Nikaya (Kindred Sayings), included by Mrs. Rhys Davids at the end of Psalms of the Sisters.

From the poems of the enlightened nuns of the Buddha's time contemporary followers of the Noble Eightfold Path can receive a great deal of instruction, help and encouragement. These verses can assist us in developing morality, concentration and wisdom, the three sections of the path. With their aid we will be able to work more effectively towards eliminating our mental defilements and towards finding lasting peace and happiness. In some respects, the inspiration from these poems may be stronger for women than for men, since these are in fact women's voices that are speaking. And when the theme of the poem is the mother-child bond, this is bound to be the case. However, at a deeper level the sex of the speakers is irrelevant, for the ultimate truths which they enunciate explain the universal principles of reality which are equally valid for men and for women.

The verses of the nuns, if systematically examined, can help serious Buddhist meditators to understand many central aspects of the Dhamma. The background to the verses, including biographical information on the nuns who uttered them, is provided by the ancient commentary on the Therigatha by the venerable Acariya Dhammapala. Mrs. Rhys Davids has included some of these background stories in Psalms of the Early Buddhists, and in the first part of this essay we will look at these stories and consider the themes they suggest that are relevant to contemporary students of Buddhist meditation.

Then we will go on to discuss a selection of the poems themselves, which deal with many specific teachings of the Buddha. We of the twentieth century who are seeking to attain liberation will find ourselves deeply grateful to these fully awakened Buddhist nuns of old for their profound assistance in illuminating the Dhamma for us in their own distinctly personal ways.

THE BACKGROUND STORIES

The ancient commentaries give us information about each nun's background and also explain the poems themselves. Two major themes of relevance to contemporary students of the Dhamma run through these stories: (1) the immeasurably long time that we have all been lost in samsara, the round of birth and death; and (2) the working of the impersonal law of kammic cause and effect which brought these women into contact with the Buddha's teachings in what was to be their final lifetime.

The Long Duration of Samsara

In the original Pali commentaries, the tales of the nuns began many, many re-births and eons prior to their final existence at the time of Buddha Gotama. We read how over ages and ages all these women had been living out the results of their old kamma and how they created powerful new kamma based on wisdom, which finally culminated in the attainment of Arahatship, full awakening. Each woman-or, more accurately, each succession of aggregates-had to undergo infinite eons of suffering in its gross and subtle forms before she was prepared to gain complete insight. But finally she gave up all clinging and was freed from the need ever again to be reborn and suffer, on any plane.

Vipassana meditators trying to develop this same understanding of the ultimate nature of conditioned existence can find inspiration if they would apply these tales to their own lives. When we realize how long we ourselves have been wandering in ignorance, constantly generating more and more unwholesome kamma, we will be able to remain patient when our early efforts to train the mind tend to falter or fail. Some of the bhikkhunis who had sufficient paramis-virtues cultivated in previous lives-even to gain Arahatship, still had to put in many years of arduous and sometimes seemingly fruitless effort before they could attain the goal.

For example, Siha entered the Sangha as a young woman but could not learn to contain her mind's attraction to external objects for seven years. Another nun worked for twenty-five years without finding any substantial peace because of her strong attachment to sense desire. But both these bhikkhunis, when all the appropriate conditions were finally fulfilled, found their patience and continued efforts fully rewarded. So too will we, if we diligently and strictly keep to the Noble Eightfold Path until we become Ariyas, noble ones. Once we have done this, we are assured that we will completely eliminate the causes of all suffering.

By making this effort to live in accordance with the Dhamma and to understand the true nature of existence, we begin to develop strong wholesome mental volitions, kamma that will have effects in future births as well as in this one. The continued efforts in this direction become easier and more natural because, as we wear away ignorance and the other defilements through insight meditation, our minds come to be more strongly conditioned by wisdom (panna). Recollecting this infinite span of time behind us, and the vast mass of wholesome volitional activities accumulated therein, will help us keep our efforts at purification balanced and strong.

These rebirth stories, illustrating the continuous suffering which every sentient being has undergone during the rounds of samsara, can also encourage us to work hard in the Dhamma. Understanding this weighty aspect of the First Noble Truth stimulates us to put forth the great effort required to overcome suffering by penetrating and uprooting its causes, which the Buddha explains are basically craving and ignorance.

Bhikkhuni Sumedha, in her poem, repeats one of the Buddha's powerful injunctions to eliminate the source of the ceaseless stream of suffering that has rushed on in our previous lives, and will otherwise continue on in the same way throughout the infinite future. Sumedha is pleading with her parents and fiance to allow her to enter the Sangha rather than force her to marry: Journeying-on is long for fools and for those who lament again and again at that which is without beginning and end, at the death of a father, the slaughter of a brother, and their own slaughter. Remember the tears, the milk, the blood, the journeying-on as being without beginning and end; remember the heap of bones of beings who are journeying-on.

Remember the four oceans compared with the tears, milk and blood; remember the heap of bones (of one man) for one eon, (as) equal (in size) to Mount Vepula. (vv. 495-497)

"Journeying-on" is samsara. In the lines beginning "Remember the four oceans compared," Sumedha is reminding her family of a discourse which they must have heard from the Buddha. Each of us, the Buddha tells us, has shed vast oceans of tears over the loss of loved ones and in fear of our own doom as the succession of aggregates has arisen and vanished throughout samsara's weary ages. During all these lifetimes, as the verse declares, we have drunk seas and seas of mother's milk, and the blood that was shed when violent death ended our lives also amounts to an immeasurable volume. How could even one gory death be anything but terrible suffering? The Buddha perceived all this with his infinite wisdom and so described it to his followers. The vastness of samsara that we endured before meeting the Dhamma in this life can easily be extrapolated from the stories of these nuns. We must also sustain the patience in our endeavour to wear down ignorance and to develop the awareness of omnipresent suffering which is life in samsara, as the First Noble Truth makes known.

Kammic Cause and Effect

The second commentarial theme that can be helpful to us in developing our own understanding of the ultimate nature of reality is the working of the law of kammic cause and effect. None of these nuns was emancipated because one day she decided, "Now I am going to cut off all craving." Nor did the grace of a guru or the power of God or the Buddha himself enlighten them. Rather, it was a very long process in the evolution of the "life continuum" that gradually permitted the conditions for liberation to develop and eventually culminate in Arahatship. Freeing the mind of ignorance, like all activities, is an impersonal cause and effect process. Natural laws of this sort are cultivated and utilized by mental volition to bring about purification. By repeatedly seeing all the phenomena of life as they are by means of concentrated Vipassana meditation, we gradually wear away the defilements that becloud the mind and cause rebirth with its attendant misery. For example, Sela took robes when she was a young woman and "worked her way to insight and because of the promise in her and the maturity of her knowledge, crushing the sankharas (conditioned phenomena), she soon won Arahatship" (p. 43). For eons, Sela had done many good deeds, such as making offerings to and looking after previous Buddhas and their monks. As a result of these meritorious actions over many lifetimes, she was reborn in the heavenly deva planes or in comfortable situations on earth. Eventually, at the time of Buddha Gotama, each of the bhikkhunis, including Sela, came into the Sangha in her own way. Because the time was right for their paramis to bear fruit, all the factors conducive to enlightenment could develop, their defilements could be effaced, and the goal could be achieved.

Sukha left the world under one of the earlier Buddhas, but she died without becoming an Ariya. Under subsequent Buddhas "she kept the precepts and was learned and proficient in the doctrine." Finally, "in this Buddha era she found faith in the Master at her own home, and became a lay disciple. Later, when she heard Bhikkhuni Dhammadinna preach, she was thrilled with emotion and renounced the world under her" (pp. 40-41).1 All her efforts in past lives then bore their appropriate fruit as Sukha attained Arahatship and became in turn a great preacher of the Dhamma. Only a small number of nuns are renowned for their skill in teaching, and it is likely that the need to develop the extra paramis to teach the Dhamma made it necessary for Sukha to study under earlier Buddhas for so long without gaining the paths and fruits.

Similar stories tell of how other bhikkhunis performed good works and put forth effort in previous lives, building various kinds of paramis which allowed them to completely give up all attachment to the world at the time of our Buddha. If we consider the process by which they gradually matured towards liberation, we can see how every mental volition and every deed of body and speech at some time or other bears fruit.

It is due to our own paramis, our own good kamma of the past, that we have the rare and great opportunity to come into contact with the teachings of a Buddha in this lifetime. It is because of wisdom already cultivated that we now have the opportunity to develop greater wisdom (pannaparami) through insight meditation.

Wisdom has the power to obliterate the results of past kamma since it comprehends reality correctly. In addition, if we continue to generate such wholesome volitions now, more good kamma is built up which will continue to bear beneficial fruit and bring us closer to the goal. However, wisdom cannot be cultivated in the absence of morality. The Buddha taught that in order to move towards liberation, it is necessary to keep a minimum of five precepts strictly at all times: abstention from killing, stealing, sexual misconduct, lying and consuming intoxicants. If the precepts are broken, the bad kamma thus created will bring very painful results. Without purity of body and speech, purity of mind cannot be developed as the mind will be too agitated by sense desires, regrets and aversion to settle on its meditation subject properly.

Some of the earlier rebirth stories of arahant bhikkhunis tell of lives in which they did not keep the precepts. Several of them suffered the results of their unwholesome deeds in animal births or in low forms of human existence. Addhakasi, for example, had a mixed background. She had become a bhikkhuni established in morality under Kassapa Buddha, the Buddha immediately preceding Gotama.

But once, due to anger, she referred to a fully liberated senior nun as a prostitute. As a result of that wrong speech, she was reborn in one of the lower realms, for to say or do anything wrong to an Ariya creates worse kamma than to say or do the same thing against a non-Ariya. When the fruit of that bad deed was mostly used up, as a residual effect she herself became a prostitute in her final life. By this time her previous good kamma was the stronger and she ordained as a nun. Keeping the bhikkhuni life pure, Addhakasi attained the goal. Causes and effects work themselves out and keep the life process going through samsara. So long as the mind is attached to anything at all, we will engage in volitional actions, make new kamma, and will have to experience their results. Cultivating good kamma will save one from much suffering and prepare the mind for the most powerful wholesome kamma of all, that born of wisdom, which can eliminate all kammic creation.

THE TEACHINGS OF THE POEMS

The actual poems composed by the nuns exhibit a wide range in tone and subject matter. They were almost all spoken after the author had realized that rebirth and all its associated suffering had been brought to an end by the perfection of insight and total elimination of defilements. So virtually all the poems contain some form of "lion's roar," an exclamation that the author has become awakened.

Trivial Incidents Spark Enlightenment

In some cases the poems describe the circumstances which brought the woman into the Sangha or which precipitated her awakening. Both of these can inspire contemporary followers of the Buddha. Sometimes the most mundane event stimulates a ripe mind to see the truth perfectly. Bhikkhuni Dhamma returned from her almsround one day exhausted from heat and exertion. She stumbled, and as she sprawled on the ground a clear perception arose in her of the utter suffering inherent in the body, bringing about total relinquishment. She describes the incident in the following lines: Having wandered for alms, leaning on a stick, weak, with trembling limbs I fell to the ground in that very spot, having seen peril in the body. Then my mind was completely released. (v.17) If someone could gain awakening based on such an event, surely there are an infinite number of potentially enlightening experiences available to all of us for contemplation. Systematic attention (yoniso manasikara) given to any subject will show up its impermanence (anicca), unsatisfactoriness (dukkha), and essenceless nature (anattā) and so encourage us to stop craving. However, unless we carefully apply our minds in Vipassana meditation under the guidance of a competent teacher, it is unlikely that we will be able to utilize our daily encounters with these basic characteristics as means towards liberation. This is because the mind's old conditioning is based on ignorance-the very inability to see things as they really are. Only concentrated mindfulness of phenomena in meditation can enable us to comprehend correctly our everyday experiences, because such methodical culture of insight through Vipassana meditation loosens the old mental tendencies by giving us direct experience of the impermanence of our mind and body.

Entering the Sangha after a Child's Death

Quite a number of women entered the Sangha after their small children had died. Grief is put to good use if it is made the motivation to develop the "path leading to the cessation of suffering." Ubbiri greatly mourned the death of her infant daughter until the Buddha pointed out to her that right in the same charnel ground where she had left this baby's body, she had similarly parted with thousands of children to whom she had given birth in previous lives. Because she had acquired strong merit in the past, this brief personalized discourse was enough to turn Ubbiri from a lamenting mother into an arahant on the spot. As she clearly saw the vastness of samsara, she was prepared to leave it behind. Her profound gratitude to the Buddha is described in these simple lines: He has thrust away for me my grief for my daughter... I am without hunger, quenched. (vv. 51, 53)

With the quenching of ignorance and craving, nothing remains but a pure mind, inherently peaceful. Ubbiri had a pliable, well-prepared mind, and thus she understood, through the Buddha's instructions, that the source of all her suffering had been craving. After countless millions of lifetimes spent rolling in samsara, Ubbiri realized how her deep motherly attachment to her children had always caused her much anguish; for sons and daughters, like everything else, are subject to the law of impermanence.

We cannot make our loved ones live beyond the span set by their own kamma. This was an insight so powerful for her that no object at all seemed worthy of interest any longer because of the potential pain permeating them all. Thus all tendency to cling was broken, never to reappear.

The life story of Patacara before she came to the Dhamma, described in considerable detail in the commentary to the Therigatha, is even more dramatic. She lost her entire family, her husband, two small children, parents and brothers in various accidents within a few days. She went insane from the sorrow, but the Buddha's compassion combined with Patacara's paramis from the past enabled her to regain her right mind.

When she came into his presence, he taught her to understand how often before she had hopelessly exhausted herself grieving for the dead. She became a stream-enterer (sotapanna), one at the first stage of irreversible progress on the path to liberation, and she was ordained. Later, as she was one day pouring water to wash her feet and watching it trickle away-as life does sooner or later for all beings-her mind became utterly free from clinging. Patacara, like Dhamma, had thoroughly developed seeds of understanding, so a very minor mundane incident at just the right moment cleared her mind of every trace of ignorance.

Many other women entered the Sangha in circumstances similar to those of Ubbiri or Patacara. A woman distraught over the death of a child must have been very common in India in those days when limited medical knowledge could not counter a very high infant mortality rate. Theri Patacara spoke to a group of five hundred such grief-stricken mothers, expressing what she had so powerfully learned from similar experience herself:

The way of which men come we cannot know; Nor can we see the path by which they go.

Why mourn then for him who came to you, Lamenting through the tears?...

Weep not, for such is the life of man.

Unasked he came and unbidden he went.

Ask yourself again whence came your child, To live on earth this little time?

By one way come and by another gone, As human to die, and pass to other births-

So hither and so hence-why should you weep?(p. 78)

In this way Patacara illustrates for these mothers the natural connection, the invisible, impersonal causal nexus between death and life, life and death. They too took robes and eventually became Arahats. Their joint "lion's roar" culminates in the lines:

Today my heart is healed, my yearning stayed, Perfected deliverance wrought in me.

I go for refuge to the Buddha, the Sangha, and the Dhamma. (p. 77)

Because of their physiology and their conditioning by family and society, women are more prone to attachment to their offspring than are men, and so will suffer all the more from their loss. However, if women train their minds to understand how clinging causes enormous suffering, how birth and death are natural processes happening as effects of specific causes, and how infinite the history of such misery is, they can utilize their feminine sufferings in the quest for awakening. In the Kindred Sayings (Vol. IV, pp. 62-163), the Buddha himself pointed out the five kinds of suffering unique to women. Three are physiological-menstruation, pregnancy, and childbirth. The other two are social, and perhaps not as widely relevant today as they were in ancient Indian society: having to leave her own family to live with her husband and in-laws, and having "to wait upon a man." All five must be the results of past unwholesome deeds, yet each one can be made a basis for insight. Women can train their minds to turn to advantage these apparent disadvantages. They can then make full use of their stronger experiences of the universality and omnipresence of suffering to condition themselves to let go of everything in the conditioned realm.

For some individuals, intense suffering is needed to make the mind relinquish its misconceptions and desires. Patacara is one example of this; Kisa Gotami is a second. The latter was so unwilling to face the truth of her child's death that she carried the dead baby around with her hoping to find one who could give her medicine to cure him. The Buddha guided her into a realization of the omnipresence of death by sending her in search of some mustard seed. This is a common ingredient in Indian kitchens, but the Buddha specified that these seeds must come from a household where no one had ever died. Kisa Gotami went looking for this "medicine" for her baby, but because of the prevalent joint family system in which three or more generations lived together under one roof, every house she went to had seen death. Gradually, as she wandered through the village, she realized that all who are born must die. Her great paramis then enabled her to understand impermanence so thoroughly that soon afterwards the Buddha confirmed her attainment of stream-entry. She then spoke these lines:

No village law is this, no city law, No law for this clan, or for that alone;

For the whole world-and for the gods too-

This is the law: All is impermanent. (p. 108)

Kisa Gotami thus transcended the limits of a woman's personal grief to understand one of the basic characteristics of all existence.

Kisa Gotami later attained Arahatship. Some of the verses she spoke on that occasion give useful lessons to any striver on the Noble Eightfold Path: Resorting to noble friends, even a fool would be wise. Good men are to be resorted to; thus the wisdom of those who resort to them increases. Resorting to good men one would be released from all pains. One should know suffering, the cause of suffering and its cessation, and the Eightfold Path; (these are) the Four Noble Truths. (vv. 213-215)

The company of the wise, especially the guidance of a teacher, is an invaluable help in getting oneself established on the path. But the company of people not involved in the Dhamma will tend to be distracting. Those who are not trying to practice the Buddha's teachings will usually lead us in the worldly direction to which their own minds incline. Thus, when we can, it is best to choose our friends from among meditators.

The Four Noble Truths

As Kisa Gotami urges in the final lines quoted above, meditators need to train their minds constantly to see the Four Noble Truths in all their ramifications.

This is wisdom, panna, the remedy for the ignorance and delusion which are at the root of all suffering as shown in the formula of dependent origination. To develop wisdom one has to ponder these four truths over and over again: (1) the Noble Truth of Suffering (dukkha) which includes all forms of suffering from severe agony to the pervasive unsatisfactoriness and instability inherent in individual existence in all planes of becoming; (2) the Noble Truth of the Cause of Suffering-craving (tanha), which drives the mind outwards after sense objects in a state of perpetual unrest; (3) the Noble Truth of the Cessation of Suffering-Nibbana, which is attained when the causes of suffering, ignorance and craving, have been utterly uprooted; and (4) the Noble Truth of the Way leading to the Cessation of Suffering-the Noble Eightfold Path discovered and taught by the Buddha, consisting in the assiduous practice of morality (sila), concentration (samadhi) and wisdom (panna).

The Four Noble Truths are concisely expressed in a verse spoken by Maha Pajapati, the Buddha's maternal aunt who brought him up when his own mother, Queen Mahamaya, died a week after his birth. It was at the insistence of Maha Pajapati that the Buddha founded the Bhikkhuni Sangha. In her poem she first praises the Buddha for the unique help he has given to so many beings by training them in the way to liberation; then she briefly sums up the Four Noble Truths which she has so thoroughly experienced as ultimate truth. It would be beneficial for modern meditators to consider these lines carefully:

Now have I understood how ill does come, Craving, the Cause, is dried up in me.

Have I not walked, have I not touched the End, Of ill-the Ariyan, the Eightfold Noble Path. (p. 89)

Buddhist meditators have to train themselves to know these truths as deeply as they can by seeing them in every aspect of existence. We follow the mundane level of the Noble Eightfold Path in order to reach the supramundane (lokuttara) path with the attainment of stream-entry. Then the constituents of the path-morality, concentration and wisdom-are cultivated to the highest degree and the end of suffering, Nibbana, is realized.

Reaching the Goal after a Long Struggle

When we read the stories of these great bhikkhunis, we see that many of them attained the highest fruits either instantaneously or soon after coming into contact with the Buddha or his Dhamma. This could have happened because they had built up paramis in many previous lives, creating pure kamma of body, speech and mind, while simultaneously wearing out the effects of past kamma. Yet not all the people whose paramis permitted them to actually hear the Buddha preach were able to become Arahats so quickly in their final lives. When we confront our rebellious minds as we try to follow his path, we can take heart from the tales of nuns who had to put forth years and years of intense persistent effort before they eliminated all their defilements.

A youthful Citta ordained at her home town of Rajagaha and spent her whole adult life as a nun striving for enlightenment. She finally attained her goal only as a weak old woman, as she laboriously climbed up the landmark of Vultures' Peak. When she had done so, she said:

Having thrown down my outer robe, and having turned my bowl upside down, I propped myself against a rock, having torn asunder the mass of darkness (of ignorance). (v. 27)

If we diligently, strictly, and vigorously practice the Noble Eightfold Path, developing insight into the true nature of existence, the opacity of delusion must eventually become completely transparent, cleared by wisdom. It may require many years or many lifetimes of work, but then patience is one of the qualities we must cultivate from the time we first set foot on the path. Another bhikkhuni who took years to reach enlightenment was Mittakali. She took robes after hearing the Satipatthana Sutta. In her "lion's roar" she describes the errors that cost her seven years to gain Nibbana. Her poem can be instructive to other meditators both within and outside the Sangha:

Having gone forth in faith from the house to the houseless state, I wandered here and there, greedy for gain and honour.

Having missed the highest goal, I pursued the lowest goal. Having gone under the mastery of the defilements, I did not know the goal of the ascetic's state. (vv. 9293)

The Buddha pointed out on many occasions that it is dangerous for monks and nuns to pursue gains or favors from the laity, as such activities nullify any attempts they may make to purify their minds. The layman gives gifts to bhikkhus and bhikkhunis to earn merit. If the mind of the recipient is pure, free from greed and other defilements, the merit accruing to the lay disciple is far greater than if the recipient's mind is filled with craving. One of the epithets given to Arahats, whose purity is permanently perfect, is "worthy of the highest offerings." All those, ordained or not, who allow craving to overtake them and waste the precious opportunity they have to practice the Dhamma, will delay their own liberation and increase their suffering.

In the simile of the poisonous snake in the Middle Length Sayings (Vol I, pp. 171-72), the Buddha points out that his teaching has only one aim, freedom from suffering. An incorrect approach that seeks to misuse the Dhamma will lead to increased suffering, just as grasping a snake by the body or tail will result in one's being bitten. The same venomous snake, if grabbed with the help of a forked stick by the neck just behind its head, will safely yield up its poison for medicinal use. The Buddha declares that similarly only those who wisely examine the purpose of his teachings will be able to gain insight and actually experience their purpose-the elimination of the causes of suffering.

When Mittakali perceived that old age and death were rapidly approaching, she finally came to realize the urgency of the task after wasting years in the pursuit of gain and honour. Since we can never be sure how much longer we will live, it is risky to put off meditation. We have come into contact with the Dhamma under conditions conducive to pursuing the Buddha's goal. Such conditions as youth and human birth will come to an end-either gradually or abruptly-so we can never be certain that the conditions to practice the Dhamma will remain ideal. Mittakali took years to comprehend that with advancing age, rigidity of mind and bodily ailments were making the job of purification ever more difficult. But once she did realize this, she was able to achieve the goal. Studying this verse of hers may help us to avoid wasting precious time: I felt a sense of urgency as I was seated in my little cell; (thinking) "I have entered upon the wrong road; I have come under the mastery of craving.

> *"My life is short. Old age and sickness are destroying it. There is no time for me to be careless before this body is broken."*
>
> *Looking at the arising and passing away of the elements of existence as they really are, I stood up with my mind completely released. The Buddha's Teaching has been done.(vv. 94-95)*

By observing the rise and fall at every instant of body, feelings, perceptions, mental formations, and consciousness, Mittakali's mind was freed from misconceptions of any lasting "I" or self. After those seven long years of being trapped in the net of desires, she saw through her foolish and dangerous interest in mundane matters. She was then able to see the elements or aggregates as they actually are: utterly transient (anicca), hence incapable of providing any satisfaction (so dukkha), working automatically without any lasting core (anatta). All her worldly involvements dropped away as she attained Arahatship and thenceforth passed beyond all sorrow and suffering.

Perhaps the most moving story of a nun who had to undergo a long struggle from the time she first ordained until she became fully enlightened is that of Punna. Under six earlier Buddhas, in the vast eons prior to the Buddha Gotama's dispensation, Punna was a bhikkhuni "perfect in virtue, and learning the three Pitakas [the Buddhist scriptures] she became very learned in the Norm and a teacher of it. But because of her tendency to pride [each time], she was unable to root out the defilements." Even at the time of Buddha Gotama, she had to work out some bad kamma and so was born as a slave. Hearing one of the Buddha's discourses, she became a stream-enterer. After she helped her master clear his wrong view, in gratitude he freed her and she ordained. After so many lifetimes of striving, the paramis she had built up as a nun under previous Buddhas ripened. Pride or conceit, always one of the last defilements to go, finally dissolved and she attained Arahatship.

By pondering the accounts of women who attained full awakening after much application and effort, we can be encouraged to continue our own exertions no matter how slow our progress may appear at a given time. In the Gradual Sayings (Vol. IV, pp. 83-84), the Buddha gives an analogy of the wearing down of the carpenter's axe handle to illustrate how the mental impurities are to be gradually worn away. Even though the woodcutter cannot say, "This much of the handle was rubbed off today, this much last week," it is clear to him that slowly, over time, the handle is being destroyed. Similarly, a meditator who has a good guide and who constantly attempts to understand the Four Noble Truths and to live in accordance with the Noble Eightfold Path, will gradually eliminate his defilements, even though the steps in the process are imperceptible. Even the Buddha declined to predict the amount of time that will elapse before the final goal is reached. This is conditioned by many interacting factors, such as the good and bad kamma built up in the past and the amount of effort put forth now and in the future. Whether it takes us millions of more lifetimes or a week, we will be sustained in our efforts by the faith that perfection of morality, concentration and wisdom will bring utter detachment and freedom from all suffering.

Liberation means renouncing attachment to oneself and to the world. We cannot rush the process of detachment; insight into the suffering brought about by clinging will do it, slowly. While trying to eliminate mental impurities, we have to accept their existence. We would not be here at all were it not for the ignorance and other defiling tendencies that brought us into this birth.

We need to learn to live equanimously with the dirt of the mind while it is slowly being cleared away. Purification, like all other mental activities, is a cause and effect process. Clarity comes slowly with the repeated application of the wisdom of impermanence. If we are patient and cheerfully bear with moments of apparent backsliding or stupidity, if we continue to work energetically with determination, not swerving off the path, the results will begin here and now. And in due time they have to ripen fully.

Contemplation on the Sangha

The Sangha, the order of monks and nuns, preserves and perpetuates the Buddha's pure teachings, and its members have dedicated their lives to practicing them. Thus contemplation on the Sangha is recommended by the Buddha to help cultivate wholesome mental states. We could begin such contemplation based on the poem of a bhikkhuni named Rohini. Her father had asked her why she thought recluses and monks were great beings. He claimed, as might many people today-particularly in the West with its strong "work ethic"-that ascetics are just lazy; they are "parasites" who do nothing worthwhile and live off the labour of others. But Rohini proclaimed her faith in the work and lives of pure recluses. She thereby inspired her father's confidence, and at her bidding he then took refuge in the Buddha, the Dhamma, and the Sangha. Her poem can also inspire us:

> *They are dutiful, not lazy, doers of the best actions; they abandon desire and hatred...*
>
> *They shake off the three roots of evil doing pure actions; all their evil is eliminated...*
>
> *Their body-activity is pure; and their speech-activity is likewise; their mind-activity is pure...*
>
> *They are spotless like mother-of-pearl, purified inside and out; full of good mental states...*
>
> *Having great learning, expert in the doctrine, noble, living in accordance with the doctrine, they teach the goal and the doctrine... with intent minds, (they are) possessed of mindfulness...*
>
> *Travelling far, possessed of mindfulness, speaking in moderation, not conceited, they comprehend the end of suffering...*
>
> *If they go from any village, they do not look back (longingly) at anything; they go without longing indeed...*
>
> *They do not deposit their property in a store-room, nor in a pot, nor in a basket, (rather) seeking that which is cooked...*
>
> *They do not take gold, coined or uncoined, or silver; they live by means of whatever turns up...*
>
> *Those who have gone forth are of various families and from various countries; (nevertheless) they are friendly to one another; therefore ascetics are dear to me. (vv. 275-285)*

The Buddhist texts speak of two kinds of Sangha, both referred to in this poem, the Ariya Sangha and the Bhikkhu Sangha. In the opening lines Rohini describes the Ariyas, "noble ones," and those striving to attain that state. The three lower kinds of Ariyas may be lay disciples or ordained monks and nuns. But because of their utter purity, the highest type, the filly liberated Arahats, can continue to live only within the Bhikkhu Sangha. It is Arahats who have completely rid their minds of greed, hatred and ignorance, the three roots of evil which Rohini mentions. Other Ariyas are striving to abandon whatever of these three still remains in their minds. All Ariyas to some extent "comprehend the end of suffering," the Third Noble Truth, for it is this experience of Nibbana which sets them apart as "noble."

Beginning with the next line, Rohini specifically talks about the behavior of monks and nuns. They wander on almsrounds through the streets with their eyes trained just a few steps ahead of them. "They do not look back" as they have no idle interest in the events that are going on around them. They do not handle money and are content with the minimum by way of the requisites-whatever their lay followers may offer them. Students of the Dhamma who are not in the monastic order would also do well to cultivate the monk's lack of interest in his surroundings. A good monk does not let his gaze wander about uncontrolled, especially when he is on almsround, because when going into the village every morning he encounters a plethora of sense objects that might entice him if he does not restrain his senses and maintain mindfulness. Attentively, the good bhikkhu goes silently from door to door and leaves when there is enough food in his bowl, without letting craving disturb his balance of mind. Such a monk is not interested in the details of the lives of those around him. His focus is always on the ultimate nature of things their impermanence, painfulness and essencelessness. As lay meditators we too need to train ourselves to be like these bhikkhus, to remain equanimous and detached amidst all the clamor and distractions of life by reminding ourselves that none of these things is worth running after.

Rohini also states that the noble monks are not greedy about money or other possessions. They do not save up their requisites out of fear for the future. Instead, they trust their good kamma to fulfill their daily needs. While, as laymen, we must work for our living, we should heed this behavior and similarly adopt a detached attitude towards wealth. We work in order to sustain our bodies and those of the people who are dependent on us. But if we can learn to do this without intense longing for the "security" that money seems to provide, we will see how the law of kamma works.

The last verse states that within the Sangha, the family, class or national background of its members does not impede their cordial relations with each other. This kind of open good will is surely useful for laymen to put into practice in their daily lives too. Since it is by ordaining that individuals can completely dedicate their lives to the Dhamma, bhikkhus and bhikkhunis offer us laymen many examples of how we should try to apply the teachings within the limitations of "the dust of household life." Rohini's poem has pointed out some of these.

The Danger of Worldly Desire

A large number of poems by the nuns emphasize the danger of worldly desire. The bhikkhuni named Sumedha shaved off her hair herself in order to force her parents to cancel her proposed marriage and permit his to enter the Sangha. But before she left home, Sumedha convinced her whole family and its retinue of the validity of the Buddha's message. To her fiance, King Anikaratta, she explained the futility of sense desires and the insatiability of the senses:

Even if the rain-god rained all seven kinds

Of gems, until earth and heaven were full,

Still senses would crave and men die unsatiated. (p. 176)

No matter how large a quantity of worldly goods we may have, if the mind has not gained insight, craving will recur. If ignorance has not been uprooted, desire will seek more and different objects, always hoping for lasting satisfaction. Durable happiness is impossible in the mundane sphere because all sense objects change and decay every moment, as does the mind itself. This perpetual state of underlying dissatisfaction-craving looking for gratification-is one of the many forms of present suffering. In addition, desire itself generates the kammic energy which propels life towards rebirth in order for it to continue its efforts at finding fulfillment. If desire is present in the mind at the moment of death, rebirth has to ensue.

After speaking the above verse, Sumedha gave a lengthy discourse to the whole assembly in her palace on the great value of a human birth in the infinity of samsara. Life in this world is precious because it provides a very rare opportunity for learning the way to put an end to rebirth and suffering, for putting into practice the teachings of the Buddha. Sumedha also spoke on the danger inherent in sensual joy and sense desire and she uttered verses about the Noble Eightfold Path as well. She enthusiastically exhorted her audience:

> *When the undying (Nibbana) exists, what do you want with sensual pleasures which are burning fevers? For all delights in sensual pleasures are on fire, aglow, seething. (v. 504)*

When craving momentarily gains its aim, mind's enjoyment of the sense object brings it to a feverish state of excitement and activity. Sumedha urges her family to look beyond such unsettling, binding pleasures and to heed the words of the Awakened One which show the way beyond all desire to utter peace. She exhorts them to keep in mind their long-term benefit and not get caught up in the fragile momentary happiness that comes with the occasional satisfaction of sense desire. She reminds them in words we too should recall: "Desires of sense burn those who do not let go" (p. 176). Clinging to pleasure always brings pain. Such agitated emotions, although perhaps pleasant in a gross way, are gone in a moment.

They arise and cease due to conditions we cannot completely control. We always tend to want the pleasant to last in spite of the fact that its nature is to change, vanish, and give way to the unpleasant. Sumedha's poem expounding this wisdom is the last one in the original Therigatha and it summarizes what the Buddha taught about the dangers of craving.

The bhikkhuni named Subha also dwells at length on the dangers of mundane wishes, using some terrifying metaphors to show the tremendous dangers inherent in attachment to the world. In the following poem taken from the Samyutta Nikaya a meditator can discover much by reflecting on Subha's intense imagery:

> *May I not meet (again) with sensual pleasures, in which no refuge is found. Sensual pleasures are enemies, murderers, like a mass of fire, pain-(ful).*
>
> *Greed is an obstacle, full of fear, full of annoyance, full of thorns, and it is very disagreeable. It is a great cause of stupefaction...*
>
> *Sensual pleasures are maddening, deceiving, agitating the mind; a net spread out by Mara for the defilement of creatures.*
>
> *Sensual pleasures have endless perils, they have much pain, they are great poisons, they give little enjoyment, they cause conflict, drying up the virtuous.(vv. 351f., 357f.)*

These lines show us the peril and suffering we must face when we allow ourselves to become entangled in mundane desires. Only personal comprehension of these dangers motivates a meditator to become truly mindful, aware of his physical and mental activities with ever-present detachment. Otherwise his "mindfulness" may be forced, suppressing reactions without helping to untie mental knots. Studying the suffering we have to encounter if we are carried away by our desires, naturally loosens their hold on the mind. We will realize along with Subha that worldly lusts are enemies and that they herald all the misery of successive births. One of our tasks in seeking liberation is to train our minds to see desire as it arises at the sense doors. We must also see desire as it persists and as it passes away. Having done this over and over again, we will understand that all desire or attachment is bound to result in unhappiness. In this way we will gradually train our minds to let go of all craving and aversions towards sense objects.

To try to practice this mindfulness without any specific training is likely to fail because the worldling, the average person, perceives no suffering in craving. A worldling can only see the expected happiness. He invariably thinks, "If only this would happen just right, all would be well." But as we purify our bodily and vocal activities through morality, still our minds through concentration, and take up insight meditation under a good teacher, we will come to see more and more clearly how all desire is suffering and brings still more suffering in the future. We will then also realize how often attaining a desired object turns out to be an anti-climax which leaves-not the anticipated happiness-but only emptiness. With a calm mind we can clearly perceive the tension, distress, and uneasiness caused by the continual dissatisfaction, which in turn is due to craving impelling the mind to various sense objects.

Thus the mind is always running-now towards what it foolishly regards as a "desirable" thing, now away from what it considers "undesirable." In Vipassana meditation, the one-pointed mind is trained to experience directly the transitory nature of body and of mind itself, and also of external sense objects. With this direct knowledge or experiential insight, the "happiness" which is so avidly sought by the worldling is seen as really just another form of suffering, and the perpetual tension caused by the ignorance and craving latent in any unliberated mind becomes evident. As sensual pleasure is understood to be the seething fire described by our bhikkhunis, the mind naturally lets go of all these different manifestations of craving. Such a mind has thoroughly learned the lesson that the nuns gleaned from their Master and passed on to us: suffering is inherent in desire.

The Danger in Attachment to One's Beauty

In ancient times as well as at present, women in all stations of life have used various means to enhance their beauty and to hide the signs of advancing age. This, however, is just a futile attempt to pretend that the body is not growing old, to keep it from showing outwardly that it is actually falling apart. But if, instead of creams and lotions, wisdom is applied to the aging process, it can deepen our understanding of impermanence on all levels. Ambapali was a wealthy and beautiful courtesan during the time of the Buddha. Before she heard the Buddha preach, her main concern had been to cultivate and maintain her renowned beauty. With the Buddha's guidance, she was able to face the inevitability of aging and the loss of her beauty and to comprehend the suffering of old age. Her verses can also stimulate our own understanding:

> *My eyes were shining, very brilliant like jewels, very black and long. Overwhelmed by old age, they do not look beautiful. Not otherwise is the utterance of the speaker of truth...*
>
> *Formerly my hands looked beautiful, possessing delicate signet rings, decorated with gold. Because of old age they are like onions and radishes. Not otherwise is the utterance of the speaker of the truth...*
>
> *Formerly my body looked beautiful, like a well-polished sheet of gold. (Now) it is covered with very fine wrinkles. Not otherwise is the utterance of the speaker of the truth...*
>
> *Such was this body. (Now) it is decrepit, the abode of many pains, an old house with its plaster fallen off. Not otherwise is the utterance of the speaker of the truth. (vv. 257, 264, 266, 270)*

Ambapali sees how all the body's charms give way to ugliness and pain as the aging process takes its toll, as the Buddha teaches it must. All physical beauty, no matter how perfect it might seem at one youthful moment, is utterly impermanent. Even at its peak, the brilliance of the eyes is already, if invisibly, starting to grow dim; the firmness of limbs is withering; the smoothness of skin is wrinkling. Impermanence and decay, Ambapali reminds us, is the nature of all bodies and of everything else in the universe as well. Khema, the queen of King Bimbisara, was another woman who had been enthralled with her own beauty prior to meeting the Buddha. But Khema had made a vow before one of the earlier Buddhas to become great in wisdom under the Buddha Gotama. During the dispensations of several of the intervening Buddhas, she had parks made which she donated to each Buddha and his Sangha.

But in her final lifetime Khema strongly resisted going to see the Buddha Gotama. Perhaps her "Mara forces" were making a last effort to keep her in samsara. They were, however, doomed to fail since by the force of her merits this was to be her final existence. King Bimbisara almost had to trick her into going to the Buddha because Queen Khema was so attached to her looks and was afraid that this would provoke the Buddha's disapproval. If we ever find ourselves resisting the Dhamma, we can use Khema's example to remind ourselves of the temporary nature of this mental state. Then we will not take it as a major personal fault. Mind's old habits are not pure, so at times it is bound to struggle against the process of purification. But the Buddha knew how to tame Khema's vanity and conceit. He created the vivid image of a woman even more attractive than she was. When she came into his presence, Khema saw this other lady fanning the Buddha. Then, before the queen's very eyes, the Buddha made the beautiful image grow older and older until she was just a decaying bag of bones. Seeing this, first Khema realized that her own beauty was not unmatched. This broke her pride. Second and more important, she understood that she herself would likewise have to grow old and decrepit.

The Buddha next spoke a verse and Khema became a stream-enterer. Then in rapid succession she went through all the stages of enlightenment to attain Arahatship on the spot. Thereupon the Buddha told King Bimbisara that she would either have to ordain or to pass away, and the king, unable to bear the thought of losing her so soon, gave her permission to ordain.

So, already an arahant, she was ordained-one of the very rare cases of a human being who had achieved Arahatship before entering the Sangha. Khema had clearly built up truly unique paramis by giving great gifts to earlier Buddhas and by learning their teachings thoroughly.2 Here again we see the great importance of creating in the present strong good kamma based on wisdom, even if we do not attain any of the paths or fruits in this lifetime. The more good deeds accompanied by wisdom that we do now, the easier will it be when the time actually comes for us to reach the goal. Meditation is, of course, the most valuable of such deeds. In the Therigatha, Khema's poem takes the form of a conversation with Mara, the being who controls and symbolizes the forces of evil. Mara praised her beauty, and her reply shows how totally her view of herself and of life had changed now that she fully understood the true nature of things:

Through this body vile, foul seat of disease and corruption,

Loathing I feel, and oppression. Cravings of lust are uprooted.

Lusts of the body and mind cut like daggers and javelins.

Speak not to me of delighting in any sensuous pleasure!

All such vanities cannot delight me any more.(p. 83)

Then she identifies Mara with those who believe that mere ritual observances will lead to mental purification. Khema states that such people, who worship fire or the constellations, etc., are ignorant of reality and cannot eliminate their defiling tendencies through such practices. This is why the belief that rites and rituals can bring about liberation has to be eliminated to attain even the stage of stream-entry. Khema concludes her verses with an exclamation of deep gratitude to the Buddha, the supreme among men. Her last line is a resounding "lion's roar":

(I am) utterly free from all sorrow,

A doer of the Buddha's teachings. (pp. 3-4)

Khema had "done," i.e., put into practice, the message of all the Buddhas, and this had taken her beyond the realms of suffering.

Further Conversations with Mara

Some of the other discourse-type verses in the Therigatha also take the form of a discussion with Mara. Typically, Mara asks the arahant nun why she is not interested in the "good things of life." Mara urged Sela, for example, to enjoy sensual pleasures while youth allowed her to do so. The theri's reply on the dangers of such delights offers similes as powerful as those used by Bhikkhuni Sumedha:

Sensual pleasures are like sword and stakes; the elements of existence are a chopping block for them; what you call 'delight in sensual pleasures' is now 'non-delight' for me. (v. 58)

Surely many of us have also heard our own internal Mara urge us to "go have a good time and never mind the long-term kammic consequences." But if we can remind ourselves often enough and early enough of the painful after-effects of such "joys"-especially of those that involve breaking moral precepts-we may see through the pleasures of the senses and so gradually lose our attachment to them. In one of the discourses from the Samyutta Nikaya, Cala tells Mara that, unlike most beings, she finds no delight in birth in spite of the so-called sensual pleasures that life makes possible. With clear simplicity she shows that ultimately all that birth produces is suffering:

Once born we die. Once born we see life's ills- The bonds, the torments, and the life cut off. (p. 186)

We too should cultivate this understanding in order to develop detachment from the poison-soaked sensual pleasures offered by mundane life.

The Doctrine of Anatta

One of the unique aspects of the Buddha's teaching is its doctrine of anatta, the impersonal, essenceless, egoless or soul-less nature of all phenomena. This universal characteristic is difficult to comprehend as it is contrary to our most deeply held assumption that "I" exist, that "I" act and "I" feel. Sakula, in the following lines of her poem in the Therigatha, briefly expresses her understanding of the impersonal quality of all compounded things:

Seeing the constituent elements as other, arisen causally, liable to dissolution, I eliminated all taints. I have become cool, quenched. (v. 101)

Sakula has attained Nibbana because she saw with total clarity that everything normally taken to be "myself" is, in fact, devoid of any such self. She knew that all these phenomena arise and dissolve every moment strictly dependent on causes.

This comprehension has rooted out all tendency to cling to the sankharas or "constituent elements" and so all the defiling mental tendencies have ceased. When Mara asks Sister Sela, "Who made this body, where did it come from and where will it go?", she gives him in reply (in one of the poems added from the Samyutta Nikaya) a discourse on egolessness:

Neither self-made the puppet is, nor yet
By another is this evil fashioned.
By reason of a cause it came to be;
By rupture of a cause it dies away.
Like a given seed sown in the field,
Which, when it gets the taste of earth,
And moisture too-by these two does grow,
So the five aggregates, the elements,
And the six spheres of sense-all of these-
By reason of a cause they came to be;
By rupture of a cause they die away. (pp.189-190)

After the seed analogy, the last four lines discuss the "self" as it actually is-a compound of conditioned, changing phenomena. The five aggregates make up nama (mentality) and rupa (materiality), each of which is turn made up of groups of ephemeral factors. Nama, the mental side of existence, consists of the four immaterial aggregates-feeling (vedana), perception (sanna), mental formations (sankhara), and consciousness (vinnana)-which arise together at every moment of experience. Rupa, which may be external matter or the matter of one's own body, consists of the four essential material qualities-solidity, cohesion, temperature, and vibration-along with the derivative types of matter coexisting with them in the very minute material groupings called kalapas, arising and passing away millions of times per second.

Each aggregate arises due to certain causes and when these causes end, the aggregate also ceases. Causes, or conditions, are connected with effects in the law of dependent arising (paticcasamuppada), which is at the centre of the

Buddha's own awakening. The refrain from Sela's poem (lines 3-4 and 10-11) is, in fact, a reformulation of the most general exposition of that law often stated thus in the suttas:

When there is this, that comes to be;

With the arising of this, that arises.

When this is absent, that does not come to be;

With the cessation of this, that ceases.

The specific link in the cycle of dependent arising most relevant to Sela's verse is: "With consciousness as condition, mentality-materiality arises." That is, at the moment of conception, nama-rupa (in this case excluding consciousness) arises due to rebirth-linking consciousness. Later on, during the course of an existence, nama, the mental aggregates, comes into being due to ignorance, past kamma, objects at the sense doors, and many other conditions. Rupa, the matter which makes up the body, arises during life because of food, climate, present state of mind, and past kamma. Sela also refers to the elements, dhatu, a word which the Buddha uses for several groups of phenomena. Let us look here at the eighteen elements. The five sense faculties (eye, ear, nose, tongue, body), their objects (sights, sounds, smells, tastes, touches), and the five types of consciousness dependent on their coming together make up fifteen of the elements. Mind as a faculty, mental objects (ideas), and the mind-consciousness that arises when those two come together are the sixth in each set, completing the eighteen.

The Buddha analyzed the totality of conditioned phenomena into ultimate constituents in a number of ways for the benefit of listeners of varying proclivities. To some, the eighteen elements are clear, to others, the five aggregates. Either way, what we need to understand as Sela did is that none of these things is "me" or "mine" or "my self." All these phenomena-the aggregates, the elements, the spheres-arise because of certain conditions, and when those conditions end, naturally they also have to end. When the relevant causes have expended their force, all these aspects of what we erroneously take to be "me" and "mine" cease. So we see with Sela that nowhere is there any real, independent, or lasting "I" with the power to create and sustain itself. There is only the concept "I am" which is conditioned by ignorance, i.e., our inability to see mind-and-body as it really is. The idea "I" is itself essenceless, it arises due to causes; and it is also inherently impermanent, bound to completely disappear when the ignorance and other supporting conditions behind it are uprooted. This is the attainment of Arahatship.

The removal of ignorance takes place step by step in Vipassana meditation. Every aspect of the mind-body complex comes to be clearly known at its ultimate level as conditioned, essenceless, transitory, oppressive. One comes to fully understand that only when the appropriate conditions come about will a so-called "being" be born. Only then will a five-aggregate life-continuum commence a new life with its bases, elements and sense organs.

If we explore Bhikkhuni Sela's seed analogy, we will see in relation to ourselves how a strict succession of causes and effects, kammic and other, governs all of life. We will discover that there is no underlying or ongoing "I" doing or experiencing anything, and will begin to loosen our attachment to this non-existent "self." Then we start to eliminate the dreadful suffering that comes attendant on this delusion.

Suffering follows from the mistaken belief in an "I," technically called sakkayaditthi, wrong view of a lasting self. On the basis of this idea the mind generates all its thoughts of craving: "I must have this," "I don't like that," "This is mine." It is basically due to this misconception of a controlling self that we have been wandering and suffering throughout eons in samsara.

If we are to eliminate all the dukkha of existence, as Theri Sela did, we must develop insight through Vipassana meditation to the point at which understanding of the ultimate truth about mind and body dissolves the mistaken belief in an "I." We can use this bhikkhuni's words to stimulate our own personal meditative experience of the essenceless nature of the five aggregates.

Men and Women in the Dhamma

The difference between the male and female in connection with the Dhamma is a minor theme running through the Therigatha. It takes two forms: poems whose subject matter is the irrelevance of one's gender for gaining insight, and instances in which a nun specifically inspires or instructs a man with a discourse. The stories of Sumedha and Rohini already discussed fit into the latter type.

An example of the first type is Soma's challenge to Mara's query about women's ability to attain Arahatship. Soma showed Mara that the capacity to gain the requisite insight for liberation need not be hindered by "woman's nature." Soma's encounter with Mara in the Therigatha proper is explained in her verses from the Samyutta Nikaya, where she rhetorically asks him:

What should the woman's nature do to them

Whose hearts are firmly set, who ever move

With growing knowledge onward in the Path?(pp. 45; 182-183)

If one is really developing morality, concentration and wisdom, it does not matter whether one was born male or female. The insight to "truly comprehend the Norm" is completely irrespective of superficial distinctions of sex, race, caste, etc. Soma adds that if one even thinks, "Am I a woman in these matter, or an I a man, or what not am I then?" one is under Mara's sway. To be much concerned with such subjects is to remain on the level of conventional truth, clinging to the non-existent self. Repeatedly worrying about which sex is better or about the "inequities" women suffer generates unwholesome kamma. Thoughts like this are rooted in attachment to "I" and "mine" and are associated with ill will or desire.

Moreover, spending time on such matters distracts us from the urgent task of self-purification. Meditators who wish to escape Mara's net need to cast off such thoughts as soon as they are noticed. We should not indulge in or expand upon them. Soma and all the other nuns follow the Buddha's advice closely when they urge us to stick exclusively to the work that will allow us to liberate ourselves from all suffering. All side issues will lose their importance and so pass away with further growth of wisdom. When we know fully that all beings are just impersonal, unstable mind-body processes, generating kamma and feeling its results, our minds will remain with the ultimate truths and have no interest in any conventional concerns. The story of the bhikkhuni known as "Vaddha's Mother" is one in which a nun specifically guides a man in the Dhamma. This woman joined the Sangha when her son Vaddha was small; thus he had been brought up by relatives. Later, he too ordained and one day went to visit his mother in the bhikkhunis' quarters. On that occasion, she exhorted and inspired him to seek and attain the highest goal:

> *Vaddha, may you not have craving for the world at any time. Child, do not be again and again a sharer in pain.*
>
> *Happy, indeed, Vaddha, dwell the sages, free from lust, with doubts cut off, become cool, having attained self-taming, (being) without taints.*
>
> *O Vaddha, devote yourself to the way practiced by seers for the attainment of insight, for the putting an end to pain. (vv. 204-205)*

From these lines Vaddha deduced that his mother had reached the goal, a fact she confirmed. She again urged him to develop "the path leading to the cessation of suffering" himself. Vaddha, being deeply inspired by his mother's words, also attained the goal and then spoke the following lines praising her:

> *Truly my mother, because of being sympathetic, applied an excellent goad to me, (namely) verses connected with the highest goal.*
>
> *Having heard her utterance, the instruction of my mother, I reached a state of religious excitement in the doctrine, for the attainment of rest-from-exertion. (vv. 210-211)*

Here we find a woman's example of perfect sainthood, combined with her timely Dhamma instruction, inspiring a man whose paramis were ripe to put forth the utmost effort and attain complete liberation.

The Five Aggregates and Nibbana

The Culavedalla Sutta (Middle Length Sayings, Vol. I) is another sutta in which a bhikkhuni instructs a man. This important text takes the form of a discourse on some fine points of the Dhamma given by the theri Dhammadinna in reply to questions put to her by her former husband, the lay disciple Visakha. They had been married for some time when he attained the third stage of holiness, that of the non-returner (anagami), by eradicating all traces of ill will and sense desire. Dhammadinna then learned from him that women too could purity their minds and she obtained his permission to take robes as a nun. By the time of this discussion, she must have already attained Arahatship, the fourth and final stage of holiness.

Visakha first asks Dhammadinna what the Buddha actually refers to when, using conventional language, he says "own self." As a non-returner, Visakha knew the answer to this basic question, but he put it by way of introduction to his progressive series of queries. Dhammadinna's reply is something for us to ponder. She says that the "five aggregates of grasping" (pancupadanakkhandha) comprise "own self." She defines the aggregates or groups of grasping as:

the group of grasping after material shape,

the group of grasping after feeling,

the group of grasping after perception,

the group of grasping after habitual tendencies,

the group of grasping after consciousness.

The aggregates are viewed and clung to as myself or mine: this is sakkayaditthi, the view that there is a lasting self. Actually, there is no lasting controller or core corresponding to the concept "me" or "I." It is merely the grasping after these five groups, which are all that actually makes up "myself," that perpetuates our illusion that there is something substantial. If we can see this, we will be attacking sakkayaditthi and will come to know that in reality there is no essence, just these five aggregates, all of whose components are continually changing.

The next question Visakha asks Dhammadinna concerns the reasons for the arising of the aggregates. Quoting the Buddha, she replies that the cause for the aggregates is "craving (that is) connected with again-becoming, accompanied by delight and attachment, finding delight in this and that, namely, the craving for sense pleasures, the craving for becoming, the craving for annihilation."

All craving contributes to the arising of the aggregates over and over again. Being attracted to the things of this world or of the heavenly planes ("craving for sense pleasures") will lead to rebirth there with renewed suffering, gross or subtle. Wanting to keep on going ("craving for becoming") strengthens clinging and ignorance to force us to continue in samsara. The belief that there is no form of life after death (rooted in "craving for annihilation") undermines the doctrine of kamma and its result, the understanding of which is essential to moral living.

After a long series of questions and answers which cover the Four Noble Truths, the attainment of cessation, feeling, etc., Visakha asks a final question: "And what, lady, is the counterpart [i.e., equal] of Nibbana?" Here Dhammadinna has to stop him: This question goes too far, friend Visakha, it is beyond the compass of an answer. Friend Visakha, the Brahmafaring is for immergence in Nibbana, for going beyond to Nibbana, for culminating in Nibbana.

Nothing can possibly be compared with Nibbana as everything else, be it mental or physical, arises and ceases due to conditions. Nibbana alone is unconditioned and unchanging. Going beyond the realm of transitory, unsatisfactory phenomena to the utter peace of Nibbana is the aim of the teaching of the Buddha and so of serious Buddhists. It is useful to keep this goal in mind even during the early stages of meditation, when it may seem remote and vague. The aspiration to attain Nibbana is cumulative. If it is frequently considered, repeated and combined with the practice of Vipassana, this aspiration will become a supporting condition for the attainment itself. Frequent recollection of the goal will also keep us from being sidetracked by the pleasurable experiences one may encounter on the path.

After this question and answer session, Dhammadinna suggests that Visakha should ask the Buddha about all this so that he is certain and learns the answers well. Visakha takes up the idea and later repeats to the Buddha his entire conversation with the theri. The Lord replies in her praise: Clever, Visakha, is the nun Dhammadinna, of great wisdom... If you had asked me, Visakha, about this matter, I too would have answered exactly as the nun Dhammadinna answered.

Kamma and its Fruit

Finally, let us look at a poem in which a bhikkhuni describes in detail a few of her previous lives and shows her questioner how she comprehended the law of kammic cause and effect working out behind her present-life experiences.

Isidasi had built up many good paramis long ago during the times of former Buddhas. But some seven lifetimes back, when she was a young man, she had committed adultery. After passing away from that existence Isidasi had to suffer the results of this immoral action:

Therefrom deceasing, long I ripened in Avici hell

And then found rebirth in the body of an ape.

Scarce seven days I lived before the great

Dog-ape, the monkey's chief, castrated me.

Such was the fruit of my lasciviousness.

Therefrom deceasing in the woods of Sindh,

Born the offspring of a one-eyed goat

And lame, twelve years a gelding, gnawn by worms.

Unfit, I carried children on my back.

Such was the fruit of my lasciviousness. (p. 157)

The next time she was born a calf and was again castrated, and as a bullock pulled a plow and a cart. Then, as the worst of that evil kamma's results had already ripened, Isidasi returned to the human realm. But it was still an uncertain kind of birth as she was the hermaphroditic child of a slave. That life too did not last long.

Next, she was the daughter of a man oppressed by debts. One of her father's creditors took her in lieu of payment. She became the wife of that merchant's son, but she "brought discord and enmity within that house."

In her final lifetime, no matter how hard she tried, no home she was sent to as a bride would keep her more than a brief while. Several times her virtuous father had her married to appropriate suitors. She tried to be the perfect wife, but each time she was thrown out. This inability to remain with a husband created an opportunity for her to break through the cycle of results. After her third marriage disintegrated, she decided to enter the Sangha. All her mental defilements were eliminated by meditation, insight into the Four Noble Truths matured, and Isidasi became an arahant.

She also developed the ability to see her past lives and thus saw how this whole causal chain of unwholesome deeds committed long ago brought their results in her successive existences:

Fruit of my kamma was it thus that they

In this last life have slighted me even though

I waited on them as their humble slave.

The last line of her poem puts the past, rebirth and all its sufferings, completely behind with a "lion's roar": "Enough! Of all that now have I made an end." (p. 163)

In Isidasi's tale we have several instructive illustrations of the inexorable workings of the law of kamma. The suffering she had to undergo because of sexual misconduct lasted through seven difficult lives. But the seeds of wisdom had also been sown and when the force of the bad kamma was used up, the powerful paramis she had created earlier bore their fruit. Hence Isidasi was able to become a bhikkhuni, purify her mind perfectly, and so eliminate all possible causes of future suffering. The beginning, the middle, and the ending of every life are always due to causes and conditions.

We have now come full circle with these stories of the theris and have returned to the theme of impersonal causes and effects working themselves out, without any lasting being committing deeds or experiencing results.

The infinite sequence of lifetimes steeped in ignorance and suffering is repeated over and over until accumulated paramis and present wisdom, aided by other factors, become sufficiently strong to enable one to see through the craving which has perpetually propelled the succession of aggregates. Through this process these bhikkhunis clearly perceived that their attachments and aversions were the source of all their suffering. Because of this insight, they were able to dissolve the knots of old delusion-based conditioning.

With their completed understanding of suffering, the First Noblc Truth, and the abandoning of craving, the Second Noble Truth, their practice of the Noble Eightfold Path, the Fourth Noble Truth, was perfected. They attained the cessation of suffering, the Third Noble Truth, in that very lifetime, and were never reborn again.

The poems of these enlightened nuns, telling how they came to meet the Buddha, how they had built up wisdom and other meritorious kamma over many previous lives, how they understood the Buddha's teachings, and how they attained Arahatship, offer us inspiration and guidance. They can help us present-day Buddhists to practice Vipassana meditation and to gain insight into suffering and its causes. Then we too will be able to give up all craving by developing wisdom. We can use the messages of the theris to assist us in putting an end to our own suffering.

Grateful for their assistance, may we all follow in the footsteps of these great nuns, true daughters of the Buddha. May our minds be perfect in wisdom, perfectly pure, and utterly free from all possibility of future suffering.

THE SANGHA

The title of this talk is a quote from William Blake from The Marriage of Heaven and Hell. It was first brought to my attention by Bhante (Sangharakshita) at the time of my ordination-ten years ago. At the time of my ordination I took a meditation practice focusing on Ratnasambhava-the archetypal Buddha of Beauty. And because I was meditating on this Buddha figure, Sangharakshita quoted this line to me from Blake. I have never quite understood it.

What does exuberance mean in this context and how does it relate to Beauty? What, for that matter, is meant by Beauty? So now, ten years later, I'm still exploring this question and I don't know whether I'm any clearer, but we'll see what happens. This talk is not really meant to address these questions anyway. The ancient Greeks spoke of the Good, the True and the Beautiful as the highest meaning in life.

In Buddhism too we can speak of the Path of Goodness, the Path of Truth and the Path of Beauty-all three need to be followed but different people may put the emphasis on one or other of these paths. Goodness is concerned with ethics and purity, Truth is concerned with wisdom and, in The Religion of Art, Bhante speaks of the Path of Beauty as the way of the artist. So here Beauty is seen in terms of creativity-artistic creativity even.

But art in this context has a very specific meaning-it must be both beautiful and meaningful in a universal sense-it must embody values that have the power to transform the individual for the better. So clearly this definition of art will exclude certain things which might be called art under other less stringent definitions. On the other hand, it might include some things which would not normally be considered works of art.

For example, Sangharakshita himself has created the FWBO and I think the FWBO could perhaps, at a stretch, be considered a work of art according to this definition. The important factors are the beauty, the meaningfulness and the creative energy that is applied. Creativity is a focussed application of energy. Energy is emotion. "Energy", to paraphrase another quote from Sangharakshita, is nothing but "the rhythm of delight in your own experience". Energy is the rhythm of delight in your own experience. Exuberance is a movement of energy-exuberance is a creative movement of energy and exuberance is Beauty.

Beauty is a creative movement of energy; that rhythm of delight in your own experience. Your own experience, of course, is an experience of the world, an experience of other people, an experience of responses to everything and everybody you come into contact with. The Path of Beauty involves taking delight in your responses to everything and everybody-it involves creativity; transforming and beautifying your responses to everything and everybody.

In this sense, exuberance is Beauty. The Sangha is characterised by "unfailing mutual delight". Sangharakshita says-Communication and taking Delight are of the essence of friendship-Sangha. The Sangha, we could say, is characterised by exuberance, an overflowing of energy into creative activity that is saturated with meaning and beauty. This is the vitality of Sangha, this is what gives life to our common pursuit, this energy, exuberance, delight that flows, pours forth in constant creative activity, creative activity that transforms ourselves and transforms the world, into something beautiful, something that is permeated by truly human values.

This overflowing of energy into creative activity-this exuberance-transforms ourselves and the world into works of art. The true artist is engaged in self-transformation which has universal application and is a source of inspiration and even admonishment to others. The Path of Beauty is the path of energy, of exuberance. Energy in Buddhist terms is Virya-energy in pursuit of the Good. Virya is exuberance.

Virya is essential to spiritual practice-it moves us from the realm of thinking it's a good idea, to actually doing it. Actually transforming ourselves. A spiritual practitioner is energetic, exuberant, creative. A spiritual practitioner is becoming beautiful by endeavouring to embody the Good and the True.

A spiritual practitioner is someone whose energy is in exuberant pursuit of the Good, the wholesome, the pure. Someone who delights in the adventure of evolving consciousness-someone who works like an artist, always making creative effort to transform their responses into something meaningful and beautiful. This is the opposite of self-obsession.

There is a teaching in the Abhidharma of the Pali Canon about 'unwise attention'. To give unwise attention to something means to focus on an object that will lead us into unskilful mental states or to focus on an object in such a way that it will lead us into unskilful mental states. Sometimes we do this with our responses to people or events. We maybe feel a bit inadequate or shy and we focus on it in such a way as to render us almost immobile-we increase our feelings of inadequacy or shyness by giving them unwise attention. Or we might feel a bit resentful and by getting obsessed with it, we develop it into a rage or fury, again giving 'unwise attention'.

We give wise attention by focussing on how to change our response-how to change our feelings of inadequacy and resentment or whatever-we take a creative approach. We also give wise attention by choosing to focus on something in our experience that is more positive. We are not 100% inadequate or resentful or unconfident-there are other aspects to our experience that we can focus on and by giving them attention they start to predominate.

So I think when we are tempted to spend time poking around in our own psyche, analysing our moods and so on, we should bear in mind this teaching about 'unwise attention' and 'wise attention' and ask ourselves are we doing something creative? Is our energy moving in the direction of the good and the beautiful? Are there aspects of our experience that we could delight in? Most people have a positive response to something-whether it's music, painting, poetry, trees, animals, the sea, mountains or whatever.

So sometimes it may be necessary to turn your attention deliberately to something you enjoy, something you have a good response to, and that will introduce another element into your experience. A more energetic, exuberant element that will help you to take a more creative approach to life's ups and downs. Exuberance is not boisterousness, it's not just mindless activity.

Exuberance in this context is an attitude and a tendency. It's an attitude of abundance, an attitude of plenty and it's a tendency to optimism. An exuberant attitude is optimistic about the universe, the law of Karma is operative, it sees the universe as basically benign. And following on from this is optimism about people and optimism about oneself.

It's a 'can do' attitude, a 'get up and go' attitude, an attitude that delights in a challenge. An attitude that sees possibilities and opportunities. And the greatest challenge, the greatest adventure that faces us at this point in human history, is the challenge of (conscious) evolution of consciousness. This is not just a Buddhist idea. This is recognised by many thinking people, the world over. Here for example is a quote from the American anthropologist—Loren Eiseley: "The need is not really for more brains, the need is for a gentler, a more tolerant people than those who won for us against the ice, the tiger and the bear.

The hand that hefted the axe, out of some old blind allegiance to the past, fondles the machine gun as lovingly. It is a habit man will have to break, but the roots go very deep." The Immense Journey-page 140 Loren Eiseley-Anthropologist/ Naturalist The triumph of evolution is the brain of mankind, a brain that increases in size by a multiple of 3 shortly after birth. This brain is an extraordinary phenomenon and it has made us the lords of nature.

However, the survival needs of mankind are now of a completely different kind and they necessitate a growth in awareness, in wisdom and compassion, which is as yet only scantily present in the world. As Loren Eiseley said, "the need is for a gentler, a more tolerant people than those who won for us against the ice, the tiger and the bear". The need now is for a recognition, an insight into our essential interconnectedness, the need is for a transcendence of selfishness, a transcendence of even the notion of self.

The need is for a transcendence of egotism, and a wholehearted embracing of egolessness-a wholehearted venture into the unknown realms of experience beyond separateness, beyond selfishness, beyond egotism. "Egotism", according to Sangharakshita, is "a centripetal tendency, a movement of contraction". "Egolessness", on the other hand, "is a centrifugal tendency, a movement of expansion towards something absolutely outside the orbit of its own being". "Something absolutely outside the orbit of our own being" is vast unknown territory for us and this is where we must go.

We must venture forth on this quest for egolessness-this is what the higher evolution of consciousness demands of us. And like all great adventures, all great endeavours, we must go alone, we must decide in our own hearts to take up the staff of spiritual practice and enter upon the path of self-transformation. Others may be travelling in the same direction, they may help us and encourage us, but in the end we must travel that path ourselves.

In plain words-we have to change ourselves. This movement of expansion towards what is beyond us, towards the unknown, is a description of the spiritual life. Expansiveness is characteristic of the spiritual life. Expansiveness is energy moving out beyond self-concern. It is above all an attitude of generosity. It is a renunciation of narrow self-interest and an understanding of the close, inseparable nature of the interests of both self and other. When we understand and recognise this truth, that our real interests and the real interests of others are identical, then there is no difficulty in being expansive, no difficulty in being generous.

The path of the higher evolution of consciousness is a path that leads us from a more thorough awareness of ourselves, a more thorough integration of our selves out to a greater and ever greater awareness and understanding of others and of the interconnectedness of all life. The path of the higher evolution of consciousness, this conscious effort to change and grow and transform ourselves; this is what life is about. This is the meaning of life. Life must live. Life must expand and grow. Life is inherently exuberant. Life is energy and we humans, with our marvellously developed brain and our capacity for self-awareness, can marshall that energy and move it ever outwards in a "centrifugal movement towards something absolutely outside the orbit of our own being".

This is truly the great wonder of this world and our dignity as human beings and possibly even our survival, depends on us individually making the decision to take up the challenge and act accordingly. The teaching of the Buddha gives us a detailed method and the teaching of Sangharakshita further clarifies and elucidates that to make it more applicable to our particular context and circumstances here in late 20th century Britain. It's a heroic task. The alternative is to live an escapist life, burying our heads beneath the trivia of a materialistic world or putting our faith blindly in some god or messiah to do our living for us. Let us then take up the challenge. Let us decide to transform ourselves. Let us allow ourselves to become part of the fabric of this exuberant, expansive life that flows through the universe. Let us give scope to our energy and creativity. Let us create ourselves anew. Let us engender in ourselves this exuberant attitude of abundance and plenty-this attitude of optimism-get up and go-can do. Let us build something beautiful together. A Sangha and the delights of a Sangha-the creations of a Sangha-beautiful spaces for meditation, beautiful spaces for living and working in.

Beauty and refinement. Joyful relationships, rich and loving friendships. Let's not complain and fight a quarrel. Life is really too short for that (Dhammapada). Let's not be fearful-there is nothing to be afraid of. Let's not have miserly, pessimistic attitudes-let's have an attitude of abundance and optimism. Let us not spend too much time wandering in the labyrinth of our own minds-let us engage with those things of beauty which will create for us new, mental states, new minds. Let us be creative, dynamic, energetic, exuberant-and let's take delight in the Buddha-for giving meaning to our lives-for revealing the meaning of our lives, let's delight in the Dharma for allowing us to change and grow and let's delight in the Sangha simply for being there. Let us delight in each other for being a living, breathing, aspiring Sangha, intent on the highest ideals and willing to wholeheartedly practice what we believe.

In practice then, here at the London Buddhist Centre, let us practice hospitality to a much greater degree. Let us be welcoming to anyone we don't know-let no one remain a stranger for long. Even if we've only been coming along for a relatively short time, let us welcome those who are newer. It is my heartfelt wish that the LBC have a reputation for simple hospitality-a welcoming, friendly, warm atmosphere. We do well in this area but I think we could do better. I had a letter from someone a while back, saying that a visitor from America who came to part of our Wesak festival in May didn't feel at all welcomed-in fact, felt excluded by a sort of cliquishness. So by all means enjoy your friends and your chats but please look out for those who are alone or who don't know anyone. Let's be welcoming and hospitable.

And going further than that, as we get more involved, let's make an effort to build friendships. Let's befriend someone. Don't wait until someone befriends you, take the initiative, go out and make friends. It requires patience, it takes time and requires commitment, but it is worth the effort, the Sangha is simply, and wholly a network of friendships. A loving, trusting friendship between two people is the basic unit of our Dharmic society. It is sometimes said that the family is the basic unit of society-perhaps it is, but friendship is the basic unit of Sangha. Without genuine friendships, the Sangha becomes a horrible, ecclesiastical shell administering meaningless institutions. With friendship the Sangha is very much part of the self-transcending path of Beauty-encouraging expansiveness, energy and an exuberant outward movement into the realms of non-separation, the realms of higher states of consciousness where the designation of yours and mine becomes increasingly meaningless and insight is no longer just an idea.

So let's work at making friends-let us seek to love rather than look for love. We will be loved if we love-we will have friends if we make friends. And this year and for 2 years here at the LBC we have a campaign to create a new retreat centre for our benefit and above all for the benefit of future generations. Let us have an optimistic, energetic, outgoing response to this vision of a new Retreat Centre, Vajrasana. Some people immediately feel a bit overwhelmed by mention of large sums of money (although what a large sum of money is, is a very relative matter) and they immediately say, "oh, it's too much-it can't be done, oh dear do we really need it" and so on. That is a sure way to failure. But we can do it.

Of course we can. We just need to raise about £300,000 between us in 2 years. That's not outlandish, that's not fantastical, it's well within the realms of possibility. And our attitude makes a big difference. If we have an exuberant, energetic, optimistic, abundant attitude, then we can create wealth and abundance. If we think creatively and in a spirit of optimism, we create an atmosphere of abundance. How we think influences how we speak and how we act and it also influences other people. Our actions obviously influence others-our words influence others-what we say creates the flavour of our world. And our thoughts influence others too.

We are not totally separate entities. Consciousness influences consciousness, thoughts have an effect. So we need to be aware of this and if we can't, for instance, support Vajrasana and the appeal for help and funds, with our actions-then let us support it with our speech and our thoughts. Let us give the project, the vision, air to breathe in. The air of optimism and energy and abundance is the atmosphere in which Vajrasana will grow into a reality and manifest in our world as a beautiful retreat centre. So if we don't have money or time or anything else to give to this project, let us at the least be generous with our thoughts and our words and give birth to the atmosphere out of which the vision can take shape. So at the LBC let us practise hospitality to a greater degree and be welcoming to newer people. Let us take action to befriend people-build the friendships which go to make up the Sangha and let us support the Vajrasana retreat centre project with our energy, our encouragement and our optimistic thoughts. There are a great many conventions, assumptions and mores in the world around us and we are affected by these conventions and assumptions. Often we are quite unconsciously affected by the ideas, views and assumptions that are so much part of the fabric of the world we live in.

We can have very conventional attitudes and beliefs, without even realising it. Exuberant, expansive, joyful, optimistic idealism is not very conventional. Cynicism is conventional. Those who regard themselves as sophisticated and worldly wise can be quite cynical and pessimistic. They can regard all idealism as fantasy, pie in the sky, never stopping to consider what the ideals actually are and how they are being put into practice. Because, of course, idealism can be pie in the sky unless it is being put into practice and unless the way it is being put into practice is permeated with the values of the ideal. For life to be at all meaningful we need to have ideals-and high ideals. Some people's ideal stops short at a good job and plenty of money.

That is a disgraceful waste of human potential. We need to have high ideals-the highest ideals-of Wisdom and Compassion perfected-and we need to put ourselves wholeheartedly into making those ideals more and more of an everyday reality. Cynicism is conventional, it is even seen as wisdom sometimes. Idealism is not so acceptable. Let us not be conventional, let's be unconventional-let's be notoriously idealistic and strive with all our hearts to practice what we believe in. And again, materialism and consumerism are conventional. Many people see their salvation in terms of shopping. Happiness and contentment can be purchased-you just have to shop around. The more we can accumulate the safer and happier we will be. Wealth brings security and pleasure. What more could you want? It's pathetic!

It is pathetic that such a large chunk of humanity spends so much of its time accumulating worthless things and destroying the environment and making life miserable for another large chunk of humanity at the same time. And we are all strongly affected by the materialistic convention of the world around us. We all want to go shopping-into those brightly lit, enticing, places of comfort and salvation. We want to be saved-from our emptiness and loneliness-and we go shopping. We pray to GAP or NEXT or M & S.

We pray to designer labels-and our prayers are never answered, but hope springs eternal in the true believer-and we go shopping-again. Living a simple life, with few possessions is less conventional. But a simple life, with few possessions, is much more conducive to spiritual practice, it is a spiritual practice and if it leaves us with surplus money we can give it away-which is another spiritual practice.

Materialism and consumerism are conventional. Living a simple life as a spiritual discipline is not. Let us not be conventional, let's be unconventional-let's stop paying obeisance to the false gods of the shopping precinct and live simply-for our own benefit and the benefit of others. It is conventional to find fault with great individuals, to debunk them, to topple them from their heights. Especially it is popular on TV, in newspapers or biographies to delve into the private lives of individuals and find bits of gossip-worthy stories that bring the great down a peg or two and show that we are all equal after all. But some people are greater than others. Some people have made a greater contribution to the life of humanity, some people have more ability, more intelligence, more talent. Some people are gifted, some people are truly great. Greatness should be recognised and applauded.

We should be grateful to those who have excelled in any field. Plato, Einstein, Shakespeare, Nelson Mandela, Michelangelo and so on-there are many, many great and worthy people who deserve our gratitude and praise. Let us recognise a hierarchy of merit, a hierarchy of ability and, of course, a spiritual hierarchy and not go along with the current practice of finding fault with the great men and women of past and present. Madeleine Bunting, the religious correspondent of The Guardian, echoes this in a recent article: "There is a curious late 20th century obsession with destroying reputations. Something almost patricidal as we metaphorically murder the figures who have framed our history and culture. Something akin to a witch-hunt about how we search out contradictions and weaknesses in people and seize upon them as evidence of hypocrisy.

Finding out such things is a legitimate pursuit of knowledge, but it is done with a judgmentalism which has echoes of bitter disillusionment." This metaphorical murder etc. is conventional. It is conventional to debunk, to bring everyone down to the same mediocre level. Hierarchies of merit, ability and spiritual insight are not so readily acceptable. Let us not be conventional, let us be unconventional. Let us recognise greatness and revere the great of past and present. It is conventional to not take any active part in public life. Society is atomised, individuals feel powerless and are apathetic. The motto is to look after number one. There is an emphasis on the private, personal world. We can have our computer at home, our TV, video player, hi-fi-we are becoming more and more self-sufficient, isolated units in society and leaving public life to the few. This is bad for democracy and in the long run bad for the society we live in. At the election and referendum last May, only 35% of the electorate in Tower Hamlets voted-it was even less in some places.

This is not a good sign. We should at least vote. But we should do more than that, we should take an interest in our local community. We should be part of the community and encourage community spirit, encourage mutual helpfulness and neighbourliness. We should not go along with the convention of self-centredness and apathy which undermines democratic public life. Let's not be conventional, let us be unconventional. Let us be outgoing, sociable, neighbourly, let us encourage and engender community spirit and a healthy public life. This is a very natural extension of the practice of loving kindness.

It is conventional to be nationalistic or to identify with some particular group. Nationalism and groupism of all kinds are more in favour than simple humanism. We hear of the gay community, the Black community, the Irish community, the business community, the countryside lobby and so on. And usually identity in terms of one group is at the expense of conflict with other groups. Nationalism is a stark example-in Northern Ireland, in Bosnia, in Kosovo, in the Middle East. This is humanity still functioning very much on a level of lower evolution—"the hand that hefted the axe"-conflict and competition to ensure survival. This is also totally stupid. Breaking into mutually exclusive groups and threatening each other is more likely to lead to human extinction than human survival. But this madness goes on. This is the depth of spiritual ignorance in the world. And we need to turn our backs on this. We need to give up identifying with little bits of humanity-we shouldn't even identify with Buddhism, as a group in opposition to others. We need to identify with humanity, we are human beings first and foremost-that is enough-where we were born, what we look like, our gender, our sexuality, our religion-all these are secondary.

And we should not be content even to identify with the human race, let us identify with all that lives, let's be sensitive to life wherever and however it manifests. Let us not be conventional, let us be unconventional. Let us give up all allegiance to groups and identify with humanity and all sentient life. It is conventional to value the romantic, sexual partnership as the most important of human relationships. It is even considered to be the basic unit of society, albeit a rather unstable basic unit.

The romantic, sexual partnership-the couple-is considered to be the closest, most intimate human relationship. It is considered to be the most fulfilling, most desirable human relationship. To be not part of a couple is to be a social misfit; you must be part of a couple or wanting to be part of a couple. This is the conventional norm. In the Sangha we value friendship more highly than the romantic, sexual relationship. We value same sex friendship as the most important and highest human relationship and we encourage and praise friendship. It is not that it is bad or wrong or unspiritual to be in a romantic couple relationship, it is just that friendship, same sex friendship is a higher form of human relationship.

It is the basic unit of our society-the basic unit of the Sangha. So let's not be conventional, let's be unconventional. Let's give highest priority to our friendships, let's give more time and energy to our friendships and let our sexual coupledom take second place, or even third place. There are no doubt many more conventions, assumptions and commonly held views that are all around us all the time-and we hardly notice.

For instance, there's the conventional notion of social drinking-drinking alcohol to be sociable. Alcohol makes you drunk not sociable! There's a big difference between being sociable and being intoxicated. But the convention has it that you must drink to be sociable. What a sham! It's a very counterfeit sociability you get when people drink alcohol. There is in fact no good reason for drinking alcohol unless getting drunk is essential to your wellbeing.

There are many good reasons for not drinking alcohol-social reasons, economic reasons, health reasons, ecological reasons, and even spiritual reasons. So again let us not be conventional, let's be unconventional. Let's be genuinely sociable and friendly and not intoxicated. No doubt you can think of more areas of conventional behaviour and ideas which we could throw out and be happier and healthier for it.

So let us not be satisfied with dull, conventional lives that have nothing of the adventurous spirit of exploring the heights of consciousness, the frontiers of consciousness. Let us be unconventional. Let us have faith in great and glorious ideals, let us have big ideas. Let's have a vision of a better world. Let's value the spiritual above the material, a simple life of few possessions above consumerism. Let's value great men and women who give substance to a vision of humanity's potential. Let's value public life and community spirit and don't shut ourselves away in atomised apathy. Let's identify with humanity rather than with any particular group. Let's value friendship above romantic, sexual relationships and let's be sociable rather than drunk. Let's break free of the bonds of convention. Let's break free of the narrow confines of accepted ideas and norms of behaviour.

Let's set our sights on a vision of beauty. Let's be creative and allow our energy to expand outwards beyond narrow self-interest, beyond narrow self-concern, beyond egotism, out beyond the orbit of what is known and comfortable. Let us be exuberant in our pursuit of the good. Let us be optimistic and exuberant. Exuberantly generous. Let's be hospitable and welcoming to strangers. Let's give time and energy to creating loving, deep friendships and let's create an atmosphere in which Sangha flourishes, an atmosphere in which the work of the Sangha flourishes-such as the Vajrasana retreat centre-an atmosphere of optimism and abundance.

Let's not stop there. Let's be even more radical-let us not accept the world as it is at all. Let's change the world-let's create a world more worthy of us, more in keeping with human dignity-a world that recognises the absurdity of nationalism, the absurdity of racism, the absurdity of materialism. The absurdity of human beings destroying or harming each other. Let's create a world that is saturated with the Wisdom of the Buddha. The Insight and Vision of the Buddha which sees clearly the interconnectedness and interdependence of all life.

Let us not be conventional, let us be unconventional. Let's be radical, let's practice the Dharma wholeheartedly. Let's build Sangha-a beautiful tapestry of friendships-and let us engage in the great adventure of the Higher Evolution of consciousness, this great, optimistic, exuberant, expansive, beautiful adventure that gives meaning to Life and to our lives.

THE PRACTICE OF SANGHA

The Arya Sangha is the noble or holy Sangha, the spiritual community of all those who have experienced some insight into the nature of reality. This is the Sangha of those who have reached a stage in their spiritual life which means that they can never fall back from the Path. They have seen into the nature of reality and what has become clear to them can never become unclear again. This is the point of Stream Entry. A Stream Entrant is a spiritual practitioner who has seen through fixed self-view, has seen through doubt and indecision and has seen through any tendency to go through the motions of spiritual practice. Bhante talks about a Stream Entrant in positive terms as someone who has transcended habit, vagueness and superficiality and attained creativity, clarity and commitment. Stream Entry occurs when we break through these three fetters of self-view, doubt, and going through the motions of practice.

The first fetter is the habit of being a particular kind of person. We act as if we have always been and will always be a particular kind of person with particular abilities and shortcomings. Consciously or unconsciously we tell ourselves stories about who we are and what we can and cannot do and we keep on telling ourselves the same stories, constantly reinforcing a particular version of 'me' with a capital M. A Stream Entrant is someone who breaks through this and has a much more creative experience of themselves and others. A

Stream Entrant is always aware of the greater potential that has yet to unfold, and the Buddha nature yet to be unveiled. The second fetter is doubt and indecision or a constant lack of clarity. This is an emotionally based avoidance of clarity and truth. This is throwing up obstacles constantly to deliberately obscure the truth about ourselves and about life. This kind of doubt and indecision is a resistance to going deeper into things, a resistance to clarifying what the Dharma is all about, a resistance to the implications of practice. It is closely related to the first fetter because this resistance is all about preserving a fixed self-view. A Stream Entrant is completely free of doubt about the Buddha, Dharma and Sangha and it is therefore no great effort for a Stream Entrant to place trust in the Three Jewels.

The third fetter is the tendency to go through the motions of practice or as it is usually put, reliance on rites and rituals as ends in themselves. When we have been practising for a while we can lose sight of the purpose of practice and then our practice of meditation, puja, study and even ethics becomes empty of deeper meaning. We may forget about the spiritual goal of becoming more aware and more compassionate-we may forget that we're trying to undermine selfishness and harshness and gain more wisdom and equanimity. We may meditate in order to have good meditations or to have strong experiences. We may do puja in order to feel good and get a bit of a buzz.

We may study simply to acquire knowledge and we may practice ethics to be a good Buddhist, but we have forgotten the higher ideal, we have forgotten about Insight and Enlightenment and we are satisfied with being a little bit happier. This is the fetter of superficiality as Bhante calls it. It keeps us on the surface of our own experience and keeps us immunised against the reality of dissatisfaction, impermanence and insubstantiality. It means we have lost creativity in our practice, we no longer have a cutting edge in our spiritual life-we're a bit lost and in need of reorientation and re-inspiring. A Stream Entrant is constantly aware of the reason for practice, constantly on a path of compassion and awareness. A Stream Entrant has broken through these fetters of fixed self-view, doubt and indecision and superficiality and has insight into the real reason for spiritual practice.

Stream Entrants and all those even more advanced make up the Arya Sangha, the noble Sangha. This is the Sangha we Go for Refuge to, this is the Sangha we can rely on. This Sangha, the Arya Sangha, is the living breathing Dharma. This is where the teachings of the Buddha leave off being concepts or images and take on human form. The teachings live in the Arya Sangha and it is because the teachings have stayed alive in this way that it is still possible for us to encounter the essential spirit of Buddhism. Currently I am reading 'Buddha in the Jungle' by Kamala Tiyavanich, (follow up to Forest Recollections) which recounts the stories of many remarkable Buddhists in Thailand in the 19th and 20th centuries.

These great Dharma farers were characterised by unremitting faith in the Three Jewels and unstained morality. Their practise of the first precept was particularly outstanding. It would appear that many of them were probably more than Stream Entrants. According to the Sangiti Sutta in the Digha Nikaya you can recognise a Stream Entrant by four characteristics: 1. Unwavering confidence in the Buddha. 2. Unwavering confidence in the Dharma. 3. Unwavering confidence in the Sangha and 4. Being possessed of morality or as the text says "he is possessed of morality dear to the noble ones, unbroken, without defect, unspotted, without inconsistency, liberating, praised by the wise, uncorrupted, and conducive to concentration". Elsewhere it says that a Stream Entrant will confess any breaches of Precepts immediately. (Kosambiya Sutta, Majjhima Nikaya 48(11)). However it is not easy to tell whether another person is spiritually developed or not; externals such as behaviour and speech can tell you something but not everything.

There is a Sutta in the Numerical Discourses entitled 'How to judge a person's character' and here's what it says: " Four facts about a person, O monks, can be known from four circumstances. What are these four? By living together with a person his virtue can be known, and this too only after a long time, not casually; by close attention, not without attention; by one who is wise, not by one is stupid. By having dealings with a person his integrity can be known, and this too only after a long time, not casually; by close attention, not without attention; by one who is wise, not by one who is stupid. In misfortune a person's fortitude can be known, and this too only after a long time, not casually; by close attention, not without attention; by one who is wise, not by one who is stupid.

By conversation a person's wisdom can be known, and this too only after a long time, not casually; by close attention, not without attention; by one who is wise, not by one who is stupid." (Numerical Discourses of the Buddha, Nyanaponika & Bodhi, No. 88) If you really want to tell whether someone is a stream entrant, you have to develop attentiveness and wisdom and then you need to live with them, work with them (have dealings with), be around them at times when things are going badly and be in communication with them.

It is not an easy matter to judge another person's character or the nature of their spiritual development. You need to have substantial experience of them, but perhaps more importantly you need to know yourself, so that your view of someone else isn't just a projection of the unconscious contents of your own mind. This is what I think is meant by a wise person or an attentive person. The Arya Sangha is a very important level of Sangha. This is where the Dharma is embodied, where the Dharma is kept alive in its essential spirit. This is the Sangha that we need to create among ourselves.

If we are intent on finding Stream Entrants or realised gurus or great spiritual beings we are probably engaged in the business of looking for a saviour. But Buddhism is the wrong place to look for saviours. The Buddha never claimed to be a saviour; he only claimed to be one who points out the path. The Arya Sangha can do no more. If we put people up on pedestals and worship them and try to turn them into saviours, we will only be disappointed. Nobody can save us. Nobody can live our life for us. Our spiritual friends are part of the conditions which help us to make an effort with spiritual practice but the effort is all our own. We can draw inspiration from the lives of others, past and present, but we have to act from that inspiration.

We need to become Stream Entrants. In that way we become a refuge unto ourselves. Sangha, or spiritual community is not an organisation, not even an ecclesiastical organisation. It is a common response to the Ideal, a shared response and a shared practice. It is being on same wavelength. It is something dynamic, something that happens, something that people do. It is not a fixed thing. We can have labels, such as Bhikku or Lama or Dharmachari/ini or Mitra or Order Member, but these are just labels. Spiritual community transcends labels; spiritual community is the actual experience of a 'coincidence of wills', an experience of resonance with the spiritual aspirations and spiritual endeavours of others. I think it is best to think of spiritual community or Sangha as a practice rather than as an institution that you become a member of. Membership is a completely unhelpful metaphor. Sangha is something you do rather than an organisation you belong to.

It is something you practise both in public and in private. You come across this phrase in the Pali canon in relation to harmony between monks; harmony is maintained and lost because of what they do and say and think 'both in public and in private'. Here's what the Sangiti Sutta says about the practice of spiritual community: " Six things are conducive to communal living. As long as monks both in public and in private show loving kindness to their fellows in acts of body speech and thought,.... share with their virtuous fellows what ever they receive as a rightful gift, including the contents of their alms bowls, which they do not keep to themselves,... keep consistently, unbroken and unaltered those rules of conduct that are spotless, leading to liberation, praised by the wise, unstained and conducive to concentration, and persist therein with their fellows both in public and in private,... continue in that noble view that leads to liberation, to the utter destruction of suffering, remaining in such awareness with their fellows both in public and in private."

There is this interesting repetition of the phrase "in public and in private" which reinforces the idea that spiritual community is a practice. In this case it is a practice of loving kindness, generosity, ethics and right view. The text goes on to say how problems arise in the spiritual community and by implication tells us what we need to avoid: " Six roots of contention: here, (a) a monk is angry and bears ill will, he is disrespectful and discourteous to the Teacher, the Dhamma and the Sangha, and does not finish his training. He stirs up contention within the Sangha, which brings woe and sorrow to many, with evil consequences, misfortune and sorrow for devas and humans. If, friends, you should discover such a root of contention among yourselves or among others, you should strive to get rid of just that root of contention. If you find no such root of contention, then you should work to prevent its overcoming you in future. Or (b) a monk is deceitful and malicious,...(c) a monk is envious and mean,...(d) a monk is cunning and deceitful,....(e) a monk is full of evil desires and wrong views,...(f) a monk is opinionated, obstinate and tenacious.

If, friends, you should discover such a root of contention among yourselves or among others, you should strive to get rid of just that root of contention. If you find no such root of contention then you should work to prevent its overcoming you in future." This points to the sort of practice we need to undertake if we want to create a spirit of Sangha among ourselves. To put it more positively we need to cultivate goodwill and be respectful to the Three Jewels and to our teachers.

We need to be honest and kindly and we need to forgive others and give freely. We need to be open in our dealings with each other. We need to study and discuss so that we develop right views about the nature of existence. We need to hold our opinions lightly and be less attached to them. We can be too literal-minded about spiritual community or Sangha. We can start to expect the ideal of spiritual community to manifest around us all the time, because of what we have read or heard.

But in order to stay on the path of Dharma, to keep our feet on the ground, we have to be able to hold in our minds and hearts the twin realities of a spiritual community that is imperfect, inadequate, stumbling and struggling and a spiritual community which is the embodiment of the Bodhisattva Ideal-a manifestation of the compassion of Avolokitesvara. These two realities are the same Reality-one is trapped in time and the literal mindedness of self-centredness and the other is free of the limitations of time and always creating itself anew in the free space of imagination.

Because we can imagine, we can respond to ideals-ideals motivate us to great endeavour as we try to realise in time and space what we have intuited. Ideals activate our deep imagination, they move us and rouse our energies and from that grows the urge, even the need, to follow the spiritual path and undergo the trials and struggles that are an inevitable part of the journey from the unawakened state to the Awakened state, from unawareness to full awareness. Sometimes it seems that the biggest trial we meet on the spiritual path is the people around us-it can seem that we would be much better off going it alone-perhaps with access to a kindly teacher whenever we needed advice.

We can feel that we would be better off without all the emotional messiness of our interaction with others on the path. But without communication with others on the path there would be no path. The path is not distinct from the practitioners and it is the communication between practitioners that keeps the Dharma alive and fully embodied, both as the way of compassion and the way of Wisdom. To progress spiritually we have to move beyond all self-centredness and it is in the practice of creating and maintaining spiritual community that ego transcendence is most potently and directly approached. We can be hindered by having expectations that ourselves and others maintain high standards of perfect ethics, meditation and wisdom all the time.

But if we are to progress we must first accept what is already there in our experience and become thoroughly familiar with the landscape of our own mind-valuing all that is worthwhile and precious there.

This is quite a crucial point-we must learn to recognise what is already of spiritual, psychological and utilitarian value in our lives and in the lives of others. From this basis of recognising and appreciating what is of value in ourselves, in others and in situations we can proceed to change or improve things, but we need this foundation of appreciation or our efforts to improve will be perverted.

There is a temptation to rush in with 'off the peg' ideas to improve ourselves or others or situations without taking the time to appreciate fully what is already there. We can expect ourselves and others to be imperfect. We can expect the spiritual community to be imperfect, we can expect Order members to be imperfect, we can expect the situations and institutions we create to be imperfect, but this need not blind us to what is of value there, what potential beauty and transcendence is there. Ideals are essential.

Imagination, the higher faculty of human consciousness, demands and creates ideals. Our intuition and imagination responds to ideals and we need to use our reason and experience to keep a perspective that includes the highest ideals and also recognises and appreciates the actual situation and its potential. We can pursue perfection but not expect perfection. We can expect imperfection but not pursue imperfection. This attitude will help us maintain a realistic perspective on our spiritual efforts and on our relationships with others. We can be realistic about the spiritual community while at the same time understanding and responding to the ideal of the spiritual community-the ideal of compassion in action.

NO CHOICE

Perhaps the greatest issue facing us in the world today is how to stop destroying the planet and how to begin to reverse some of the damage we have already done. One of the reasons we have done this to ourselves and to our home, the planet Earth, is because we, the human race, have been and continue to be ignorant of the connections between things, ignorant of how all life is interconnected and interdependent.

We have been ignorant of the very existence of an ecosystem. And it would be a great mistake for us to continue this ignorance into our search for solutions. It would be a mistake for us to think of environmentalism as concerned with a particular aspect of life. It would be a mistake to think that environmental issues were separate from issues of war or poverty or economics or politics or leisure or work or spiritual life. To think of environmental issues as separate in that way would be to continue the ignorance that has brought us into this plight in the first place.

The social, the spiritual and the ecological are not separate spheres of knowledge and activity, they are intimately and irrevocably interconnected and it is ignorance of this that leads us to behave in ways that are destructive to the planet and therefore destructive to ourselves. This ignorance comes about because human beings have developed self-reflexive consciousness. We are aware and we are aware that we are aware.

This consciousness, which is what distinguishes us from the animals, is our greatest asset, and our greatest gift and perhaps our greatest curse. Because of this consciousness of self there is a consciousness of other and a consciousness of insecurity in relation to other. The consciousness of self is crude, rudimentary even, and is closely identified with the body, with things, with people as things and with a rigid world view. This self is constantly buffeted by the winds of change externally and internally by the primitive forces of survival and reproduction. So a sense of insecurity is an inevitable accompaniment of emerging self-consciousness. As Subhuti says in The Buddhist Vision "the rudimentary self or immature ego tries to find security by using the same instincts as those by which the animal preserves itself.

Just as the animal hunts for the food which will nourish its organism, so the ego tries to possess those things it considers as securing its identity. And as the animal will attack and destroy whatever threatens its survival, so the ego seeks to destroy whatever undermines its integrity. Aided and amplified by the human power of imagination, these reactions can reach the monstrous proportions of ruthless empire-building and of mass destruction through war."

So the immature ego is ignorant of interconnection and experiences itself as separate, and as fixed and unchanging. This according to Buddhism is the basic spiritual ignorance, experiencing ourselves as separate and as fixed and unchanging. It is this basic spiritual ignorance that gives rise to the greed for possessions and people to give us a sense of security and it is this basic spiritual ignorance which gives rise to hatred and a violent rejection of anything that appears to threaten this separate fixed and unchanging self.

Here we can see the source of all human conflict, the source of consumerism, the source of overpopulation, the source of our blind destruction of our own environment. This is what is depicted at the centre of the Tibetan Wheel of Life. There are three animals, a cock, a snake and a pig biting each other's tails and going round and round in circles. The cock symbolises greed, the snake hatred and the pig ignorance.

They symbolise the animal within us which is covered over with a thin veneer of civilisation. Animals of course are not destructive; it is only the animal in conjunction with self-consciousness that is destructive. So this picture is not saying anything about animals, it is a mirror for us to look into and if we are honest we will recognise, perhaps with the shock, that what we see is our own inner self, motivated by greed for possessions, for sex, for status, motivated by aversion to discomfort or criticism and motivated by the yearning for security. This is what the first circle on the Wheel of Life shows.

It is directly confronting us with our spiritual ignorance and spiritual immaturity. Because we are dealing with symbolism here it is perhaps better not to or over conceptualise. Concepts can become a barrier between us and the truth. It is better just to look in the mirror and see what we see; a cock, a snake and a pig; pecking, strutting, crawling, hissing, rooting, snuffling animals. However we are self conscious, we are human beings and that spark of consciousness is what can save us from the excesses of ignorance. We have the choice to eat from the fruit of the tree of knowledge, to borrow an image from elsewhere.

We have the choice to do something with our awareness. What we can do with our awareness is develop it. We can evolve further. We can make the choice to evolve our awareness and dissolve the fetters of ignorance, neurotic greed and hatred. We can embark on what has been called the path of the higher evolution, that is the evolution of consciousness or awareness.

This is what the spiritual life is about, you could say this is what the truly human life is about and this is the long term and fundamental solution to the problem of human destructiveness. This is the radical solution in that it goes to the roots of the problem.

The second circle on the Wheel of Life is about this choice we have. A choice we make whether we want to or not because even doing nothing is a choice. This circle of the Wheel is divided into two segments, one white and one black. In the black segment, naked and anguished men and women tumble downwards tormented by demons, in the white segment men and women wearing bright garments and performing various benign activities are ascending.

The message of this section of the Wheel of Life is that we experience the consequences of our actions. This is what is known in Buddhism as the law of Karma, a much used and often misunderstood term. To understand what Karma is we need to understand a very fundamental Buddhist teaching, the teaching of conditionality. After the Buddha's Enlightenment experience he tried to communicate what he had seen and understood in many different ways.

One of the ways he used to explain his insight is formulated as the law of conditionality, which very simply states that everything arises in dependence upon conditions. In the texts it says "this being that becomes, from the arising of this that arises. This not being that does not become, from the ceasing of this that ceases." so everything comes into being in dependence upon preceding conditions. This applies to everything: a thought, a giraffe, a mountain, a war, a planet, a universe. So this would appear to be a very obvious and simple assertion, that everything arises in dependence upon conditions. However, simple and obvious as it may seem, it is the most fundamental teaching of Buddhism and it has vast implications. Karma is just one kind of conditionality.

There are five kinds; there is conditionality on the inorganic level, the level covered more or less by the laws of physics. There is conditionality on the organic level, the level of biology. There is conditionality on the lower mental level involving such things as perceptions and instincts.

Then there is conditionality on the level of intentional action which is the Karmic level and above that is the transcendental, Dharmic level of conditionality. The reason I have enumerated this rather technical list is simply to make the point that Karma does not explain everything that happens to us.

There are a multitude of conditions at work all the time and it is impossible to separate out what results from our own intentional actions and what results from other kinds of conditionality. So we need to beware of simplistic understandings of Karma. It is not a model of linear cause and effect and it is not an exhaustive explanation of everything that happens to everyone. Everything arises in dependence upon conditions but not all conditions are Karmic.

Put simply Karma is intentional action. Buddhism teaches an ethics of intention. Traditional ethical systems in the West speak in terms of 'good' and 'bad'.

Buddhism doesn't think in terms of good and bad actions. It focuses instead on the intention behind the action. Indeed the terms good and bad are alien to Buddhist ethical teaching, instead we use the terms skilful and unskilful. A skilful or ethical action is one that arises out of a mind that is loving, generous and wise and an unskilful or unethical action is one that arises out of a mind that is selfish, hateful and ignorant. Actions are understood to be of thought, speech and body. So the law of Karma states that unskilful actions have negative consequences and skilful actions have benign and positive consequences.

Difficulties, suffering and unhappiness which we experience may be due to our unskilfulness in the past i.e. may be due to our past Karma, or may be due to other conditions.

Happiness and good fortune may be due to our skillfulness in the past, i.e. may be due to our past Karma, or to other conditions. But the importance of the law of Karma is not that it may explain our present circumstances or help us to analyse the past. The importance of the law of Karma is that it allows us to shape the future and, because all things are interconnected, how we shape our own future inevitably affects others and even the whole planet. Skilful or ethical action of thought, word and deed is the best way to create a happy and satisfying life.

Skilful action is based in mental states of kindness, generosity and wisdom which are by nature expansive, outgoing and compassionate.

This has a beneficial effect on everybody we encounter and on all the creatures and plant life. When we are experiencing kindness, love, generosity and wisdom we do not harm the world around us, we enjoy and protect it. So the choice we have to make is whether to embark on the difficult task of overcoming our natural instinct to seek security for our fragile ego sense or go beyond that natural instinct by deliberately evolving consciousness that is expansive and self-less.

It would seem that the obvious answer would be to say yes, lets go for it. However that is not a choice that the majority of people make. Most people decide to stay within the confines of their narrow self interest and seek as much security as they can from the world around them. This is because the spiritual path, the path of the higher evolution of consciousness, is truly difficult. It is not the work of a day or a week or year but of twenty, thirty, or more years and even then the fruits are gathered slowly.

The truly spiritual life goes against the whole trend and logic of ordinary life. I have to make the effort, I have to change, I have to be transformed even, but ultimately it is not about any acquisition for me, not even the acquisition of wisdom. Certainly we must use our natural self interest to get started. We can be legitimately motivated by a desire for happiness and well-being. But ultimately all self-centredness is transcended, and our sense of self and other is radically transformed, so that to act in the interests of others is no different from acting in the interests of self. This is something that can be understood intellectually, but intellectual understanding is not sufficient to sustain consistent effort over many years.

We need to have a heart response to the possibilities open

to us, the possibilities of great wisdom and compassion that transcend all hankering after security all desire for personal gain, status, happiness even.

We need to have a heart response to the ideal of becoming more truly human so that we come to value co-operation above competition, to value simplicity above wealth, value harmony above gain, value peace above revenge, and the welfare of all beings above our own life.

We need to have a heart response because the heart or the emotions are where our energy is where our motivation is and we will need energy and motivation to make progress on the spiritual path.

Because if we are not motivated strongly enough we will not be able to overcome the many obstacles and struggles that we will inevitably meet along the way. For instance we will want to meditate but may get discouraged when we experience nothing but distraction for weeks or months on end. We will want to be loving and kind but may get discouraged when we meet people, especially Buddhists, were not nice kind people and who perhaps don't even like us.

We will want to be wise but may get discouraged when nobody wants to listen to our wisdom and they even laugh of us. We will want to be ethical but may get discouraged when others take advantage of us.

We will want to be more aware but may get discouraged when we become more aware and realise that we are not as good and truthful and kind as we liked to believe. We will want to transcend selfishness but may get discouraged by the tenacity of our egotism. Spiritual life is not easy, it is not for the faint-hearted. It is a tough choice but it is worthwhile and it works.

The alternative is to continue to seek security and happiness in ways that cannot ever deliver happiness and security. It may be difficult to make progress on a spiritual path but wisdom, happiness and compassion do arise in dependence upon the effort made. The mundane path of material success and status may appear easier but it is an illusion from top to bottom and it only brings sorrow and pain. This doesn't need any great elucidation, it is plain to see all around us and it is evident in the history of the human race down through all the generations.

The great difference that has occurred over the last couple of centuries is that the world has become smaller due to the advances in technology and the human race is capable of massive destructiveness also due to the advances in technology. So our choice to pursue the life of material gain, power and status has greater implications now than ever before.

And those implications are becoming more visible in such things as climate change, radioactive waste, weapons of mass destruction, large scale poverty and starvation and overpopulation.

The implications of choosing a life of awareness, simplicity, ethical behaviour and compassion for all sentient life are also greater than ever before because of the possibilities of global communication and because of the spiritual vacuum at the heart of the world.

When we choose a life of spiritual quest within a Buddhist context, we undertake to live by five specific principles. These are the principle of non-violence, principal of generosity, the principle of contentment, the principle of truthfulness and the principle of awareness. The practice of meditation helps us to live by these principles. The first principle underlies all the other principles and is the cornerstone of the whole edifice of Buddhist philosophy and practice.

This is the principle of non-violence or to put it more positively, the principle of love. This love is what we call Metta, a love that is sustained, consistent, spontaneous and seeks no reward.

This principle has implications for every aspect of our lives; most obviously it implies cooperative, forgiving and kindly relations with other people, even those we disagree with or dislike. So it rules out revenge, it rules out prejudice, it rules out persecution, it rules out discrimination, it rules out character assassination, it rules out slander, it rules out doing anything to others that they don't wish us to do.

It rules out all kinds of manipulation and exploitation. All of these things appear in gross forms in the world around us, but as we become more ethically sensitive we will discover their more subtle forms in our own hearts and minds.

We will begin to notice the edge of competitiveness or malice in our humour, we will begin to notice the subtle emotional blackmail between lovers, we will notice all the little ways we have of undermining the achievement of others and so on. Here we find our working ground and it is here in our everyday relations with others that we can begin the process of cultivating a compassionate mind.

The principle of non-violence has implications beyond our relations with other people. It applies to our relations with all living things: animals, birds, insects, trees, flowers etc. Before the Chinese invasion in 1950, Tibet was a safe haven for wildlife, and vast herds of antelope and musk deer roamed the plains together with bears, wolves, foxes and wild sheep.

But all that has changed now. The American photographer and author Galen Rowell in his essay" The Agony of Tibet", writes, "the invaders made a sport of shooting indiscriminately at wildlife.

In 1973, Dhondub Choedon, a Tibetan now in exile in India, reported that "Chinese soldiers go on organised hunts using machine guns. They carry away the meat in lorries and export the musk and furs to China".

Important habitat for vast herds of animals was soon over grazed as the Chinese forced nomadic families into communes to raise livestock for export instead of their own subsistence. Tibetans, including the children, were forced to kill 'unnecessary animals' such as moles and marmots that vied with humans for grain and dug up valuable grazing land.

Children were given a qouta for small animals to kill that, if not met, resulted in beatings and other forms of punishment." It is so sad to think of the children being conditioned to kill animals. A stark illustration of how totally different a materialistic outlook is from a spiritual and non-violent outlook.

The principle of non-violence or love extends also tc our attitude to the natural world.

The Thai monk Prayudh Payutto has said that it is best to avoid using the word 'environment' in our concerns for ecology. He feels the word 'environment' betrays its origins in Western attitudes that separate human beings from the rest of nature. Nature includes us. Ecology includes us.

When we really begin to understand and see this then we see that the effort we make to transform ourselves is ecological work and that all our activities have ecological implications. If a river dries up it is relatively easy to see the ecological implications. If human hearts dry up the ecological implications are far greater.

We must keep our hearts moist with the life-giving waters of love. Prayudh Payutto has written an essay entitled "Buddhist solutions for the 21st century". In it he states that modern human civilisation is in the grip of three harmful and tenaciously held views, these are: "1. The perception that mankind is separate from nature, that mankind must control, conquer, or manipulate nature according to his desires. 2. The perception that fellow human beings are not fellow human beings. Rather than perceiving the common situations or experiences shared among all people, human beings have tended to focus on the differences between themselves. 3. The perception that happiness is dependent on an abundance of material possessions.

The first perception is an attitude toward nature; the second perception is an attitude toward fellow human beings; the third perception is an understanding of the objective of life." He goes on to say that for a human beings to live happily there must be freedom on three levels: physical freedom, social freedom, and inner freedom.

Inner freedom is the ability to live happily and contentedly within ourselves without needing to manipulate and exploit the world around us. Without inner freedom human happiness is totally dependent on manipulation of the external environment and social exploitation. So this inner freedom, which is freedom from neurotic craving, freedom from hatred and freedom from spiritual ignorance is essential to the ecology of our planet. Without this inner freedom we are at the mercy of forces which push us into over-consumption and violent competition and a search for happiness and security where happiness and security cannot be found. These are some of the implications of this first principle of Buddhism, the principle of non-violence.

The other four principles are, as I said, based on this one. The principle of generosity extends the principle of love into our relationship to property and possessions. Generosity is basically an attitude to possessions, property and money which sees sharing and giving as more important than acquiring and owning. It is an attitude that holds things lightly, regarding ourselves as only temporary owners of whatever we have. In fact it is even better if we can see ourselves not as owners but as stewards, we are simply looking after something until it passes on to someone else.

The Buddha said that a strong possessiveness about things or people lead to suffering; all things are impermanent and the stronger we hold on to them the more painful is the inevitable letting go. This applies to everything including our own body and sense of identity.

The principle of generosity runs completely counter to what has been called the 'religion of consumerism', with its scriptures and liturgies dedicated to exciting greed and its places of worship designed to entice us to acquire things we neither need nor want. Consumerism could be said to be the dominant ethic in the developed world today and this makes the principle of generosity all the more radical. Generosity as a practice in a society and world which is dedicated to its opposite is not an easy practice.

To develop a truly generous attitude, an attitude of non-ownership, non-possession, non-acquiring, an attitude of sharing, stewardship and giving requires a big effort to overcome the constant conditioning and brainwashing that we are subjected to and have been subjected to since childhood.

Another Thai monk, Sulak Sivaraksa, writes "consumerism

supports those who have economic and political power by rewarding their hatred, aggression, and anger. And consumerism works hand-in-hand with the modern educational system to encourage cleverness without wisdom.

We create delusion in ourselves and call it knowledge. Until the schools reinvest their energy into teaching wholesome, spiritual values instead of reinforcing the delusion that satisfaction and meaning in life can be found by finding a higher-paying job, the schools are just cheerleaders for the advertising agencies, and we believe that consuming more, going faster, and living in greater convenience will bring us happiness.

We don't look at the tremendous cost to ourselves, to our environment, and to our souls. Until more people are willing to look at the negative aspects of consumerism, we will not be able to change the situation for the better.

Until we understand the roots of greed, hatred, and delusion within ourselves, we will not be free from the temptations of the religion of consumerism, and we will remain stuck in this illusory search for happiness." The third principle is the principle of contentment and this is traditionally related to our sexual activity.

On the one hand we are enjoined to refrain from any form of exploitation or manipulation to satisfy our sexual desires and on the other hand we are encouraged to practise contentment with our current sexual status, instead of constant neurotic seeking after new experiences. Ultimately this principle aims at what is referred to as a state of stillness, simplicity and contentment which frees us to a large extent from any neurotic dependence on sex.

For most of us this principle will in practice mean trying not to use subtle, or even not so subtle, manipulation or emotional blackmail to get others to behave as we want them to and it will also mean meditating to attain to more tranquil and contented states of mind. The fourth principle of Buddhist ethics is truthfulness. Truthfulness is essential to the functioning of any society. Without truthfulness there can be no trust and without trust human relations fall apart and we are left with an atmosphere of suspicion and hatred.

Truthfulness as an ethical principle has to be based on loving kindness and not used as a weapon to hurt others. And truthfulness, like all these ethical principles, begins with ourselves.

We need to be honest with ourselves about what we think, what we feel, what we do and what we say. To be honest with oneself is not necessarily an easy matter, it may entail facing up to unpleasant aspects of our character and it may seriously dent our pride and even possibly put us in the position of needing to apologise to others. Truthfulness means, firstly, being factual in what we say or write.

It also means steering clear of exaggeration for effect. Exaggeration is one of the great building bricks of egotism. Truthfulness means not understating things and it means not deliberately omitting relevant information. Omissions can distort a narrative to the point of falsehood. And of course, truthfulness means not deliberately lying. When we tamper with the truth it is usually because we want to be seen in a particular light or we want to gain some advantage: we want to be liked, we want to be popular and bending the truth can seem to be an easy way to get attention and approval or get whatever we want.

Of course if we do that habitually the person who gets attention and approval will be a fiction and in our hearts we will be lonelier than ever. For friendship to exist, for any loving human relationships to exist, there has to be honesty, otherwise we only have fictions relating to fictions, facades relating to facades, which is, to say the least, unsatisfactory.

The fifth principle of Buddhist ethics is the principle of awareness or mindfulness. You could say that awareness is just as fundamental as love.

We need awareness that is saturated with love and compassion and our love and compassion needs to be as aware as possible. Love and compassion without awareness can degenerate into sentimentality and pity and awareness without love can be cold and alienated. So these two qualities, love and awareness, need to be developed in tandem.

That is why we teach the two meditation practices, Mindfulness of Breathing and the Metta Bhavaṇa. The Mindfulness of Breathing cultivates awareness and the Metta Bhavana practice develops loving kindness. Awareness begins with ourselves.

We need to become more aware of our bodies and our actions, we need to become aware of our thoughts and of our emotions. This forms the basis for awareness of other people, awareness of the world around us and ultimately awareness of reality. Sangharakshita has said "awareness is revolutionary. It is revolutionary in that it brings about change of a far reaching and profound nature.

Awareness is naturally expansive. As we become more and more aware become more expansive and full of life. Our energy becomes more focused and more available to us and we become more capable of taking responsibility for our lives. Our normal state is not really one of being aware, we don't really know what we're thinking, feeling, doing or saying and other people are just projections of our unconscious needs, desires and aversions.

We think we're being original when all our views and opinions are received. We think we are independent of influence when our whole life is a constant swinging from one influence to the next.

Awareness gives us the possibility of a genuine individuality and more real relationships with other people. It is revolutionary in that it throws the light of truth onto our lives and wakes us up to what is really going on.

Awareness transforms us. The greater the awareness the more far reaching the transformation and there is no limit to how aware we can become. Buddhahood or Enlightenment could be said to be a state of perfected awareness. Awareness of other people and awareness of the world around us shows us that we are one with humanity and one with nature. It shows us that there is beauty everywhere. Lack of awareness, which is self-centredness, is narrow in perception and sees threat and ugliness everywhere. Awareness sees beauty and optimism even in the most unlikely places.

Awareness of reality is a constant immersion in the reality that all life is process, all life is flux and change, all life is interconnected and interdependent. To be constantly immersed in this vision, to experience this all the time is to be free from all ill-will and possessiveness.

This awareness gives life a quality of lightness and a vast prospective that turns all personal fears and anxieties into absurdities and makes much of what seems important in the world around us look ridiculous.

Perhaps that is why the Dalai Lama is always laughing so heartily! However because of the presence of compassion there is no arrogance or impatience in this awareness. There is rather a tender regard for the suffering of the world which is one's own suffering too when one ceases to separate oneself from others and the world.

These then are the five principles that we undertake to live by when we embark on the spiritual path: non-violence, generosity, contentment, truthfulness and awareness.

These are the principles that we train ourselves in over and over again in order to transcend the poisons of neurotic greed, ill-will and spiritual ignorance, which are the cause of human suffering, both on the personal level and the global level. By training ourselves to live by these principles we contribute to our own well-being and to the well-being of the whole world. Perhaps all this gives some little explanation of the symbolism of the inner two circles of the Wheel of Life.

The Wheel of Life is an ancient symbol over two thousand years old. In one Buddhist text, which dates from 100 years BC, the Buddha is depicted as telling his followers to paint the Wheel of Life at the entrance to every monastery and to have a monk on standby to explain the imagery to visitors and novices. In this essay then we are taking part in an age-old ritual. Buddhism was wiped out in India, so that only one ancient image of the wheel of life survives in India, at the caves of Ajanta.

But Tibet inherited the riches of Indian Buddhism and the Wheel of Life is still very much used in Tibetan temples. It is the nature of symbolism that it cannot be tied down to concepts and that there is always more to say.

The Wheel of Life is a mirror of truthfulness and in it we see ourselves, warts and all. We also see the seeds of our happiness, the seeds of our Enlightenment even.

Sometimes our vanity leads us to the mirror and sometimes our vanity keeps us away from a mirror, but this mirror shatters our vanity so that we can begin to see things as they are really are and so that we can make the choice to embark on the path of the higher evolution of consciousness, which is in reality no choice, because we cannot live by choosing death, we can only live by choosing life.

To conclude here is a little story from 'The Snow Leopard' by Peter Matheson which perhaps illustrates this point quite well, "the Lama of the Crystal monastery appears to be a very happy man, and yet I wonder how he feels about his isolation in the silences of Tsakang, which he has not left in eight years now and, because he's crippled may never leave again.

Since Jang-bu, the interpreter, seems uncomfortable with the Lama or with himself or perhaps with us, I tell him not to inquire on this point if it seems to him impertinent, but after a moment Jang-bu does so.

And this holy man of great directness and simplicity, big white teeth shining, laughs out loud in an infectious way at Jang-bu's question.

Indicating his twisted legs without a trace of self-pity or bitterness-they belong to all of us-he casts his arms wide to the sky and the snow mountains, the high sun and the dancing sheep, and cries, "Of course I am happy here! It's wonderful! Especially when I have no choice!"

"NON-THEISTIC ETHICS" AND "BUDDHISM AND PHENOMENOLGY"

Non-Theistic Ethics

Presenters:

- Edward Ted Slingerland (University of Colorado, Boulder): "Confucius as Virtue Ethicist.
- Presenters Sallie B. King (James Madison University): "From Is to Ought: Natural Law in Theravada"

In her paper, Professor King explores the role of the natural law (Pali: dhamma) in Theravada Buddhist ethics and argues that such an ethics, especially in the interpretation of Phra Prayudh Payutto, supports democratic systems of government and individual rights.

King commences her argument by citing Stephen Buckle's definition of natural law as "an unchanging normative order that is part of the natural world." Thus defined, natural law grounds ethics in the order of the cosmos as the natural rather than supernatural source of normative behavior.

Similarly, King argues, Theravada Buddhism grounds ethical reasoning in the dhamma, which Buddhadasa Bhikkhu paraphrases as "nature itself," "the laws of nature," and "a person's duty to act in accordance with the laws of nature." Payutto further distinguishes between "saccadhamma" as "the conditions... of dhamma" and "cariyadhamma" as the "knowledge pertaining to the application of saccadhamma."

That which harmonizes human behavior with the conditions of reality Buddhadasa calls "sila." Thus defined morality constitues normalcy, that is, harmony with the nature of things, individually and socially. In this sense, Theravada Buddhism replaces the moral extremes of "bad" and "good" with "unskillful" and skillful."

The natural law, specified as the law of conditioned origination (paticca-samuppada) and the law of karma is merely desciptive rather than normative. King argues that Theravada Buddhist ethics differs from the Confucian natural law theory in that the latter is normative in character while the former is predominantly descriptive. The moral imperative as implied in the law of karma explicates this descriptive nature of Theravada ethics. King explains: "if one violates the moral law, or in other words, behaves in an anti-dhammic fashion, it is inevitable that unpleasant consequences will follow, since that is how the universe is constructed."

Morality, then, becomes a matter of conforming to and harmonizing with "the way things are." Metta, love, karuna, compassion, upekkha, equanimity, and samaggi, unity, constitute the appropriate response to the world and its order. Buddhism comprises the observation that humans tend to be in disharmony with nature and experience suffering (dukkha) and provides a "cure" for this problem, as formulated in the four noble truths.

In the second half of her paper, King asks how such an ethics based on the observation of the natural law and an "emphatic, caring, compassionate response" to the human predicament, can support the value of the individual and respond to unjust governments?

She argues that the notions of causal interdependence and harmony with "the way things are" does not justify tyranny as one aspect of the interdependence between government and its people but rather implies "non-egocentricism" and harmony with the natural law (not that of "a particular social system"). To the contrary, a government that does not harmonize with the dhamma violates the natural order itself and "could be easily challenged on that ground, simply for the sake of putting an end to suffering." Even Buddhadasa argues that a violation of the dasarajadhamma (the ten virtues of a ruler) justifies rebellion.

However, while Buddhadasa and Payutto agree that independent critical thinking is necessary, they disagree in their interpretation of the relationship between individuals and society. Buddhadasa, who proposes a "dhammic socialism," argues that liberalism and individualism underestimate the power of human defilements (kleseas) and, therefore, interprets non-egocentricism to privilege society over the individual.

Payutto, on the contrary, argues that the freedom of the individual is interrelated to the freedom of other individuals and thus is important to society. Based on his interpretation of interdependence, Payutto formulates the idea of a "dhammic democracy" which "balances the interests of individual and society."

Thus Buddhadasa seems to emphasize the importance of human defilements, on the one hand, while Payutto stresses human potential, on the other. King argues that Payuttto's view is both "more philosophically adequate" and "truer to the values of Shakyamuni Buddha."

Professor Twiss commences his response by outlining the three different kind of complexities involved in a comparative study.

Comparative studies face methodological complexities insofar as they apply, critique, or dialogue categories across cultures and traditions; they face social complexities insofar as they cross cultural and religious boundaries; and they face the problem of having to negotiate complexities with individual traditions. Since both, Slingerland and King refrain from a cross-cultural critique of ethical categories, Twiss concludes they are "implicitly rather than self-consciously comparative."

Finally, he acknowledges his bias in favour of an interpretation of Buddhist ethics as virtue ethics and thus against King's reading of Theravada Buddhist ethics as a natural law theory.

Nevertheless, he acknowledges that King's interpretation is "plausible" and decides to focus on King's definition of natural law. By the same token, he suggests that while he contends that King's interpretation of Confucianism as natural law ethics is "not utterly off-the-wall," he definitely leans towards an interpretation of Confucian ethics as value ethics.

In general, Twiss argues that Kings definition of the natural law neglects "an emphasis on the role of reason" and " the socio-moral functions of natural law ethics." Central to a natural law theory are general and specific principles which enable a moral life, a social order, and a critique thereof.

These principles are found in "the natural cosmic order," in what it means to be human, by "general consensus," or in divine revelation. Based on this expanded notion of natural law, Twiss argues, that a consideration of the "epistemic warrants" of the Theravada position could highlight "the uniqueness of the Buddhist view" and would engage in a "fruitful dialogue with natural law positions in other traditions." At the heart of this issue, however, lies the question, whether a natural law or a law of karma, for this matter, can serve as the basis for a moral theory if it is purely descriptive and devoid of any normative character. It is the answer to this question which will determine the value of the Buddhist natural law theory for the reconstruction of a Buddhist social ethics.

5

MEDICAL AND SPIRITUAL ETHICS

Abstract: This article provides an introduction to some contemporary issues in medical ethics and the literature which addresses them from a Buddhist perspective. The first part of the article discusses Buddhism and medicine and outlines some of the main issues in contemporary medical ethics. In the rest of the paper three subjects are considered: i) moral personhood, ii) abortion, and iii) death, dying and euthanasia. The bibliographic references appended to the article will be updated periodically (contributions are welcome), and the latest version of the bibliography will be available from the journal's "Resources" directory.

BUDDHISM AND MEDICINE

It has not gone unnoticed that the Buddhist aim of eliminating suffering coincides with the objectives of medicine (Duncan et al, 1981; Soni, 1976). The Buddhist emphasis on compassion finds natural expression in the care of the sick, and according to the Vinaya the Buddha himself stated "Whoever, O monks, would nurse me, he should nurse the sick" (Zysk, 1991:41). Buddhist clergy and laity have been involved with the care of the sick for over two thousand years. The Indian Buddhist emperor Asoka states in his second Rock Edict that provision has been made everywhere in his kingdom for medical treatment for both men and animals, and that medicinal herbs suitable for both have been imported and planted. Birnbaum (1979) and Demieville (1985) provide good general introductions to Buddhism and medicine. Buddhism appears to have played an important role in the evolution of traditional Indian medicine (Zysk, 1991), and there are many parallels between Buddhist medicine, as recorded in the Pali canon, and Aayurveda (Mitra, 1985).

There are short monographs by Haldar on the scientific (1977) and public heath aspects (1992) of medicine in the Pali sources. It is likely that as Buddhism spread through Asia it would have interacted with indigenous medical traditions promoting the cross-fertilization of ideas. Redmond (1992) discusses the relationship of Buddhism to medicine from Theravada and Mahayana perspectives and compares Buddhist and Daoist concepts of disease. Discussions of Tibetan medicine may be found in Clifford (1984), Dhonden (1986), and Rechung (1976), while Ohnuki-Tierney (1984) discusses illness and culture in contemporary Japan. Buddhism's holistic understanding of human nature encourages a psychosomatic approach to the pathology of disease (Soni, 1976), something to which Western medicine is now increasingly attuned. It may also be suggested that the Buddhist philosophy of origination in dependence is both a fruitful diagnostic model and a philosophy which encourages a preventive approach to healthcare. However, disquiet has been voiced recently about how natural" certain forms of traditional Buddhist medicine are-notably the Tibetan "black pill"-some recipes for which specify rhinoceros horn and bear-bile among the ingredients (Leland, 1995).

MEDICAL ETHICS

Despite Buddhism's long association with the healing arts, little attention has been paid to the ethical issues which arise from the practice of medicine. A small number of monographs provide introductions to the issues and dilemmas which arise in medical practice. These are Ratanakul (1986), Nakasone (1990) and Keown (1995), and these volumes should be consulted in conjunction with the sources listed under the specific subject-headings below. Also relevant is the unpublished Masters thesis by Shoyu Taniguchi (1987a). For general discussions in the periodical literature see Taniguchi (1987b), Mettanando (1991), and Ratanakul (1988; 1990). A useful discussion of Buddhism in terms of the "four principles" approach to medical ethics developed by Beauchamp and Childress (1989) is provided by Robert Florida (1994). The Encyclopedia of Bioethics contains articles on medical ethics in India (Jaqqi, 1987), Asia (Unschuld, 1987), and Japan in the nineteenth century (Kitagawa, 1987). Also on Japan see Umezawa (1988). On medical ethics in imperial China see Unschuld (1979) and on Thailand Violette Lindbeck (1984) and Ratanakul (1988; 1990).

The principal issues to be addressed in contemporary medical ethics may be summarised as moral personhood (the question of who is and who is not entitled to moral respect), abortion, embryo experimentation, genetic engineering, consent to treatment, resource allocation, defining death, organ transplantation, living wills, the persistent vegetative state, and euthanasia. Little systematic attention has yet been directed to these subjects by Buddhist practitioners or scholars, and some subjects have not been discussed at all from a Buddhist perspective. The arrangement of the topics below is neither comprehensive nor final. It is inevitable there will be overlap between the sections, and items which appear under one category may contain discussion of issues or principles which have broader relevance. At this time, however, it seems useful to identify three groups of issues and related literature. These concern: moral personhood, issues surrounding life at its beginning, and issues surrounding life at its end. There is insufficient literature on resource-allocation, socio-economic issues, or other questions about general medical practice to justify a category on those topics in this review. There are signs, however, that a Buddhist perspective on certain aspects of medical treatment is beginning to appear, for example Epstein (1993) and Kabat-Zinn's (1990, 1994) integration of Buddhist meditation into medical practice, and the growing literature on Buddhism and social justice, such as Jones (1989) and Sizemore and Swearer (1993).

MORAL PERSONHOOD

Personhood is both a central problem for Buddhist ethics and Western medical ethics, and consequently a very promising area for a dialogue between the two. The problem for Buddhist ethics has always been why should people act ethically if there is no act, no actor and no consequences of action (Collins, 1982). If there is no self or other, how can there be karmic consequences, responsibility, loyalty, or even compassion? Theravadin scholars continue to be divided over whether Buddhism suggests different ethics for those who persist in the illusion of self (kammic ethics) and for those who would transcend the illusion of self (nibbanic ethics). The paradoxical unity of compassionate ethics and nihilistic insight into selflessness has been the central koan of Mahayana Buddhism. Tantra and Zen suggest that the person who sees that there is no "I" is beyond good and evil. For bioethics, struggles over abortion, animal rights and brain death have brought personhood to the forefront (Nelkin, 1983). Opponents of abortion and euthanasia, and advocates for the disabled and animals, on the other hand, assert that mere humanness or merely being alive should bestow a "right to life."

But most bioethicists believe that human beings and animals take on ethical significance to the extent that they are "persons." Some, such as Tooley (1984), would set a standard which would exclude almost all animals, newborns, and the severely retarded or demented. When they specify which elements of sentience and neurological integrity create the illusion of personhood, Western bioethicists begin to sound remarkably Buddhistic: "the awareness of the difference between self and other; the ability to be conscious of oneself over time; the ability to engage in purposive actions" (see, for instance, Fletcher, 1979). At the same time, Western bioethicists have become increasingly troubled by questions about the autonomy, continuity and authenticity of the self. Do anti-depressants create an inauthentic self, or is the self more authentic when its cheerful? Is one respecting a patient's autonomy by respecting the treatment preferences they expressed when healthy, or those they express in the throes of illness? Is it ever possible for a patient to givc truly free and informed consent to treatment?

The most radical challenge to Western ethics of self-determination came in 1984 with the publication of British philosopher Derek Parfit's Reasons and Persons. In this meticulously argued tome, Parfit rejects the existence of continuous selves and concludes that an individual is as discontinuous from itself at some later time as it is from other individuals. Consequently, working for the future welfare of all beings is the same as working for one's own future welfare, since there will be no "I" to benefit in the future.

Bioethicists are only now incorporating Parfit's argument. For instance, researchers find that is impossible to accurately anticipate one's state of mind when one is sick or dying, much less when one is unconscious, undercutting the assumption of continuous personhood undergirding "living wills." From a Buddhist/Parfitian perspective, the search for "real" preferences, central to the identity of the person, is a pointless one. With this acknowledgement, it is less troubling to place our trust in our family and friends to make decisions for our future selves (Kuczewski, 1994). More to the point, a Buddhist/Parfitian would encourage citizens to look beyond their personal preferences in dying, which may be to "die with dignity" but may also be to use as many resources as possible to stave off death, and instead participate in creating a health care system that served the needs of everyone in society.

Another area of potential dialogue is in the efforts to go beyond Cartesian (and Hindu etc.) mind-body dualism in defining life and death. Over the last twenty years the West has slowly accepted that a "person" is dead if their brain is destroyed, even if the body continues to function.

Yet it still troubles many Westerners and Buddhists to declare the permanently unconscious "dead," believing that this is an example of inappropriate mind-body dualism. Other Westerners and Buddhists believe that only a "neocortical" definition of death recognizes the centrality of consciousness and personhood in ethics (Gervais, 1986). More challenging, some Western ethicists have begun to discuss the status of personhood as future technologies make possible the continuity of personality from one body to another (More, 1994). When medical technology offers reincarnation, Buddhist bioethics will certainly flourish.

ABORTION

Buddhism, like all religious and secular philosophies, focuses on two central questions concerning abortion: (a) when does the embryo or fetus acquire the property which makes termination of pregnancy "killing"?; and (b) is termination of a pregnancy, before or after this point, ever justifiable?

While there was a minority tradition in classical Hindu embryology that held that incarnation does not occur till as late as the seventh month (Lipner, 1989), most Buddhist commentators have adopted classical Hindu teachings that the transmigration of consciousness occurs at conception, and therefore that all abortion incurs the karmic burden of killing. Before modern embryology, however, in both Buddhist countries and the West, ideas about conception were scientifically inaccurate, and often associated the beginning of life with events in the third or fourth month of pregnancy (for a discussion of traditional Tibetan embryology, see Dhonden, 1980 and Lecso,1987).

Another problem in early Buddhists' embryology is their assumption that the transmigration of consciousness is sudden rather than gradual. Based on the findings of modern neuro-embryology Buddhists today might maintain that the fetus does not fully embody all five skandhas and the illusion of personhood until after birth; this is the argument developed by most Western ethicists to defend abortion (Tooley, 1984; Flower, 1985; Bennett, 1989).

If the fetus is not yet a fully embodied person, then the karmic consequences of abortion would be even less than the killing of animals, which Buddhism teaches do have moral status. This neurological interpretation of the skandhas may be more consistent with Western Buddhism, which often sees the doctrine of rebirth as peripheral or interprets rebirth metaphorically rather than literally (Batchelor, 1992; King, 1994).

The second question is whether abortion always generates bad karma, or in Western terms, is it ever "justified." This relates to the debate about whether Buddhist ethics are absolutist, utilitarian or "virtuist," i.e. seeing the good in the development of personal qualities. The absolutist would hold that bad karma is incurred from any act of murder, whatever the justifications. The utilitarian would argue that murder can be a compassionate act with positive karmic consequences, taking into account factors such as the health of the fetus or mother, the population crisis, and the readiness of the parents to raise a child.

A virtue-oriented Buddhist would argue that the attitude and motivations of the pregnant woman and her collaborators would determine the ethics of an abortion. Along this line, Tworkov (1992) argues that the karmic skilfulness of an abortion is related to whether the person became pregnant and made her decision to abort without serious mindfulness. From this perspective, aborting a fetus conceived without an effort at contraception would be more karmically significant than an abortion necessitated in spite of contraception.

The much discussed Japanese tolerance for, and ritualization of, abortion appears to combine both utilitarian and virtue approaches. The Japanese believe that abortion is a "sorrowful necessity," and Buddhist temples sell rituals and statues intended to represent parents' apologies to the aborted, and wishes for a more propitious rebirth. The Japanese have reached these accommodations consensually, with little debate, and without discussion of the rights of women or the unborn (LaFleur, 1990, 1992).

The Theravadin commentator Buddhaghosa appears to have combined all three views. He held that killing produces karma jointly through the mental effort and intensity of the desire to kill, and the virtue of the victim (Florida, 1991). Since killing big animals required more effort, and was therefore worse than killing small animals, the karma of feticide would be less than murder of adults, and less in earlier stages of pregnancy. On the other hand, for Buddhaghosa, the karma of feticide would be greater than that of killing villains in self-defence.

Buddhists have thus far given little thought to the third important question, the connection between morality and law, specifically how, and on what grounds, the state should regulate abortion. Some Buddhists have adopted the stance of many moderates in the West: abortion is murder of a person, but women should have that choice (for instance, Imamura, 1984 and Lecso, 1987). Since most Buddhists have no problem with laws to discourage and punish murder in general, implicit in this position is that murder is either justifiable when it conflicts with bodily autonomy or, since few Buddhists would imprison butchers, that fetuses are closer in status to animals. Clearly there is much room for clarification of the relationship between religious ethics and law in pluralistic societies.

Some scholars (such as Ling, 1969, and LaFleur, 1992) have looked beyond the strictly ethical concerns with abortion to examine the cultural aspects of the question. From this perspective it is sometimes pointed out that Buddhism is not "pro-natalist," i.e. does not hold that reproduction is a religious duty-quite the reverse in fact-and does not advocate "family values," at least in the sense that Confucianism did. Buddhist skepticism about family and reproduction was a central cause of Confucian and Shinto persecution. The Sinhalese embrace of contraception and abortion was so enthusiastic in the 1960s, compared to Sri Lanka's Muslims, Catholics and Hindus, that racialist monks began to argue that Buddhists had an obligation to "race-religion-nation" to reproduce.

DEATH, DYING AND EUTHANASIA

The themes of impermanence, decay and death are omnipresent in Buddhist literature. In many Asian cultures Buddhism is identified as the authority par excellence on matters pertaining to death, and is closely linked to the rites and ceremonies associated with the transition from this life to the next. Buddhist literature emphasises the importance of meeting death mindfully since the last moment of one life can be particularly influential in determining the quality of the next rebirth.

General reflections on death will be found in Philip Kapleau's 1972 anthology The Wheel of Death and his 1989 The Wheel of Life and Death. Stephen Levine is the author of several books dealing with the subject of death from a Zen perspective while a contemporary Tibetan perspective is provided by Sogyal Rinpoche's popular Tibetan Book of Living and Dying, Glenn H. Mullin (1986) and John Powers (1995, Ch.10). James Whitehill (1974) discussed what can be learned from the death of the Buddhist masters, and the development of a corpus of "Great Death" stories of various Buddhist masters is examined by LaFleur (1974). Other writings on death in Buddhism include Smart (1968), Amore (1974), and Bowker (1991).

In a 1993 monograph on the subject of death in Buddhism, Becker asserts that the Buddhist tradition, especially in Japan, is very tolerant of suicide and euthanasia. Evidence of this is the Buddha's tolerance of suicide by monks (Wiltshire, 1983) and Japanese stories praising suicide by monks, samurai and laypeople. Becker suggests that Buddhism values self-determination and praises those who decide when and how they will die when they do so in order to have a dignified conscious death. Becker also concludes that the key point is not whether there is still warmth or reflexes (as suggested by some readings of the Visuddhimagga) but whether the patient's skandhas have permanently left, i.e. the patient is permanently unconscious. In other words, Buddhism would endorse a brain death definition of death. On the understanding of death in Japanese religion see also Picken (1977).

A number of issues in medical ethics turn upon the problem of defining death, but few writers have addressed the question of a Buddhist definition of death directly. Only van Loon (1978), Keown (1995), and Mettanando (1991) have argued for a specific definition: van Loon equates death with neocortical death whereas Keown and Mettanando support the "whole brain" criterion.

There has been considerable resistance to the adoption of the brain death standard in Japan, both from the public and within the medical profession, due in no small measure to its association with organ transplantation. The brain death criterion allows organs to be harvested with the minimum delay, thereby enhancing the prospects for a successful transplant.

Japanese tradition, however, requires the performance of rituals over a lengthy period before an individual is regarded as having passed on, and is also reluctant to countenance plundering the bodily organs of future ancestors. Some commentators suggest that public acceptance of brain death is growing as professional groups and universities develop criteria, and as pressure from potential beneficiaries grows. Also, countries such as the Philippines have raised objections to Japanese patients going abroad for transplants rather than building an organ retrieval system of their own.

The best analysis available (in English) of the Japanese situation is Hardacre (1994), but relevant material may also be found in Lock and Honde (1990), Feldman (1988), Becker (1990), and Nudeshima (1991). For discussions of the issue outside of Japan see Ratanakul (1988, 1990), Sugunasiri (1990), and Nakasone (1994).

A more positive attitude towards transplantation is revealed in Tsomo (1993). The author surveyed teachers from many different traditions about their attitudes to donation. All were very positive, and emphasized that the corpse is merely an empty vessel, and that to give of oneself is a great thing, and an act of compassion.

EUTHANASIA

There are no monographs devoted specifically to euthanasia in Buddhism. There are a few periodical articles and the subject is dealt within one or two books. Relevant issues are the distinction between various forms of euthanasia (e.g. "active" and "passive") and the use of narcotics in palliative care which may cloud the mind and interfere with the process of dying (Keown, 1995; Kapleau, 1989; Lecso, 1986; Ratanakul, 1988, 1990).

Kapleau's volume The Wheel of Life and Death (1989) contains a short discussion of euthanasia in conjunction with suicide and it is suggested that Buddhism would reject the practice of either. Ratanakul concurs, reporting "a growing consensus among the Thai public that euthanasia (passive or active) is morally unjustifiable" (1990:27). Keown and Keown

(1995) explore Buddhist and Christian attitudes to euthanasia and suggest both oppose it for similar reasons. Nakasone, however, is of the opinion that "Evidence indicates that Buddhists would favour the 'right-to-die' position" (1990:76). Jennifer Green's short article "Death with Dignity: Buddhism" (1989:40-41) discusses only the practicalities of funeral arrangements and does not mention euthanasia. Neuberger (1987) is likewise concerned with practical as opposed to moral issues.

Euthanasia has been a special feature in two Buddhist magazines, Raft, and Tricycle. London-based Raft, the Journal of the Buddhist Hospice Trust, devoted its No. 2 Winter 1989/90 issue to Euthanasia. Sixteen pages in length it contains short pieces by authors such as Elisabeth Kubler-Ross, Ajahn Sumedho, Dame Cicely Saunders and David Stott, exploring the cases for, against, and in terms of a middle way. A similar range of opinions will be found in the Winter 1992 edition of Tricycle, which contains short articles by Patricia Anderson, Jeffrey Hopkins, Philip Kapleau, Chogyam Trungpa, and an interview with author Stephen Levine.

TRIPITAKA

The Tipitaka (Pali ti, "three," + pitaka, "baskets"), or Pali canon, is the collection of primary Pali language texts which form the doctrinal foundation of Theravada Buddhism. The Tipitaka and the paracanonical Pali texts (commentaries, chronicles, etc.) together constitute the complete body of classical Theravada texts.

The Pali canon is a vast body of literature: in English translation the texts add up to thousands of printed pages. Most (but not all) of the Canon has already been published in English over the years. Although only a small fraction of these texts are available on this website, this collection can be a good place to start. The three divisions of the Tipitaka are:

VINAYA PITAKA

The collection of texts concerning the rules of conduct governing the daily affairs within the Sangha-the community of bhikkhus (ordained monks) and bhikkhunis (ordained nuns). Far more than merely a list of rules, the Vinaya Pitaka also includes the stories behind the origin of each rule, providing a detailed account of the Buddha's solution to the question of how to maintain communal harmony within a large and diverse spiritual community.

SUTTA PITAKA

The collection of suttas, or discourses, attributed to the Buddha and a few of his closest disciples, containing all the central teachings of Theravada Buddhism. (More than nine hundred sutta translations are available on this website.)

The suttas are divided among five nikayas (collections):

- Digha Nikaya-the "long collection"
- Majjhima Nikaya-the "middle-length collection"
- Samyutta Nikaya-the "grouped collection"
- Anguttara Nikaya-the "further-factored collection"
- Khuddaka Nikaya-the "collection of little texts":
    - Khuddakapatha
    - Dhammapada
    - Udana
    - Itivuttaka
    - Sutta Nipata
    - Vimanavatthu
    - Petavatthu
    - Theragatha
    - Therigatha
    - Jataka
    - Niddesa
    - Patisambhidamagga
    - Apadana
    - Buddhavamsa
    - Cariyapitaka

* Nettippakarana (included only in the Burmese edition of the Tipitaka)
* Petakopadesa (" ")
* Milindapanha (" ")

ABHIDHAMMA PITAKA

The collection of texts in which the underlying doctrinal principles presented in the Sutta Pitaka are reworked and reorganized into a systematic framework that can be applied to an investigation into the nature of mind and matter.

VINAYA PITAKA

The Basket of the Discipline

The Vinaya Pitaka, the first division of the Tipitaka, is the textual framework upon which the monastic community (Sangha) is built. It includes not only the rules governing the life of every Theravada bhikkhu (monk) and bhikkhuni (nun), but also a host of procedures and conventions of etiquette that support harmonious relations, both among the monastics themselves, and between the monastics and their lay supporters, upon whom they depend for all their material needs.

When the Buddha first established the Sangha, the community initially lived in harmony without any codified rules of conduct. As the Sangha gradually grew in number and evolved into a more complex society, occasions inevitably arose when a member would act in an unskillful way. Whenever one of these cases was brought to the Buddha's attention, he would lay down a rule establishing a suitable punishment for the offense, as a deterrent to future misconduct. The Buddha's standard reprimand was itself a powerful corrective: It is not fit, foolish man, it is not becoming, it is not proper, it is unworthy of a recluse, it is not lawful, it ought not to be done. How could you, foolish man, having gone forth under this Dhamma and Discipline which are well-taught, [commit such and such offense]?... It is not, foolish man, for the benefit of un-believers, nor for the increase in the number of believers, but, foolish man, it is to the detriment of both unbelievers and believers, and it causes wavering in some.-The Book of the Discipline, Part I, by I.B. Horner (London: Pali Text Society, 1982), pp. 36-37.

The monastic tradition and the rules upon which it is built are sometimes naively criticized-particularly here in the West-as irrelevant to the "modern" practice of Buddhism. Some see the Vinaya as a throwback to an archaic patriarchy, based on a hodge-podge of ancient rules and customs-quaint cultural relics that only obscure the essence of "true" Buddhist practice. This misguided view overlooks one crucial fact: it is thanks to the unbroken lineage of monastics who have consistently upheld and protected the rules of the Vinaya for almost 2,600 years that we find ourselves today with the luxury of receiving the priceless teachings of Dhamma. Were it not for the Vinaya, and for those who continue to keep it alive to this day, there would be no Buddhism.

It helps to keep in mind that the name the Buddha gave to the spiritual path he taught was "Dhamma-vinaya"-the Doctrine (Dhamma) and Discipline (Vinaya)— suggesting an integrated body of wisdom and ethical training. The Vinaya is thus an indispensable facet and foundation of all the Buddha's teachings, inseparable from the Dhamma, and worthy of study by all followers-lay and ordained, alike. Lay practitioners will find in the Vinaya Pitaka many valuable lessons concerning human nature, guidance on how to establish and maintain a harmonious community or organization, and many profound teachings of the Dhamma itself. But its greatest value, perhaps, lies in its power to inspire the layperson to consider the extraordinary possibilities presented by a life of true renunciation, a life lived fully in tune with the Dhamma.

SUTTAVIBHANGA

The Suttavibhanga contains the basic training rules for bhikkhus and bhikkhunis, along with the "origin story" for each one.

These rules are summarized in the Patimokkha, and amount to 227 rules for the bhikkhus, 311 for the bhikkhunis. The Patimokkkha rules are grouped as follows:

- Parajika: rules entailing expulsion from the Sangha (Defeat) (4 for bhikkhus, 8 for bhikkhunis)
- Sanghadisesa: rules entailing an initial and subsequent meeting of the Sangha (13, 17)
- Aniyata (indefinite) rules (2, 0)
- Nissaggiya pacittiya: rules entailing forfeiture and confession (30, 30)
- Pacittiya: rules entailing confession (92, 166)
- Patidesaniya: rules entailing acknowledgement (4, 8)
- Sekhiya: rules of training (75, 75)
- Adhikarana samatha: rules for settling disputes (7, 7)

II. Khandhaka

 * A. Mahavagga-in addition to rules of conduct and etiquette for the Sangha, this section contains several important sutta-like texts, including an account of the period immediately following the Buddha's Awakening, his first sermons to the group of five monks, and stories of how some of his great disciples joined the Sangha and themselves attained Awakening.
 * B. Cullavagga-an elaboration of the bhikkhus' etiquette and duties, as well as the rules and procedures for addressing offences that may be committed within the Sangha.

III. Parivara-A recapitulation of the previous sections, with summaries of the rules classified and re-classified in various ways for instructional purposes.

SUTTA PITAKA

The Basket of Suttas

The Sutta Pitaka, the second division of the Tipitaka, consists of more than 10,000 suttas (discourses) delivered by the Buddha and his close disciples during and shortly after the Buddha's forty-five year teaching career, as well as many additional verses by other members of the Sangha. More than nine hundred sutta translations are available on this website. The suttas are grouped into five nikayas, or collections:

Digha Nikaya

The "Long" Discourses (Pali digha = "long") consists of 34 suttas, including the longest ones in the Canon. The subject matter of these suttas ranges widely, from colourful folkloric accounts of the beings inhabiting the deva worlds (DN 20) to down-to-earth practical meditation instructions (DN 22), and everything in between. Recent scholarship suggests that a distinguishing trait of the Digha Nikaya may be that it was "intended for the purpose of propaganda, to attract converts to the new religion."

Majjhima Nikaya

The "Middle-length" Discourses (Pali majjhima = "middle") consists of 152 suttas of varying length. These range from some of the most profound and difficult suttas in the Canon (e.g., MN 1) to engaging stories full of human pathos and drama that illustrate important principles of the law of kamma (e.g., MN 57, MN 86).

Samyutta Nikaya

The "Grouped" Discourses (Pali samyutta = "group" or "collection") consists of 2,889 relatively short suttas grouped together by theme into 56 samyuttas.

Anguttara Nikaya

The "Further-factored" Discourses (Pali anga = "factor" + uttara = "beyond," "further") consists of several thousand short suttas, grouped together into eleven nipatas according to the number of items of Dhamma covered in each sutta. For example, the Eka-nipata ("Book of the Ones") contains suttas about a single item of Dhamma; the Duka-nipata ("Book of the Twos") contains suttas dealing with two items of Dhamma, and so on.

Khuddaka Nikaya

The "Division of Short Books" (Pali khudda = "smaller," "lesser"), consisting of fifteen books (eighteen in the Burmese edition):

1. Khuddakapatha-The Short Passages

2. Dhammapada-The Path of Dhamma
3. Udana-Exclamations
4. Itivuttaka-The Thus-saids
5. Sutta Nipata-The Sutta Collection
6. Vimanavatthu-Stories of the Celestial Mansions
7. Petavatthu-Stories of the Hungry Ghosts
8. Theragatha-Verses of the Elder Monks
9. Therigatha-Verses of the Elder Nuns
10. Jataka-Birth Stories
11. Niddesa-Exposition
12. Patisambhidamagga-Path of Discrimination
13. Apadana-Stories
14. Buddhavamsa-History of the Buddhas
15. Cariyapitaka-Basket of Conduct
16. Nettippakarana (Burmese Tipitaka only)
17. Petakopadesa (Burmese Tipitaka only)
18. Milindapanha-Questions of Milinda

DIGHA NIKAYA

The Long Discourses

The Digha Nikaya, or "Collection of Long Discourses" (Pali digha = "long") is the first division of the Sutta Pitaka, and consists of thirty-four suttas, grouped into three vaggas, or divisions:

1. Silakkhandha-vagga-The Division Concerning Morality (13 suttas)
2. Maha-vagga-The Large Division (10 suttas)
3. Patika-vagga-The Patika Division (11 suttas)

An excellent modern translation of the complete Digha Nikaya is Maurice Walshe's The Long Discourses of the Buddha: A Translation of the Digha Nikaya (formerly titled: Thus Have I Heard) (Boston: Wisdom Publications, 1987). A fine anthology of selected suttas is Handful of Leaves (Vol. 1), by Thanissaro Bhikkhu (distributed by the Sati Centre for Buddhist Studies).

The translator appears in the square brackets []. The braces {} contain the volume and starting page number in the PTS romanized Pali edition.

- DN 2: Samannaphala Sutta-The Fruits of the Contemplative Life {D i 47} [Thanissaro]. King Ajatasattu asks the Buddha, "What are the fruits of the contemplative life, visible in the here and now?" The Buddha replies by painting a comprehensive portrait of the Buddhist path of training, illustrating each stage of the training with vivid similes.
- DN 9: Potthapada Sutta-About Potthapada {D i 178} [Thanissaro]. The wandering ascetic Potthapada brings to the Buddha a tangle of questions concerning the nature of perception. The Buddha clears up the matter by reviewing the fundamentals of concentration meditation and showing how it can lead to the ultimate cessation of perception.
- DN 11: Kevatta (Kevaddha) Sutta-To Kevatta (Kevaddha) {D i 211} [Thanissaro]. This discourse explores the role of miracles and conversations with heavenly beings as a possible basis for faith and belief. The Buddha does not deny the reality of such experiences, but he points out that-of all possible miracles-the only reliable one is the miracle of instruction in the proper training of the mind. As for heavenly beings, they are subject to greed, anger, and delusion, and so the information they give-especially with regard to the miracle of instruction-is not necessarily trustworthy. Thus the only valid basis for faith is the instruction that, when followed, brings about the end of one's own mental defilements. The tale that concludes the discourse is one of the finest examples of the early Buddhist sense of humor. [This summary provided by Thanissaro Bhikkhu]
- DN 12: Lohicca Sutta-To Lohicca {D i 224} [Thanissaro]. A non-Buddhist poses some good questions: If Dhamma is something that one must realize for oneself, then what is the role of a teacher? Are there any teachers

who don't deserve some sort of criticism? The Buddha's reply includes a sweeping summary of the entire path of practice.

- DN 15: Maha-nidana Sutta-The Great Causes Discourse {D ii 55} [Thanissaro]. One of the most profound discourses in the Pali canon, which gives an extended treatment of the teachings of dependent co-arising (paticca samuppada) and not-self (anatta) in an outlined context of how these teachings function in practice. An explanatory preface is included.
- DN 16: Maha-parinibbana Sutta-The Last Days of the Buddha {D ii 72} [Vajira/Story (complete text) | Thanissaro (chapters 5-6)]. This wide-ranging sutta, the longest one in the Pali canon, describes the events leading up to, during, and immediately following the death and final release (parinibbana) of the Buddha. This colorful narrative contains a wealth of Dhamma teachings, including the Buddha's final instructions that defined how Buddhism would be lived and practiced long after the Buddha's death-even to this day. But this sutta also depicts, in simple language, the poignant human drama that unfolds among the Buddha's many devoted followers around the time of the death of their beloved teacher.
- DN 20: Maha-samaya Sutta-The Great Meeting {D ii 253} [Piyadassi | Thanissaro]. A large group of devas pays a visit to the Buddha. This sutta is the closest thing in the Pali canon to a "who's who" of the deva worlds, providing useful material for anyone interested in the cosmology of early Buddhism.
- DN 21: Sakka-panha Sutta-Sakka's Questions (excerpt) {D ii 263} [Thanissaro]. Śakka, the deva-king, asks the Buddha about the sources of conflict, and about the path of practice that can bring it to an end. This discourse ends with a humorous account about Sakka's frustration in trying to learn the Dhamma from other contemplatives. It's hard to find a teacher when you're a king.

- DN 22: Maha-satipatthana Sutta-The Great Frames of Reference (The Great Discourse on the Foundations of Mindfulness) {D ii 289} [Thanissaro]. This sutta offers comprehensive practical instructions on the development of mindfulness in meditation. The Buddha describes how the development of continuous mindfulness of the four satipatthana ("foundations of mindfulness" or "frames of reference")-mindfulness of the body, of feelings, of the mind, and of mind-objects-can lead ultimately to full Awakening. [The text of this sutta is identical to that of the Satipatthana Sutta (MN 10), except that the Majjhima version omits the exposition of the Four Noble Truths (sections 5a,b,c and d in part D of this version).]
- DN 26: Cakkavatti Sutta-The Wheel-turning Emperor (excerpt) {D iii 58} [Thanissaro]. In this excerpt the Buddha explains how skillful action can result in the best kind of long life, the best kind of beauty, the best kind of happiness, and the best kind of strength.
- DN 31: Sigalovada Sutta-To Sigala/The Layperson's Code of Discipline {D iii 180} [Narada | Kelly/Sawyer/Yareham]. The householder's code of discipline, as described by the Buddha to the layman Sigala. This sutta offers valuable practical advice for householders on how to conduct themselves skillfully in their relationships with parents, spouses, children, pupils, teachers, employers, employees, friends, and spiritual mentors so as to bring happiness to all concerned.
- DN 32: Atanatiya Sutta-The Discourse on Atanatiya {D iii 194} [Piyadassi]. One of the "protective verses" (paritta) that are chanted to this day for ceremonial purposes by Theravada monks and nuns around the world. See Piyadassi Thera's The Book of Protection (Kandy: Buddhist Publication Society, 1999).

MAJJHIMA NIKAYA

The Majjhima Nikaya, or "Middle-length Discourses" of the Buddha, is the second of the five nikayas (collections) of the Sutta Pitaka. This nikaya consists of 152 discourses by the Buddha and his chief disciples, which together constitute a comprehensive body of teaching concerning all aspects of the Buddha's teachings.

An excellent modern translation of the complete Majjhima Nikaya is The Middle Length Discourses of the Buddha: A New Translation of the Majjhima Nikaya, translated by Bhikkhu Nanamoli and Bhikkhu Bodhi (Boston: Wisdom Publications, 1995). The Introduction to that book contains an extraordinary synopsis of the Buddha's teachings in general, and of their expression in the Majjhima in particular. A fine anthology of selected suttas is Handful of Leaves (Vol. 1), by Thanissaro Bhikkhu (distributed by the Sati Centre for Buddhist Studies).

The sutta summaries appearing below that are marked "[BB]" were adapted from Bhikkhu Bodhi's summaries (in The Middle Length Discourses of the Buddha) and are used with permission. Those marked "[TB]" were provided by Thanissaro Bhikkhu.

The translator appears in the square brackets []. The braces {} contain the volume and starting page number in the PTS romanized Pali edition.

- MN 1: Mulapariyaya Sutta-The Root Sequence {M i 1} [Thanissaro]. In this difficult but important sutta the Buddha reviews in depth one of the most fundamental principles of Buddhist thought and practice: namely, that there is no thing-not even Nibbana itself-that can rightly be regarded as the source from which all phenomena and experience emerge.
- MN 2: Sabbasava Sutta-All the Fermentations {M i 6} [Thanissaro]. The Buddha teaches seven methods for eliminating from the mind the deeply rooted defilements (sensuality, becoming, views, and ignorance) that obstruct the realization of Awakening.
- MN 4: Bhaya-bherava Sutta-Fear & Terror {M i 16} [Thanissaro]. What would it take to live in solitude in the wilderness, completely free of fear? The Buddha explains.

- MN 7: Vatthupama Sutta-The Simile of the Cloth {M i 36} [Nyanaponika]. With a simple simile the Buddha illustrates the difference between a defiled mind and a pure mind. [BB]
- MN 8: Sallekha Sutta-The Discourse on Effacement {M i 40} [Nyanaponika]. The Buddha explains how the unskillful qualities in the heart can be eradicated through meditation.
- MN 9: Sammaditthi Sutta-Right View {M i 46} [Nanamoli/Bodhi | Thanissaro]. A discussion of right view demonstrating how the four noble truths, dependent co-arising, and the knowledge that ends mental fermentation all build on the basic dichotomy between skillful and unskillful action.
- MN 10: Satipatthana Sutta-Frames of Reference/ Foundations of Mindfulness {M i 55} [Nyanasatta | Soma | Thanissaro]. The Buddha's comprehensive practical instructions on the development of mindfulness as the basis for insight. [The text of this sutta is identical to that of the Maha-satipatthana Sutta (DN 22), except that the latter contains a more detailed exposition of the Four Noble Truths (sections 5a,b,c and d in part D of that version).]
- MN 11: Cula-sihanada Sutta-The Shorter Discourse on the Lion's Roar {M i 63} [Nanamoli/Bodhi]. The Buddha declares that only through practicing in accord with the Dhamma can Awakening be realized. His teaching is distinguished from those of other religions and philosophies through its unique rejection of all doctrines of self. [BB]
- MN 12: Maha-sihanada Sutta-The Great Discourse on the Lion's Roar {M i 68} [Nanamoli/Bodhi]. The Buddha expounds the ten powers of a Tathagata, his four kinds of intrepidity, and other superior qualities which entitle him to "roar his lion's roar in the assemblies." [BB]
- MN 13: Maha-dukkhakkhandha Sutta-The Great Mass of Stress {M i 83} [Thanissaro]. In deliciously graphic

terms, the Buddha describes the allures and drawbacks of sensuality, physical form, and feeling. What better incentive could there be to escape samsara once and for all?

- MN 14: Cula-dukkhakkhandha Sutta-The Lesser Mass of Stress {M i 91} [Thanissaro]. What mental qualities must be abandoned in order to free oneself of greed, aversion, and delusion? Can painful austerities be used to purify oneself and burn away the karmic fruit of past misdeeds? Through skillful question-and-answer dialogues with the lay follower Mahanama and with a group of Jain ascetics, the Buddha lays these questions to rest.
- MN 18: Madhupindika Sutta-The Ball of Honey {M i 108} [Thanissaro]. A man looking to pick a fight asks the Buddha to explain his doctrine. The Buddha's answer mystifies not only the man, but also a number of monks. Ven. Maha Kaccana finally provides an explanation, and in the course of doing so explains what is needed to bring the psychological sources of conflict to an end.
- MN 19: Dvedhavitakka Sutta-Two Sorts of Thinking {M i 114} [Thanissaro]. The Buddha recounts the events leading up to his Awakening, and describes his discovery that thoughts connected with sensuality, ill-will, and harmfulness do not lead one to Awakening, while those connected with their opposites (renunciation, non ill-will, and harmlessnes) do.
- MN 20: Vitakkasanthana Sutta-The Relaxation of Thoughts {M i 118} [Thanissaro | Soma]. The Buddha offers five practical methods of responding wisely to unskillful thoughts (thoughts connected with desire, aversion, or delusion).
- MN 21: Kakacupama Sutta-The Simile of the Saw {M i 122} [Buddharakkhita (excerpt) | Thanissaro (excerpt)]. The Buddha tells the story of a wise slave who deliberately tests her mistress's patience. The Buddha invokes several memorable similes here to illustrate the correct way to develop patience.

- MN 22: Alagaddupama Sutta-The Snake Simile {M i 130} [Nyanaponika | Thanissaro]. Using two famous similes, the Buddha shows how the development of right view calls for the skillful application both of grasping and of letting-go. The sutta includes one of the Canon's most important expositions on the topic of not-self.
- MN 24: Ratha-vinita Sutta-Relay Chariots {M i 145} [Thanissaro]. Using the simile of a set of relay chariots, Ven. Punna Mantaniputta explains the relationship of the factors of the path to the goal of the holy life. [TB]
- MN 26: Ariyapariyesana Sutta-The Noble Search {M i 160} [Thanissaro]. Most of us spend a good part of our lives looking for happiness in all the wrong places. In this sutta the Buddha recounts the story of his own search and points out where a true and lasting happiness can be found.
- MN 27: Cula-hatthipadopama Sutta-The Shorter Elephant Footprint Simile {M i 175} [Thanissaro]. At what point do you know for sure that the Buddha's awakening was genuine? [TB]
- MN 28: Maha-hatthipadopama Sutta-The Great Elephant Footprint Simile {M i 184} [Thanissaro]. An explanation of the four noble truths, focusing on the aggregate of physical form and showing (1) how all the aggregates are interrelated and (2) how all four noble truths, together with the principle of dependent co-arising, are related to the aggregates. [TB]
- MN 33: Maha-gopalaka Sutta-The Greater Cowherd Discourse {M i 220} [Thanissaro]. Eleven factors that are conducive to spiritual growth, and eleven that are obstructive. (Apart from the preamble, this sutta is identical to AN 11.18.)
- MN 34: Cula-gopalaka Sutta-The Shorter Discourse on the Cowherd (excerpt) {M i 225} [Olendzki]. In this brief excerpt the Buddha urges his monks to cross over to the lasting safety of Nibbana.

- MN 36: Maha-Saccaka Sutta-The Greater Discourse to Saccaka (excerpt) {M i 237} [Thanissaro]. In this excerpt, the Buddha recounts his early meditation practices and austerities that led him finally to discover the path to Awakening.
- MN 39: Maha-Assapura Sutta-The Greater Discourse at Assapura {M i 271} [Thanissaro]. With characteristic clarity and concision the Buddha outlines the full course of training by which a meditator may earn the right to call him-or herself a true contemplative. As presented here, the training begins with conscience and concern for the results of one's actions, and leads progressively onward through the cultivation of virtue, sense-restraint, moderation, wakefulness, mindfulness, alertness, the four jhanas, finally culminating in the realization of the insight knowledges.
- MN 41: Saleyyaka Sutta-The Brahmans of Sala {M i 285} [Nanamoli]. The Buddha explains to a group of brahman householders how one's present actions-by body, speech, and mind-determine one's future fortune.
- MN 43: Mahavedalla Sutta-The Greater Set of Questions-and-Answers {M i 292} [Thanissaro]. Ven. Sariputta answers questions dealing with discernment, right view, and the higher meditative attainments.
- MN 44: Culavedalla Sutta-The Shorter Set of Questions-and-Answers {M i 299} [Thanissaro]. Dhammadinna the nun fields a series of Dhamma questions put to her by her former husband: questions on self-identification, cessation, penetration into the true nature of feeling, and the attainment of Nibbana.
- MN 45: Cula-dhammasamadana Sutta-The Shorter Discourse on Taking on Practices {M i 305} [Thanissaro]. Is something right because it feels right? [TB]
- MN 52: Atthakanagara Sutta-To the Man from Atthakanagara {M i 349} [Thanissaro]. Ven. Ananda describes eleven modes of practice that can lead to the Deathless. (Apart from the preamble, this sutta is identical to AN 11.17.)

- MN 53: Sekha-patipada Sutta-The Practice for One in Training {M i 353} [Thanissaro]. "Consummate in clear-knowing and conduct" is a standard epithet for the Buddha. This sutta explains what it means, and shows that it can be used to describe an arahant as well. [TB]
- MN 54: Potaliya Sutta-To Potaliya (excerpt) {M i 359} [Thanissaro]. Using seven graphic similes for the drawbacks of sensual passions, the Buddha teaches Potaliya the householder what it means, in the discipline of a noble one, to have entirely cut off one's worldly affairs. [TB]
- MN 57: Kukkuravatika Sutta-The Dog-duty Ascetic {M i 387} [Nanamoli]. Act like a dog, and that's what you'll become. Choose your actions with care!
- MN 58: Abhaya Sutta-To Prince Abhaya (On Right Speech) {M i 392} [Thanissaro]. The Buddha explains the criteria for determining whether or not something is worth saying. This discourse is a beautiful example of the Buddha's skill as teacher: not only does he talk about right speech, but he also demonstrates right speech in action.
- MN 59: Bahuvedaniya Sutta-Many Things to be Experienced/The Many Kinds of Feeling {M i 396} [Nyanaponika | Thanissaro]. The Buddha discusses the range of possible pleasures and joys, and concludes by advocating a pleasure that goes beyond feeling. [The text of this sutta is almost identical to that of SN 36.19.]
- MN 61: Ambalatthika-rahulovada Sutta-Advice to Rahula at Mango Stone {M i 414} [Thanissaro]. The Buddha admonishes his son, the novice Rahula, on the dangers of lying and stresses the importance of constant reflection on one's motives. (This is one of the suttas selected by King Asoka (r. 270-232 BCE) to be studied and reflected upon frequently by all practicing Buddhists. See That the True Dhamma Might Last a Long Time: Readings Selected by King Asoka, by Thanissaro Bhikkhu.)

- MN 62: Maha-Rahulovada Sutta-The Greater Exhortation to Rahula {M i 420} [Thanissaro]. The Buddha delivers meditation instructions to his son, the novice Rahula.
- MN 63: Cula-Malunkyovada Sutta-The Shorter Instructions to Malunkya {M i 426} [Thanissaro]. Ven. Malunkyaputta threatens to disrobe unless the Buddha answers all his speculative metaphysical questions. Using the famous simile of a man shot by a poison arrow, the Buddha reminds him that some questions are simply not worth asking.
- MN 66: Latukikopama Sutta-The Quail Simile {M i 447} [Thanissaro]. Fetters are strong, not because of their own tensile strength, but because of the tenacity of our unwillingness to let them go. [TB]
- MN 70: Kitagiri Sutta-At Kitagiri {M i 473} [Thanissaro]. A discourse on the importance of conviction in the Buddhist path. Not only is conviction a prerequisite for listening to the Buddha's teachings with respect, but-as is shown by the unusual discussion here categorizing the types of noble disciples-it can underlie the practice all the way to the Deathless. [TB]
- MN 72: Aggi-Vacchagotta Sutta-To Vacchagotta on Fire {M i 483} [Thanissaro]. The Buddha explains to a wanderer why he does not hold any speculative views. Using the simile of an extinguished fire he illustrates the destiny of the liberated being. [BB] [For more on the use of fire imagery in early Buddhist texts, see the book Mind Like Fire Unbound.]
- MN 74: Dighanakha Sutta-To LongNails {M i 497} [Thanissaro]. A discussion of how to abandon doctrinaire views of radical acceptance, radical rejection, and any combination of the two. [TB]
- MN 75: Magandiya Sutta-To Magandiya (excerpt) {M i 501} [Thanissaro]. In this passage, the Buddha teaches a member of a hedonist sect about the nature of true pleasure and true health. [TB]

- MN 78: Samana-Mundika Sutta-Mundika the Contemplative {M ii 22} [Thanissaro]. The highest attainment is not simply the abandoning of unskillful actions and a reversion to childlike harmlessness. It requires first developing skillful habits and skillful resolves, and then letting them go. [TB]
- MN 82: Ratthapala Sutta-About Ratthapala {M ii 54} [Thanissaro]. A two-part story about the monk who, the Buddha said, was foremost among his disciples in ordaining on the power of pure conviction. In the first part of the story, Ratthapala deals with his parents' opposition to his ordaining, and their attempts, after ordination, to lure him back to lay life. In the second part, he recalls the four observations about the world that inspired him, as a healthy and wealthy young man, to ordain in the first place.
- MN 86: Angulimala Sutta-About Angulimala {M ii 97} [Thanissaro]. A murderous bandit takes refuge in the Buddha, develops a heart of compassion, and becomes an arahant. [TB]
- MN 87: Piyajatika Sutta-From One Who Is Dear {M ii 106} [Thanissaro]. King Pasenadi of Kosala figures prominently in many discourses as a devout follower of the Buddha. In this discourse we learn how-thanks to Queen Mallika's astuteness-the king first became favorably disposed toward the Buddha. [TB]
- MN 90: Kannakatthala Sutta-At Kannakatthala {M ii 125} [Thanissaro]. A case study in how social advantages can be a spiritual liability. The discussion focuses on the factors needed for release-attainable by all people, regardless of caste or race-while the gently satirical frame story shows how the life of a king, or any highly placed person, presents obstacles to developing those factors. [TB]
- MN 95: Canki Sutta-With Canki (excerpt) {M ii 164} [Nanamoli (excerpt) | Thanissaro (excerpt)]. A pompous brahman teenager questions the Buddha about safeguarding, awakening to, and attaining the truth. In

the course of his answer, the Buddha describes the criteria for choosing a reliable teacher and how best to learn from such a person. [TB]

- MN 101: Devadaha Sutta-To Devadaha {M ii 214} [Thanissaro]. The Buddha refutes a Jain theory of kamma, which claims that one's present experience is determined solely by one's actions in past lives, and that the only way to undo the effects of past unskillful actions is to "burn them away" through severe practices of austerity. The Buddha here outlines one of his most important teachings on kamma: that it is both the results of past deeds and present actions that shape one's experience of the present. It is precisely this interaction of present and past that opens up the very possibility of Awakening.
- MN 105: Sunakkhatta Sutta-To Sunakkhatta {M ii 252} [Thanissaro]. The Buddha addresses the problem of meditators who overestimate their progress in meditation. The sutta ends with a warning: anyone who claims enlightenment as license for unrestrained behavior is like someone who fails to follow the doctor's orders after surgery, who knowingly drinks a cup of poison, or who deliberately extends a hand toward a deadly snake. [TB]
- MN 106: Anenja-sappaya Sutta-Conducive to the Imperturbable {M ii 261} [Thanissaro]. Advanced meditation instruction: how the fourth jhana and the formless attainments can be developed and used as a basis for the realization of Nibbana.
- MN 107: Ganaka-Moggallana Sutta-The Discourse to Ganaka-Moggallana {M iii 1} [Horner]. The Buddha sets forth the gradual training of the Buddhist monk and describes himself as a "shower of the way." [BB]
- MN 108: Gopaka-Moggallana Sutta-Moggallana the Guardsman {M iii 7} [Thanissaro]. Ven. Ananda explains how the Sangha maintains its unity and internal discipline after the passing away of the Buddha. [BB]

Interestingly, this sutta also shows that early Buddhist practice had no room for many practices that developed in later Buddhist traditions, such as appointed lineage holders, elected ecclesiastical heads, or the use of mental defilements as a basis for concentration practice. [TB]

- MN 109: Maha-punnama Sutta-The Great Full-moon Night Discourse {M iii 15} [Thanissaro]. A thorough discussion of issues related to the five aggregates. Toward the end of the discussion, a monk thinks that he has found a loophole in the teaching. The way the Buddha handles this incident shows the proper use of the teachings on the aggregates: not as a metaphysical theory, but as a tool for questioning clinging and so gaining release. [TB]
- MN 110: Cula-punnama Sutta-The Shorter Discourse on the Full-moon Night {M iii 20} [Thanissaro]. How to recognize-and become-a person of integrity.
- MN 111: Anupada Sutta-One After Another {M iii 25} [Thanissaro]. A description of how insight can be developed either while in, or immediately after withdrawing from, the different levels of jhana.
- MN 116: Isigili Sutta-The Discourse at Isigili {M iii 68} [Piyadassi]. The Buddha enumerates the many paccekabuddhas who lived on Isigili mountain.
- MN 117: Maha-cattarisaka Sutta-The Great Forty {M iii 71} [Thanissaro]. On the nature of noble right concentration, and its interdependence with all the factors of the noble eightfold path.
- MN 118: Anapanasati Sutta-Mindfulness of Breathing {M iii 78} [Thanissaro]. One of the most important texts for beginning and veteran meditators alike, this sutta is the Buddha's roadmap to the entire course of meditation practice, using the vehicle of breath meditation. The simple practice of mindfulness of breathing leads the practitioner gradually through 16 successive phases of development, culminating in full Awakening.

- MN 119: Kayagata-sati Sutta-Mindfulness Immersed in the Body {M iii 88} [Thanissaro]. This sutta serves as a companion to the Anapanasati Sutta [Thanissaro]. and explains the importance of establishing a broad awareness of the body in meditation to develop jhana.
- MN 121: Cula-sunnata Sutta-The Lesser Discourse on Emptiness {M iii 103} [Thanissaro]. The Buddha instructs Ven. Ananda on the practice that leads to the "entry into emptiness," the doorway to liberation. [TB]
- MN 122: Maha-sunnata Sutta-The Greater Discourse on Emptiness {M iii 109} [Thanissaro]. The Buddha instructs Ananda on several practical aspects of the meditative dwelling in emptiness, a mode of awareness that can ultimately bring the meditator to the threshold of Awakening.
- MN 125: Dantabhumi Sutta-The Discourse on the "Tamed Stage" {M iii 128} [Horner]. By analogy with the taming of an elephant, the Buddha explains how he tames his disciples. [BB]
- MN 126: Bhumija Sutta-To Bhumija {M iii 138} [Thanissaro]. Does the desire for Awakening get in the way of Awakening? According to this discourse, the question of desiring or not desiring is irrelevant as long as one develops the appropriate qualities that constitute the path to Awakening. The discourse is also very clear on the point that there are right and wrong paths of practice: as a geographer might say, not every river flows to the sea. [TB]
- MN 131: Bhaddekaratta Sutta-An Auspicious Day {M iii 187} [Nanananda | Thanissaro]. In this stirring discourse the Buddha underscores the vital urgency of keeping one's attention firmly rooted in the present moment. After all, the past is gone, the future isn't here; this present moment is all we have.
- MN 135: Cula-kammavibhanga Sutta-The Shorter Exposition of Kamma {M iii 202} [Thanissaro | Nanamoli]. Why do some people live a long life, but

others die young? Why are some people born poor, but others born rich? The Buddha explains how kamma accounts for a person's fortune or misfortune.

- MN 136: Maha-kammavibhanga Sutta-The Greater Exposition of Kamma {M iii 207} [Nanamoli]. The Buddha reveals some of the subtle complexities in the workings of kamma. [BB]
- MN 137: Salayatana-vibhanga Sutta-An Analysis of the Six Sense-media {M iii 215} [Thanissaro]. A discussion of the emotions: where they come from, how they function in the path of practice, and how they manifest in an awakened person who is fit to teach others. [TB]
- MN 138: Uddesa-vibhanga Sutta-An Analysis of the Statement {M iii 223} [Thanissaro]. How to attend to outside objects without letting the mind become externally scattered, and how to focus in strong states of absorption without becoming internally positioned. It's not easy, but it can be done. [TB]
- MN 140: Dhatu-vibhanga Sutta-An Analysis of the Properties {M iii 238} [Thanissaro]. A poignant story in which a wanderer, searching for the Buddha, actually meets the Buddha without realizing it. He recognizes his mistake only after the Buddha teaches him a profound discourse on four determinations and the six properties of experience. An excellent illustration of the Buddha's statement, "Whoever sees the Dhamma sees me." [TB]
- MN 141: Saccavibhanga Sutta-Discourse on The Analysis of the Truths {M iii 248} [Piyadassi | Thanissaro]. Ven. Sariputta gives a detailed elaboration on the Buddha's teaching of the Four Noble Truths.
- MN 143: Anathapindikovada Sutta-Instructions to Anathapindika {M iii 258} [Olendzki (excerpt) | Thanissaro]. Ven. Sariputta offers a deep teaching on non-clinging to the ailing lay-follower Anathapindika.
- MN 146: Nandakovada Sutta-Nandaka's Exhortation {M iii 270} [Thanissaro]. Ven. Nandaka discusses

impermanence with a large group of nuns, driving his point home with particularly vivid similes. It must have been an effective teaching: soon afterwards, these nuns all become enlightened.

- MN 147: Cula-Rahulovada Sutta-The Shorter Exposition to Rahula {M iii 277} [Thanissaro]. The Buddha leads his son, Ven. Rahula, to arahantship.
- MN 148: Chachakka Sutta-The Six Sextets {M iii 280} [Thanissaro]. How the contemplation of the six senses leads to an understanding of not-self and, ultimately, to Awakening.
- MN 149: Maha-salayatanika Sutta-The Great Six Sense-media Discourse {M iii 287} [Thanissaro]. How a clear understanding of the six senses leads to the development of the Wings to Awakening and to final release.
- MN 152: Indriya-bhavana Sutta-The Development of the Faculties {M iii 298} [Thanissaro]. What qualifies as full mastery of the senses?

SAMYUTTA NIKAYA

The Grouped Discourses

The Samyutta Nikaya, the third division of the Sutta Pitaka, contains 2,889 suttas grouped into five sections (vaggas). Each vagga is further divided into samyuttas, each of which in turn contains a group of suttas on related topics. The samyuttas are named according to the topics of the suttas they contain.

For example, the Kosala Samyutta (in the Sagatha Vagga) contains suttas concerning King Pasenadi of Kosala; the Vedana Samyutta (in the Salayatana Vagga) contains suttas concerning feeling (vedana); and so on.

An excellent modern print translation of the complete Samyutta Nikaya is Bhikkhu Bodhi's The Connected Discourses of the Buddha: A New Translation of the Samyutta Nikaya (Boston: Wisdom Publications, 2000; originally published in two volumes, but now available in a single volume). A fine anthology of selected suttas is Handful of Leaves (Vol. 2), by

Thanissaro Bhikkhu (distributed by the Sati Centre for Buddhist Studies).

The suttas are numbered here by samyutta and sutta, with the suttas numbered sequentially from the start of each samyutta, using as a guide the Rhys Davis & Woodward PTS English translations of the Samyutta Nikaya (The Book of the Kindred Sayings).

The braces {} that follow each sutta and samyutta title contain the corresponding volume and starting page number, first in the PTS romanized Pali edition of the Samyutta Nikaya, then in Bhikkhu Bodhi's Connected Discourses of the Buddha ("CDB"). The translator appears in the square brackets [].

6

Ethics of Buddhism

Essentially, according to Buddhist teachings, the ethical and moral principles are governed by examining whether a certain action, whether connected to body or speech is likely to be harmful to one's self or to others and thereby avoiding any actions which are likely to be harmful. In Buddhism, there is much talk of a skilled mind. A mind that is skilful avoids actions that are likely to cause suffering or remorse. Moral conduct for Buddhists differs according to whether it applies to the laity or to the Sangha or clergy. A lay Buddhist should cultivate good conduct by training in what are known as the "Five Precepts". These are not like, say, the ten commandments, which, if broken, entail punishment by God. The five precepts are training rules, which, if one were to break any of them, one should be aware of the breech and examine how such a breech may be avoided in the future. The resultant of an action (often referred to as Karma) depends on the intention more than the action itself. It entails less feelings of guilt than its Judeo-Christian counterpart. Buddhism places a great emphasis on 'mind' and it is mental anguish such as remorse, anxiety, guilt etc. which is to be avoided in order to cultivate a calm and peaceful mind. The five precepts are:

(1) To undertake the training to avoid taking the life of beings. This precept applies to all living beings not just humans. All beings have a right to their lives and that right should be respected.

(2) To undertake the training to avoid taking things not given. This precept goes further than mere stealing.

One should avoid taking anything unless one can be sure that is intended that it is for you.

(3) To undertake the training to avoid sensual misconduct. This precept is often mistranslated or misinterpreted as relating only to sexual misconduct but it covers any overindulgence in any sensual pleasure such as gluttony as well as misconduct of a sexual nature.

(4) To undertake the training to refrain from false speech. As well as avoiding lying and deceiving, this precept covers slander as well as speech which is not beneficial to the welfare of others.

(5) To undertake the training to abstain from substances which cause intoxication and heedlessness. This precept is in a special category as it does not infer any intrinsic evil in, say, alcohol itself but indulgence in such a substance could be the cause of breaking the other four precepts.

These are the basic precepts expected as a day to day training of any lay Buddhist. On special holy days, many Buddhists, especially those following the Theravada tradition, would observe three additional precepts with a strengthening of the third precept to be observing strict celibacy. The additional precepts are:

(6) To abstain from taking food at inappropriate times. This would mean following the tradition of Theravadin monks and not eating from noon one day until sunrise the next.

(7) To abstain from dancing, singing, music and entertainments as well as refraining from the use of perfumes, ornaments and other items used to adorn or beautify the person. Again, this and the next rule.

(8) To undertake the training to abstain from using high or luxurious beds are rules regularly adopted by members of the Sangha and are followed by the layperson on special occasions.

Laypersons following the Mahayana tradition, who have taken a Bodhisattva vow, will also follow a strictly vegetarian diet. This is not so much an additional precept but a strengthening of the first precept; To undertake the training to avoid taking the life of beings. The eating of meat would be considered a contribution to the taking of life, indirect though it may be.

The Buddhist clergy, known as the Sangha, are governed by 227 to 253 rules depending on the school or tradition for males or Bhikkhus and between 290 and 354 rules, depending on the school or tradition for females or Bhikkhunis. These rules, contained in the Vinaya or first collection of the Buddhist scriptures,, are divided into several groups, each entailing a penalty for their breech, depending on the seriousness of that breech. The first four rules for males and the first eight for females, known as Parajika or rules of defeat, entail expulsion from the Order immediately on their breech. The four applying to both sexes are: Sexual intercourse, killing a human being, stealing to the extent that it entails a gaol sentence and claiming miraculous or supernormal powers. Bhikkhunis' additional rules relate to various physical contacts with males with one relating to concealing from the order the defeat or parajika of another. Before his passing, the Buddha instructed that permission was granted for the abandonment or adjustment of minor rules should prevailing conditions demand such a change. These rules apply to all Sangha members irrespective of their Buddhist tradition.

The interpretation of the rules, however differs between the Mahayana and Theravada traditions. The Theravadins, especially those from Thailand, claim to observe these rules to the letter of the law, however, in many cases, the following is more in theory than in actual practice. The Mahayana Sangha interprets the rule not to take food at an inappropriate time as not meaning fasting from noon to sunrise but to refrain from eating between mealtimes. The fasting rule would be inappropriate, from a health angle, for the Sangha living in cold climates such as China, Korea and Japan. When one examines the reason that this rule was instituted initially, the conclusion may be reached that it is currently redundant. It was the practice in the Buddha's time for the monks to go to the village with their bowls to collect food. To avoid disturbing the villagers more than necessary, the Buddha ordered his monks to make this visit once a day, in the early morning. This would allow the villagers to be free to conduct their day to day affairs without being disturbed by the monks requiring food. Today, of course, people bring food to the monasteries or prepare it on the premises so the original reason no longer applies. As many of you would be aware, in some Theravadin countries, the monks still go on their early morning alms round, but this is more a matter of maintaining a tradition than out of necessity. Also, a rule prohibiting the handling of gold and silver, in other words-money, is considered by the Mahayana Sangha a handicap were it to be observed strictly in today's world. They interpret this rule as avoiding the accumulation of riches which leads to greed. Theravadin monks tend to split hairs on this rule as, although most will not touch coins, many carry credit cards and cheque books.

Let me now deal briefly with the Buddhist attitude to violcncc, war and peace. The Buddha said in the Dhammapada:

* Victory breeds hatred. The defeated live in pain. Happily the peaceful live giving up victory and defeat.(Dp.15,5) and
* Hatreds never cease by hatred in this world; through love alone they cease. This is an eternal law. (Dp.1,5)

The first precept refers to the training to abstain from harming living beings. Although history records conflicts involving the so-called Buddhist nations, these wars have been fought for economic or similar reasons. However, history does not record wars fought in the name of propagating Buddhism. Buddhism and, perhaps, Jainism are unique in this regard. His Holiness, the Dalai Lama has never suggested armed conflict to overcome the persecution and cruelty perpetrated by the Communist Chinese occupation forces. He has always advocated a peaceful and non-violent solution. Venerable Maha Ghosananda, the Supreme Patriarch of Cambodia has urged Cambodians to put aside their anger for the genocide of the Khmer Rouge and to unify to re-establish their nation. He has written: The suffering of Cambodia has been deep. From this suffering comes great compassion. Great compassion makes a peaceful heart. A peaceful heart makes a peaceful person. A peaceful person makes a peaceful family. A peaceful family makes a peaceful community. A peaceful community makes a peaceful nation. A peaceful nation makes a peaceful world.

Going back to the early history of Buddhism, Emperor Asoka, who, after a bloody but successful military campaign, ruled over more than two thirds of the Indian subcontinent, suffered great remorse for the suffering that he had caused, banned the killing of animals and exhorted his subjects to lead kind and tolerant lives. He also promoted tolerance towards all religions which he supported financially. The prevalent religions of that time were the sramanas or wandering ascetics, Brahmins, Ajivakas and Jains. He recommended that all religions desist from self praise and condemnation of others. His pronouncements were written on rocks at the periphery of his kingdom and on pillars along the main roads and where pilgrims gathered. He also established many hospitals for both humans and animals. Some of his important rock edicts stated:

1. Asoka ordered that banyan trees and mango groves be planted, rest houses built and wells dug every half mile along the main roads.
2. He ordered the end to killing of any animal for use in the royal kitchens.
3. He ordered the provision of medical facilities for humans and beasts.
4. He commanded obedience to parents, generosity to priests and ascetics and frugality in spending.
5. All officers must work for the welfare of the poor and the aged.
6. He recorded his intention to promote the welfare of all beings in order to repay his debt to all beings.
7. He honours men of all faiths.

Not all Buddhists follow the non-violent path, however. A Buddhist monk, Phra Kittiwutthi of the Phra Chittipalwon College in Thailand, is noted for his extreme right-wing views.

He said that it was not a breech of the first precept to kill communists. He said that if Thailand were in danger of a communist takeover, he would take up arms to protect Buddhism. Sulak Sivaraksa, a Thai peace activist, reports in his book, "Seeds of Peace" that Phra Kittiwutthi has since modified his stance by declaring "to kill communism or communist ideology is not a sin". Sulak adds that the monk confessed that his nationalist feelings were more important than his Buddhist practice and that he would be willing to abandon his yellow robes to take up arms against communist invaders from Laos, Cambodia or Vietnam.

By doing so, he said, he would be preserving the monarchy, the nation and the Buddhist religion. In contrast to the views of Phra Kittiwutthi, Sulak Sivaraksa reports that the Vietnamese monk, Thich Nhat Hanh is of the view that 'preserving Buddhism does not mean that we should sacrifice people's lives in order to safeguard the Buddhist hierarchy, monasteries or rituals. Even if Buddhism as such were extinguished, when human lives are preserved and when human dignity and freedom are cultivated towards peace and loving kindness, Buddhism can be reborn in the hearts of human beings.

In conclusion, I will briefly mention some other issues mentioned in the Syllabus.

The third precept on training in restraint of the senses includes sexuality. A Buddhist should be mindful of the possible effects on themselves and on others of improper sexual activity. This precept would include adultery because this also breeches the precept of not taking what does is not freely given. A relationship with someone who is committed to another is stealing. Similarly in cases of rape and child abuse, one is stealing the dignity and self respect of another. One is also the cause of mental pain, not to mention physical pain so one is causing harm to another living being. Therefore, such behaviour is breaking several precepts. Marriage is not a sacrament in Buddhism as it is in other religions. Marriage is governed by civil law and a Buddhist is expected to observe the prevailing law in whatever country they live. In the Theravadin tradition, monks are prohibited by their Vinaya rules to encourage or perform a marriage ceremony. The rule states:

Should a Bhikkhu engage to act as a go-between for a man's intentions to a woman or a woman's intentions to a man, whether about marriage or paramourage, even for a temporary arrangement, this entails initial and subsequent meeting of the Sangha. In many Theravadin countries, the couple will, following their marriage in a civil ceremony, invite the monks to their home to perform a blessing ceremony. They will offer food and other requisites to the monks and invite their family and friends to participate. In the Mahayana tradition the same rule conveys an entirely different meaning. It reads:

Should a Bhikkshu, seek to establish a conducive situation by means of which a man and a woman engage in sexual misconduct, either by himself, by order, or by means of messages, and as a result of his activities the man and woman should meet, he has committed an offence.

This rule does not preclude marriage but, rather, deals with the monk assuming the role of a procurer for immoral purposes. In Western countries, following the Christian precedent, many Mahayana monks become registered marriage celebrants so that, if called upon, a marriage ceremony can be performed in the temple. Generally, in countries where the law allows, Buddhists accept de-facto relationships. Promiscuity would be frowned upon as sexual misconduct but an ongoing relationship between two people, either within or outside of marriage would be considered moral conduct. As one of the essential Buddhist teachings is that everything is impermanent and subject to change, the irrevocable breakdown of a relationship between a couple would be understood in this light, so divorce would not be considered improper.

As far as bioethical questions are concerned, it is mainly a matter of the attitude of the different traditions or schools of Buddhism. This is tied to the concept of rebirth and when it occurs. According to the Theravadin tradition, rebirth occurs immediately upon death. The body of the deceased is no longer considered as a part of the former being, so such things as autopsies, organ transplants etcetera are allowable. In fact, many Theravadins, especially in Malaysia, encourage the donation of human organs as being the highest form of giving. Often, especially at Vesak, the celebration of the birth, enlightenment and passing away of the Buddha, blood donations are performed in the temple grounds. The Mahayana, on the other hand, believes that there is an intermediate state between incarnations, known as Antarabhava. Most people following this tradition try to avoid touching or moving the body for, at least eight hours after death. This, of course, means that the organs would by then be useless for transfer to another human being. The Buddhist work ethic and business and professional ethics would, ideally be closely tied to respect for the environment. It is well described in E. F. Schumacher's book "Small is Beautiful":

"While the materialist is mainly interested in goods, the Buddhist is mainly interested in liberation. But Buddhism is the Middle Way and therefore in no way antagonistic to physical well being. The keynote of Buddhist economics is simplicity and non-violence. From an economist's point of view, the marvel of the Buddhist way of life is the utter rationality of its pattern-amazingly small means leading to extraordinarily satisfying results."

Ken Jones in a paper called "Buddhism and Social Action" comments: "Schumacher outlines a 'Buddhist economics' in which production would be based on a middle range of material goods (and no more), and on the other a harmony with the natural environment and its resources.

The above principles suggest some kind of diverse and politically decentralised society, with co-operative management and ownership of productive wealth. It would be conceived on a human scale, whether in terms of size and complexity or organisation or of environmental planning, and would use modern technology selectively rather than being used by it in the service of selfish interests. In Schumacher's words, 'It is a question of finding the right path of development, the Middle Way, between materialist heedlessness and traditionalist immobility, in short, of finding Right Livelihood'".

Despite the theory surrounding Buddhist business practice, greed still seems to be the order of the day in many Buddhist countries. In Thailand, a monk in the north, Acharn Ponsektajadhammo, has been leading a campaign against the environmental vandalism of the timber industry. Tree felling in Northern Thailand has caused erosion, flooding and has economically ruined small farmers. For his environmental efforts, Acharn Ponsektajadhammo has had death threats and was recently arrested. In Japan, another country where the majority of the population is Buddhist, the killing of whales and dolphins is still prevalent. Animals seem to find no place in the group culture of Japanese society.

As may be seen from the foregoing, Buddhist ethical principles are very noble and in an ideal world their practice would lead to peace and harmony but, unfortunately, as the Buddha has taught, people are motivated by greed hatred and delusion-even Buddhists.

THE ETHICS OF BUDDHISM

It is well-known that Buddhism is the most ethical of "religions". An important part of the Noble Eightfold Path relates to the development of ethical conduct; for many a layperson Buddhist practice consists mainly in the "keeping of the precepts"; many Bhikkhus see in the Vinaya rules the essence of the religious life; and even many of the paramitas expected of those aspiring to Buddhahood are ethical in nature. Yet to present the teaching of the Buddha as being solely and exclusively concerned with ethics could serve as a detraction from the real objective of the Buddha-Dhamma, which is to serve as a path or vehicle leading to Enlightenment. While conforming to the norms of Buddhist ethics is essential for this purpose this alone will not guarantee the elimination of ignorance (avijja), which is the real meaning of Enlightenment. The tendency of some exponents of the Dhamma to represent Buddhism as just another ethical system is misleading, especially when put before a newcomer to the Dhamma who may not be able to distinguish between Buddhist ethics and the precepts of other ethical teachers, and may conclude that

Buddhism has nothing new to offer. All religions inculcate some basic ethics, whether relating to individual or to social conduct. Indeed the advocacy of an ethical system does not need a religious framework, and some: of the great ethical teachers of the world (e.g. Socrates or Confucius) did not feel the need for one. The religion-surrogates of the modern world, like Humanism, rationalism, or Communism, have all evolved their own norms of ethics, however inadequate we may consider them to be. Wherein, then, lies the uniqueness of Buddhist ethics? This question could be answered in many ways, but here we shall look at it from the standpoint of three criteria.

First of all there are the ethical rules themselves. When we consider what actions are considered "good" and what are deemed to be "bad", it might appear that there is a great deal of agreement between the different ethical Systems. Such actions like killing, theft, sexual misconduct, and falsehood seem to be condemned universally. The differences emerge when we examine the question more closely, e.g. when we investigate the rationale for these rules, whether they are absolute or are relative to some other end, and so on. The rule against killing could be taken as an example. Many ethical systems proscribe only the killing of humans (i.e. murder), but Buddhism applies the rule to all sentient existence. Furthermore even in the case of humans, exceptions are sometimes allowed, e.g. for "holy" or "just" war. Buddhism admits of no such exemptions. In Buddhism the ethical quality of actions depends on the mental factors associated with their commission or even contemplation, and on the impact they have on the well-being of others. If action is committed with greed, aversion or delusion it is unwholesome (akusala), but the degree of moral reprehensibility (and karmic consequence) depends on a whole host of factors. Even an "accidental" killing could have adverse consequences if it was caused through negligence and unmindfulness, which is a kind of "Delusion" (moha). What has been said of the rule regarding killing, may also be extended to the other ethical precepts as well. Furthermore Buddhist ethics does not stop at the Five Precepts (panca siila), which provides only the very minimum for the proper conduct of lay persons.

The second criterion that could be adduced for the evaluation of ethical Systems relates to the motivation for adhering to the ethical rules of the system, religious or secular. In Buddhism the goal of ethical conduct is self-control, self-understanding, and self-development. It is an essential prerequisite for the training of the mind, the elimination of ignorance and the attainment of Enlightenment. Theistic religions usually require the adherence to their ethical precepts as a means to the union with God, whether in an abstract metaphysical sense or more directly as entry into a kingdom ruled by God, or even the enjoyment of pleasures in a heavenly paradise. In such a system the most important rule, precept or commandment is not usually an ethical one, but belief in, love of, submission and obedience to, and veneration of God. This is thus placed at the head of the Judeo-Christian decalogue, with the ethical rules coming subsequently. When we look at "secular" ethics, such as those embodied in legal systems, the objective is usually the avoidance of social conflict, the regularization of property rights, and the like. Of course, some secular laws (e.g. those relating to the so-called "victimless crimes") are more directly "moral" in nature, but these too usually are indirect social objectives. The pursuit of Buddhist ethics too leads to social harmony, but this harmony is achieved through individual perfection, rather than through the compulsory observance of legalistic rules. But because of the non-compulsive nature of Buddhist ethics, they are not intended to replace the laws of society, but neither are those of other ethical systems erected on religious and philosophical foundations.

The third aspect of the question relates to the way in which "good" and "bad" conduct results in appropriate consequences. This is the question of the "policing of the rules". Here two approaches may be distinguished. One is where some kind of trial and punishment (or reward) is instituted individually for each person. The supreme judicial authority could be God to the theist; or simply the normal judicial processes of society in the case of the secularist and the materialist. The second approach relies on the workings of an impersonal law (like the Law of Karma in its Buddhist and Hindu-Jam forms). The legal model of trial-and-punishment is best suited to the enforcement of the laws of society, such as are necessary for the preservation of the authority of the State and the well-being of society. When this model is used to evaluate personal moral conduct and behaviour, as in the theory of divine judgement, several curious features arise. One that could be mentioned is the doctrine of the "forgiveness of sins". According to this doctrine the exercise of divine grace could wipe out "sins" and negate the principle that actions bring their own reward. In such a system the ultimate factor which determines the destiny of an individual is not the scrupulous observance of the ethical rules of the system, but the element of blind faith in its dogmas.

In Buddhism the operation of the law of kamma (karma) is all-pervasive and universal. Its exact modus operandi is not detailed, and may not be immediately obvious. Unlike in some other versions of the karmic hypothesis, in Buddhism there is no mechanical equivalence between action and result (vipaka). As mentioned above the karmic quality of an act depends on a whole host of circumstances. In the accumulation of kammas, good and bad, the fruiting of some may be postponed or delayed while that of others could be immediate. What is certain is that the law of kamma makes divine authority, divine grace, etc. redundant.

Thus in spite of superficial similarities, Buddhist ethics differs from other ethical systems when analysed in detail. In the Noble Eightfold Path the elements corresponding to morality and ethics are Right Speech, Right Action and Right Livelihood. These three together constitute siila. The cultivation of siila normally proceeds alongside progress in the other two great constituents of the Path, namely mental training (bhavana) and wisdom-insight (panna). Because of the mutually supportive nature of the three components of morality, mental development and wisdom, it is difficult to argue about the relative importance of these three components. Nonetheless it has long been the generally accepted view that panna is both the threshold as well as the culmination of Buddhist practice, with the other two components of sla and bhavana being the chief means to the realization of this great objective.

The distinction between ends and means is very important in the understanding of the true place of ethics in Buddhism. For the ordinary person (putujjana) ethical conduct may appear to be an end in itself, but for the adept (sekha) it is a means to the realization of a greater end. Because of the Buddha's custom of proclaiming the Dhamma according the varied capacities of his listeners, there are diverse references to the importance of siila in the Buddha's discourses which at first sight might appear to be inconsistent or even contradictory. This apparent inconsistency, however, disappears when the actual context is considered. By way of illustration we can consider two places in the Pali Cannon of Buddhism which seem to attach different degrees of importance to morality (siila) in the Buddha's system.

"The first of these comes from the Brahmajala Sutta. This is the first discourse in the Sutta Pitaka (the section dealing with Buddhist doctrines), and this exalted position accorded to it reflects its importance to the early Buddhists, perhaps to the Buddha himself. This discourse was occasioned by a report brought to the Buddha of derisive commuents made on him, his Doctrine and the Sangha by a wandering teacher called Suppiya, and the equally unfounded praise bestowed on him by Brahmadatta a follower of Suppiya. This had led to conflict between teacher and pupil, and disquiet amongst the followers of the Buddha. The Buddha commences the discourse by advising his followers to consider all statements made about him, whether favourable or unfavourable, in an objective manner, with equanimity and even-handedness, and then to reject what was wrong, whether it be unfounded blame or unfounded praise, and to point out these errors in a calm and reasoned manner.

The Buddha anticipated that much of the praise heaped on him would be for the wrong reasons: "It is in respect only of trifling things (appamattaka.m) or matters of little value (oramattaka.m), or mere morality (siilamattaka.m) that an unconverted man (putujjana) when praising the Buddha would speak". What is interesting from our point of view is that the

Buddha considers the mere keeping of ethical rules to be a matter not worthy of any real praise. In this sutta the Buddha groups ethical rules into three categories. The first of these (the cula siila) contains the basic ethical precepts (like the "killing of living things") which are usually included amongst the Five Precepts laid down for the guidance of lay persons. The other two categories (the majjhima and maha siilas) contain, ethical rules of lesser importance or those specially laid down for monks. As against these "moralities", none of which is deserving of real praise, the Buddha describes those things that are deserving of real praise.

These are the "things profound difficult to realize, hard to understand, tranquillising, sweet, not to be grasped by mere logic, subtle, comprehensible only to the wise". More specifically they turn out to be the realization of Right View (samma di.t.ti), and the refutation of wrong views, in which connection the Buddha outlines the famous list of sixty-two schools of thought, ranging from theism to materialism, which then as now, were the main contenders with the Dhamma. Even though the Brahmajala was mainly concerned with what was praiseworthy in a Buddha, it does provide a clear statement of the principle that wisdom-insight (panna) ranks above siila and bhavana in the accomplishments necessary for the realization of the Buddhist goal of Nibbana. The second extract from the Dhama which we shall consider seems to paint a slightly different picture. This is probably the best known stanza in the Dhamapada, itself the best-known of the Buddhist books. This Stanza (No.183) with its usual translation is as follows:

Sabbapapassa akara.na.m, kusalassa upasamapda,
sacittapariyodapana.m eta.m Buddhana sasana.m

Not to do any evil, to do good, To purify one's mind, this
is the teaching of the Buddhas.]

The ethical import of this Stanza is obvious. It seems to claim that the Buddha's teaching is threefold: avoid unethical conduct, cultivate good deeds, and train one's mind. There is no question of the ethical purport of the first two postulates. "Training the mind" could also be interpreted as an ethical postulate, especially when we consider the Buddhist view that evil thoughts generated by an unguarded mind are karmically effective.

The last phrase of this Stanza is usually taken to mean that the three ethical postulates constitute the whole (or at least the most important part) of the Dhamma. However it could be taken to mean that these ethical principles are part of the teachings of the Buddha, and not necessarily the part that constitutes the Buddha's unique discovery. In the Commentary to the Dhammapada it is stated that this and the two following Stanzas constituted the admonition (ovadagata) delivered by the previous legendary Buddhas to bhikkhus on the uposatha days.

In the explanation of the meaning of the terms in this Stanza, the Commentator says that "to do good" really means the "generation and development of skillful acts from ordination until the realization of the path of Arahat-hood", while "purifying the mind" means the elimination of the five "hindrances" which are obstacles to the realization of jhanic states during meditation. All this is in keeping with the general purpose of these stanzas, which was to serve as exhortations to Bhikkhus on the uposatha day, and not to serve as a summary of the Buddha-Dhamma.

The uniqueness of Buddhist ethics lies in its many outstanding qualities. It is all-embracing and comprehensive without being impractical or impossible to follow. It is free from taboos relating to diet, dress, behaviour etc. which very often pass as ethical principles. It serves the needs of the worldling as well as those of the recluse. It is useful to the rich and to the poor; to the powerful as well as to the powerless. To conform to Buddhist ethics one need not have to be a "buddhist"; and it serves as a norm to measure the ethical standard of other teachings. But Buddhist ethics is only the threshold for those who wish to pursue the Buddha's path to Enlightenment and the end of all ill.

BUDDHIST ETHICS AND SOCIAL CRITICISM

Buddhism arose in India during a period of intense intellectual and social ferment. It was a period during which the authority of the Vedas had been placed in doubt, the concept of god as a supreme being and creator was in question, the hereditary restrictions on caste mobility were under attack, and the efficacy of Brahminical rituals was being challenged. The authors of the Upanishads had opened the door for various heterodox currents to emerge in society, and amongst the most significant of these were the Lokayatas who polemicized against religious charlatans, and the Nyayavadis whose rational epistemology created the foundation for intense philosophical debate and encouraged the investigation of the real world based on reason and logic, freed from the burden of superstition and irrational adherence to burdensome rituals.

Various ideological sects competed for the attention and acceptance of the ruling elites and the public. The most important amongst these were the Jains and the Buddhists. Although each of the various sects made original and interesting contributions to philosophy, it was the early Buddhists who attempted to provide a unified philosophical system where ethical conduct and social criticism lay at the very core of their ideological system.

Although today, Buddhism is viewed as a religion by many of its followers, the early Buddhists sects were either strongly atheistic or agnostic.

The atheists believed that rather than "God having created man in his own image" it was man who had created "God" in his image. In their view, the liberation of humanity was contingent upon humanity shedding the delusion that "God" existed. Other parables from surviving Buddhist texts indicate agnosticism. For instance, there is a suggestion that Buddhist followers ought not to waste their time on unsolvable metaphysical questions such as "does god exist". The search to identify the "one true god" or to speculate on the nature of god was seen as an exercise in futility.

But the most frequently cited argument against god by the Buddhists was that if an omnipotent and omniscient being such as "God" truly existed, and who was also all good, there could not be the kind of dukkha (suffering) that was so widespread in the real world. These shlokas (verses) from the Bhuridatta Jataka illustrates this point:

If the creator of the entire world they call "God" be the lord of every being, why does he order such misfortune, and not create concord?

If the creator of the entire world they call "God" be the lord of every being, why let prevail deceit, lies and ignorance, why create such inequity and injustice? If the creator of the entire world they call "God" be the lord of every being, then an evil master is he, knowing what's right did let wrong prevail!

Unlike religions that ascribed earthly miseries to human sinfulness that brought upon the wrath of a vengeful god who needed to be feared, Buddhism saw the root of human suffering in ignorance that could only be ended through the acquisition of wisdom. Rather than expect some supernatural entity to end human suffering, the Buddhists argued that it was in human hands to end their sorrows through conduct and action driven by knowledge and correct understanding of human nature and the physical world. Hence, the aspiration for knowledge (jigyasa) was seen as the answer to blind faith. Although the Buddhists were not alone in developing this view, the elaboration of this point of view became pivotal to early Buddhist philosophy.

Central to Buddhist philosophy was an understanding of human nature and what caused dukkha-i.e. human suffering. They saw human personality as constituting five attributes, i.e. body, feeling, perception, disposition and consciousness, and used this framework to develop their understanding of human suffering. Citing examples of conditions that led to human suffering, such as aging, sickness and death, or association with the unpleasant, (or separation from the pleasant), or the inability to get what one wished-they concluded that suffering was a condition of stress and conflict inherent within human existence and interaction with the world. They also connected suffering to the very impermanence of things. They observed how people lamented over the loss of a loved one, or experienced sorrow when something or someone that had once given them happiness became separated from them. They noted that even human pleasures were not immune from suffering because they didn't last forever, and the loss of pleasure inevitably left people feeling deprived. Seeing as how clinging to things (that were necessarily impermanent) was one of the primary causes of dukkha, they cautioned against excessive attachment. At the same time, they recognized a recurring and more general type of existential unease and anxiety (aniccha) that arises from the very transience of life, and our inability to control or comprehend all worldly phenomenon, which they characterized as viparinama-dukkha. But the Buddhists did not see dukkha only emanating from the difficulties of an individual. They also saw suffering emerge on a much larger scale from hostile social conditions such as poverty, war, and social oppression which they described as dukkha-dukkha.

As a formula (char-mulya) for addressing these different types of suffering, the Buddhists advocated a four-fold scheme of (a) recognizing the problem i.e. suffering (dukkha); (b) identifying the cause of the suffering-such as craving stemming from ignorance (samudaya); (c) establishing the goal of ending the problem (nirodha)-i.e. the cessation of suffering (nirvana); (d) conducting life in a manner that was consistent with the cessation of suffering-following the right path or engaging in the right practice (marga).

Followers were thus goaded into developing both a sense of personal ethics and a social conscience:

> *"He who has understanding and great wisdom does not think of harming himself or another, nor of harming both alike. He rather thinks of his own welfare, of that of others, of that of both, and of the welfare of the whole world. In that way one shows understanding and great wisdom." Anguttara Nikaya-(Gradual Sayings)*
>
> *"By protecting oneself (e.g., morally), one protects others; by protecting others, one protects oneself." Samyukta Nikaya (Kindred Sayings)*

Human actions (kamma, kaama, or karma) in the Buddhist framework were to be judged based on both the intention or motive (chetanaa) and the consequences (vipaaka) of the action. Altruistic actions which helped in the establishment and promotion of a just society were encouraged in the dharmaniyama (moral duty code). {The discourses, or suttas in the Digha Nikaya, illustrate how there was deep concern with the creation of social conditions favourable to the cultivation of Buddhist values and the expansion of social equity and justice. These views undoubtedly influenced the creation of a "welfare state" during the reign of emperor, Ashoka (B.C. 274-236)}

In their theories of causality Buddhists challenged the view that human destiny was unaffected by the ethics or morality of human actions. They countered the doctrine of amoral causation (akriyavaada) whose adherents argued that there was no merit in doing good and no demerit for doing evil. (An extreme expression of such thinking was seen in philosophers who denied all morality and saw no crime in the killing of any person.)

Realizing that such a world-view could lead to the rejection of moral distinctions and personal responsibility for ones actions, they argued strenuously against such beliefs. They also argued against the theory of Makkali Ghosha (or Ghoshala) who believed that human fate was predetermined, and therefore denied that human actions had any bearing on the results of things (ahetuvaada) and maintained that human intention and effort were essentially powerless in changing human destiny, and therefore advocated fatalism (niyati).

They also countered philosophers from the school of "absolute skepticism" who doubted everything and never committed themselves to any specific position in doctrinal debates. Philosophers from this school such as Sanjaya Belarthaputra (who was known as a theorist of endless equivocation or an equivocationist (amraavikkhepavaadin)) were criticized in the Brahmajaala Sutta (or Sutra) as "eel-wrigglers" who were incapable of taking a definitive stance on the vital philosophical questions of the day. Such skepticism was seen as emanating from both the fear of being in error and the lack of knowledge (or inability) to provide reasonable answers to question put forward for discussion. Such all-pervading doubt coupled with a cynical skepticism (vichikicchaa) was viewed as a serious mental hindrance, a fetter in the path to wisdom.

Other theories that contradicted the notion that human actions mattered were theories of accidentalism (ahetu-apachayavaada), theistic determinism (ishvaranimmaanavaada) and past-action determinism (purvaketavaada or purvekatahetu). All of these were opposed by the Buddhists. Accidentalism was an indeterminist theory which held that whatever was experienced was uncaused and unconditioned by human intervention. Theistic determinism was a determinist theory, which held that whatever was experienced was due to God's will or by plan of a "Supreme-Being". Past-action determinism was also a determinist theory, but it held the belief that whatever was experienced, whether pleasurable or painful or indifferent was entirely due to ones past actions (from a previous life), and ones present actions had no relevance. The danger in each of these theories was highlighted in these words: "Thus for those who fall back on these three erroneous views as essential dogma, there is neither the will to do what is ought to be done, or not to do what is ought not to be done, nor necessity to do this deed or abstain from that deed. No moral improvement or intellectual culture can be expected from them."

Some of the theories in circulation at that time built on a germ of truth but generalized to the point of absurdity. For instance the accidentalists were correct only to the extent that certain things did indeed appear to happen by random chance or accident. But they failed to recognize that sometimes what may have seemed to be accidental was more due to inadequate understanding or improper or incomplete perception, and that other activities had a clearly discernible cause. To deal with the extreme generalizations of such theorists, they introduced a middle standpoint for their epistemology and ethics.

They thus rejected the theory admitting that everything exists (sabba atthii ti) and in permanence-i.e. the extreme of eternalism (sassatavaada), and its opposite which advocated that nothing actually exists (sabba natthii ti) i.e. nihilism (the denial of all reality in real-world phenomenon) or the extreme of annihilationalism (ucchedavaada). Related to their critique of the eternalist and nihilist philosophies was their rejection of both hedonism and self-mortification (attakilamathaanuyoga) which they viewed as painful, fruitless, unprofitable and ignoble.

Buddhist texts also expressed suspicion about claims by heretical teachers of being constantly "all-knowing" and "all-seeing" and in possession of "all-embracing knowledge-and-vision." Such claims were countered with arguments relating to the actual behaviour of such charlatans in different situations. For instance, they wondered why such "all-knowing" and "all-seeing" spiritual teachers lost their way in an unfamiliar place or why they were unable to escape from trouble while countering a fierce animal such as dog, elephant, horse or bull. Moreover, if they were really omniscient, they wouldn't need to ask for people's names, clans, or the name of a village or market town or make enquiries about anything. That they did such things indicated that their knowledge was evidently limited just like that of any average worldly person (puthujjana).

Unlike religions that were based on revealed truth or the sanctity of every word in a holy textbook, the Buddhist belief system prescribed reasoning based on investigation as the means of determining ones dhamma, (or dharma as in Hindu practise). In a parable in the Kaalaama Sutta, followers of Budhism are advised not to accept any moral codes on the following ten grounds: (1) Vedic authority (anussava), (2) tradition (paramparaa), (3) hearsay or report (itikiraa), (4) textual authority (pittakasampadaa), (5) apparent agreebility of the view (sama o no garu), (6) authority of the holder of the view (takkahetu), (7) apparent logicality of the view (nayahetu), (8) the fact that the view is an accepted standpoint (aakaaraparivitakka), (9) inadequate reflection on reasons (bhabbaruupataa), or (10) the fact that the view agrees with one's own.

In this manner, the Buddhism developed a very sophisticated philosophical system in which social ethics were integrated with rational investigation of human nature, social organization and the physical world. Buddhist ideas and concepts left a powerful impression on other Indian philosophical and religious belief systems, and over time, many commonalities developed amongst the competing ideologies.

However, there were also certain problems with the Buddhist world view which prevented its complete acceptance by intellectuals committed to the scientific method. For instance, although the Buddhists rejected the theory of past action determinism, they did posit the existence of a soul which survived a person's death and carried with it the merits and demerits of a person's past lives. Presumably this concept was essential to the Buddhist goal of encouraging right conduct but it was rejected by those who considered the soul as inseparable from the body and did not believe that the soul survived death. Those who rejected the concept of transmigration of the soul naturally couldn't accept the idea that human destiny had anything to do with merits and demerits accumulated in previous incarnations of the "soul". In their view, morality and ethics were entirely social constructs and had to be dealt with accordingly. The realists (such as the Nyayavadis) who shared the Buddhist concern for morals and ethics in society argued that while morals and ethics ought to be encouraged, they could only be enforced through societal laws and judicial codes.

Another problem facing the Buddhists was that in many ways, their views were too advanced for their times. Society had not yet developed to the point where education was universal, and knowledge of the real world sufficient to prevent superstitions and irrational beliefs from being completely abandoned by the masses. In an era where society had only limited control over nature, it was inevitable that sections of society would continue with beliefs in deities and supernatural phenomenon in the hope that they may be spared from natural disasters or that their crops might withstand attacks from pests and disease. Thus although the Buddhists had a very important and salutatory effect on Indian society, the most advanced Buddhist concepts could be understood and practised by only a minority in society.

Over time, the spirit of inquiry and rational investigation that had spurred the early Buddhist scholars towards dialectical thinking and critical social analysis became more and more replaced by narrow and literalist interpretations of the earlier texts. For instance, advice against accepting something that appeared "logical" without personal verification was taken to mean that logic could be rejected. Advice against wasting ones time on unsolvable metaphysical questions was also taken too literally and many Buddhist scholars remained aloof from the metaphysical debates pursued by other philosophical schools such as those of the Jains and the Nyaya Vaisheshikas. What they didn't anticipate was that some of these debates might lead to useful advances in mathematics or deeper understanding of human thought processes and new insights on human memory and psychology. These led to valuable advances in the interpretation of moods and emotions-thus benefiting Indian art, literature and music.

In addition, later Buddhist monks lapsed into some of the very things that had been attacked by the early Buddhists such as indulgence in unnecessary and elaborate rituals, belief in supra-natural phenomenon, and alienation of the priests from the masses. Activities such as meditation which were encouraged as a means to gaining wisdom became ends in themselves, and were turned into idealistic fetishes. Although Buddhist monks dutifully delivered sermons on right conduct and right action, they often failed to engage in relevant and timely social criticism-and did not always connect the textual suggestions to concrete practice. Intra-Buddhist disputes developed around less significant details, even as some of the most important ideas that had initially shaped the philosophy were pushed into the background. As a result Buddhism as it was practised came to be associated with idealism and inaction. Whereas the early Buddhists saw no merit in worshipping god or its images, later Buddhism developed a pantheon of deities not very different from other Indian religions. Thus even as Buddhism had spread almost throughout Asia by the 5th-6th C AD, it gradually began to lose its distinct edge and liberating influence on much of Indian society. Within the Indian subcontinent, strains of Buddhism survived in Sri Lanka, Bengal, Bhutan, Sikkim, parts of Bihar and Nepal, and parts of Sindh, Punjab, Kashmir and Afghanistan. In parts of Orissa and adjoining regions (such as Chhattisgarh and Telengana), Tantric (and other) influences reshaped the practice of Buddhism. Yet, Buddhism continued to have an impact outside India and developed pockets of influence as far West as Syria, as well as in much of Central Asia (including what is now Uzbekistan, Tajikistan, Kyrgyzia, Kazakhstan) and Tibet. In the East, its influence was felt on virtually every nation including Burma, Thailand, Malaya and Indonesia, Laos, Cambodia, Vietnam, China, Korea and Japan.

As noted earlier, the vast literature of Buddhism (like much of Hindu or Jain literature) was not a literature of revelation and authority. Its essays on social ethics and moral responsibilities, its treatises on philosophy and science, its art and poetry were but pointers to a path to wisdom. This gave Buddhism both flexibility and adaptability. Owing to its non-hegemonic character and humanist appeal, Buddhism was adopted without coercion or force. It was also successfully fused with Hinduism in many parts of South East Asia just as elements of it had been integrated into Hindu practices in India. In China, it was integrated with Taoism and Confucian principles; in Japan with Shinto beliefs. For several centuries, within India and outside, several people followed multiple faiths and identified as both Buddhists and Hindus, or as both Buddhists and Tantrics, (or Buddhists and Taoists) and so on. During the Gupta period (and in other reigns), philosophers from various schools of thought received royal patronage and temple grants were conferred for the construction of Buddhist and Hindu monuments alike. It is also important to recognize that the form of Buddhism that was embraced in each nation was often quite different. For instance, in Western and Central Asia, it was not the philosophical or intellectual aspects of Buddhism that were popularized, but rather, its personal moral codes. Buddhist prosletysers imbued their stories of the Buddha with examples of miraculous healing and super-natural compassion so as to win more followers.

While such tendencies were also to be seen as Buddhism travelled within India or outwards, in Burma, Sri Lanka and Thailand, Buddhism developed organizational structures that appear to have been much more resilient. It was perhaps realized that the development of Buddhist virtue would require leadership and constant interaction with the community. In these nations, Buddhism did not degenerate into the extremes of mysticism or retreatism that became commonplace in certain parts of India (such as in the foothills of the Western Himalayas). Burmese and Thai monks maintained a practical and benevolent connection with the community, and thus retained a measure of respect within the community. This also appears to be the case in Japan. In Korea, the emphasis on gaining wisdom was taken very seriously, and Buddhist monks took the lead in promoting mass literacy. This propelled the growth of technologies associated with the production of paper, writing instruments, inks, and furniture. And unlike in India, (where due to Upanishadic influences, "inner" wisdom came to be favoured over outer wisdom), Buddhist concern for disseminating the writings of the Buddha had significant positive secular impact. In Korean (and other Eastern) Buddhism, there was the correct realization that a Buddhist mindset, or that a Buddhist society could not be constructed overnight. There was thus the emphasis on the (helical) upgradation of individuals and society towards greater "Buddhahood". This philosophical element was perhaps signficant in that it prevented the sort of philosophical stagnation that occurred in India, where followers too often sought immediate succuor, and thus not only became divorced from reality, but also lost sight of the strategic potential of the philosophy.

In addition, it ought to be noted that Buddhism in India also had to contend with strongly anarchic and ultra-democratic tendencies. Precisely because its philosophical structure emphasized the relative and changing nature of truth, different tendencies under the Buddhist mantle competed for leadership through argument and debate. Initially, this led to important advances in democratic practices within the Sanghas. But over time, it also led to clashes of egoes, hair-splitting and deadlock. While some Buddhist sects compromised and fused with other tendencies (even alien tendencies), others remained fiercely autonomous. To survive, Buddhism had to confront both the tendency to be co-opted, as well as the tendency to atomize.

However, the catastrophic demise of Buddhism in India was triggered by the onslaught of Islam which first obliterated the remnants of Buddhism in Central Asia, and then later in Afghanistan and India. By and large, Buddhism survived only in those countries that escaped invasions by Islamic conquerors.

As a gentle faith that encouraged its followers to abjure violence, it was perhaps unable to protect itself from iconoclasts and proselytizers who intended to enforce a new religio-political order. Accustomed to centuries of peaceful co-existence, India's Buddhists had not anticipated the need to develop viable strategies for self-defence that could have combated the violence of India's Islamic conquerors who virtually obliterated Buddhism from the land of its birth.

Yet, it also appears that (in large part) later Buddhism had deviated considerably from the rational principles outlined in the early texts. Monasteries often became isolated from mainstream society, and monks who focused exclusively on meditative practices and idealistic or esoteric philosophical speculation contributed little to social progress.

Some have even argued that the monastic orders had degenerated into sheer parasitism and were becoming a heavy social drain. Consequently, value judgements on the demise of Buddhism and the rise of Islam in India need to be made with a measure of caution. Nevertheless, it must be acknowledged that the ascent of Islam was concomitant with the eclipse of Buddhism, and since the influence of Buddhism was greatly dependant on the existence of the monastic orders, the destruction of monasteries and their conversion to mosques and institutions of Quranic learning simply lead to mass conversions to Islam.

In the long term, this could have had the effect of stunting India's future intellectual development, since the destruction of important institutions of Buddhist learning also led to a notable decline in the opportunity (and social sanction) to study secular subjects such as logic and epistemology (which were also taught at Buddhist universities-such as Bhagalpur).

It might also be observed that the destruction of Buddhist centres of learning coincided with the destruction of extremely valuable textual materials-which could have been potentially rediscovered, and revived or reinterpreted by future generations of Indians so as to achieve a society that was more thoughtful and learned. Islamic texts did not offer anything comparable in terms of causality or epistemology.

Nor did they offer the psychological, sociological, or moral insights that had been developed under the ambit of Buddhism. Nor was there any comparable stress on seeking knowledge or constantly updating ones understanding of nature and human society. One can, therefore, only speculate as to the full consequences of this profound sociolgical and cultural loss (and discontinuity).

But East of India, Buddhism did survive, and in countries such Korea, Thailand and Burma, it continued to enjoy a loyal popular following. Philosophical innovations also took place, and as noted earlier, Buddhist scholars in China, Korea and Japan offered their own commentaries and somewhat individual interpretations of Buddhist concepts and formulations outlined in later (5-7th C.) Indian texts. And although the sacking of monasteries and centres of learning (such as Nalanda and Vikramshila in Bihar) led to records of the original Buddhist texts being permanently destroyed, it has been possible to reconstruct some of them from translations that survived outside India such as in Thailand and Tibet. Notwithstanding the virtual erasure of Buddhism in India, it is possible to infer from these reconstructed texts and other archaeological records (and surviving monuments and artifacts) that Buddhism had a very powerful impact in shaping the destiny of India, and in triggering a social and cultural renaissance that would take Indian and other Asian civilizations to a higher level of social, cultural and material development.

BUDDHIST ETHICS

PAI LU-TIEN, a famous Chinese poet, author, and statesman who lived in the thirteenth century of the Christian era, once went to see an eminent Buddhist monk whose saintly life was known far and near, and asked him if he would instruct him in the essentials of Buddhist doctrine. The monk assented and recited the following gatha:

> *"Commit no wrong, but good deeds do, And let thy heart be pure, All Buddhas teach this truth, Which will for aye endure."*

The statesman-poet was not at all satisfied with this simple moral teaching, for he expected to have something abstruse, recondite, and highly philosophical from the mouth of such a prominent and virtuous personality. Said the poet, "Every child is familiar with this Buddhist injunction. What I wish to learn from you is the highest and most fundamental teaching of your faith." But the monk retorted, "Every child may know of this gatha, but even a silvery-haired man fails to put it into practice." Thereupon, it is said, the poet reverentially bowed and went home meditatively.

If we are requested today to state what is the most fundamental in Buddhist ethics, we have to make the same assertion. There may be and in fact are many schools and denominations in Buddhism, each claiming to have transmitted the true spirit of Buddha; but they will be unanimous in declaring that the gatha aforementioned is one of the common grounds on which they all stand.

"Sabba papassa akaranam" is heard in all Southern monasteries, and the lines "Chu wo mo tso, etc.," are seen everywhere in the Eastern lands of Buddhism. If Buddhism were called a sort of ethical culture society on account of this simple code of morality, its followers would make no objection to it, for the recognition of a personal God, or the conception of original sin, or belief in a risen Christ is not thought indispensable to Buddhist salvation. Let a man do what is good and avoid what is bad and have his heart as pure as he can of all egotistic impulses and desires, and he will be delivered from the clutches of ignorance and misery. What ever his dogmatic views on religion, he is one of the enlightened who are above bigotry, intolerance, vanity, conceit, pedantry, and prejudice. He must truly be said to be one whose spiritual insight has penetrated into the depths of existence.

Now, the question is: What is good? What is evil? And how is the heart to be cleansed? I am not going to discuss here these great ethical and religious problems from a mere theoretical point of view. Buddhism has nothing to do with utilitarianism or intuitionalism or hedonism or what not. Buddhism is most practical in its announcement of what constitutes goodness. It dogmatically and concretely points out good deeds one by one. First, negatively, it enumerates ten deeds of goodness (kusalam) as most fundamental in Buddhist ethics; while, positively, it considers the six paramitas (virtues of perfection) or eightfold path as the route leading to a virtuous life.

The ten deeds of goodness are: (1) Not to kill any living being; (2) Not to take anything that does not belong to oneself; (3) Not to look at the other sex with an unclean heart; (4) Not to speak falsehood; (5) Not to calumniate; (6) Not to use vile language; (7) Not to make sensational utterances; (8) Not to be greedy; (9) Not to be out of temper; and lastly, (10) Not to be confused by false doctrines.

Later Buddhists, however, make ten affirmative propositions out of those just mentioned, thus: It is good (1) to save any living being, (2) to practise charity, (3) to be clean-minded, (4) to speak truth, (5) to promote friendship, (6) to talk softly and gently, (7) to be straightforward in speech, (8) to be content with one's own possessions, (9) to be meek and humble, and (10) to think clearly and rightly.

The six paramitas or virtues of perfection are: (1) Charity, which includes the giving away of worldly possessions as well as the proclamation of the Good Law, (2) The observation of the moral precepts as formulated by Buddha, (3) Meekness, (4) Strenuosity, (5) Contemplation, (6) Spiritual enlightenment.

The eightfold path is: (1) Right view, (2) Right reflection, (3) Right speech, (4) Right deed, (5) Right livelihood, (6) Right striving, (7) Right understanding, (8) Right contemplation. In these various enumerations of Buddhist virtues, what is most unique are perhaps the virtues of strenuosity and those of contemplation and enlightenment.

To be good Buddhists, we must never be indolent, whiling away our time to no purpose. Mere piety will not do, so long as there is some work to be accomplished for the sake of humanity and civilization. Love, again, must be accompanied with enlightenment, for the affection is very frequently wasted on account of its blindness. God-fearing is recommendable, but without contemplation we fail to recognize the purport of our own position in the system of the universe. Mere passion leads to fervour and violence if not properly guided by contemplation which brings enlightenment, revealing the reason of existence and purifying the heart of ignorance. Ignorance, according to Buddhism, is the root of all evil, and therefore it advises us in strong terms to have ignorance completely destroyed. And it is only then that the all-illuminating light of enlightenment guides us gloriously to the destination of all beings, where we gain purity of heart, and whatever flows from this eternal fountain of purity is good.

It is evident, then, that by purity of heart is meant absence of ignorance and self-will. But it is not a negative condition, for the most essential postulate of Buddhism is that in each of us there abide the indwelling reason of the universe, which, when released from the temporal bondage of ignorance and self-will, becomes the master of itself by reducing everything to subjection and restoring it to its right place. In a pure heart, therefore, the universal reason manifests itself in its full glory and works its own destiny unmolested. What one with such a heart wills is what makes the bird sing and the flower smile, what has raised the mountain and makes the water flow. He is hungry and the universe wishes to eat; he is asleep and all the world hybernates.

This sounds extraordinary, but the enlightened understand it perfectly well. We cannot make the blind see what we ourselves see. The blind may protest that we are deceiving them; but could we do otherwise, inasmuch as they are deprived of the sense we have, or they have not yet learned how to make use of it? It is declared by Buddhists, therefore, that to realize fully the sanctity of religious life one must have Buddha-wisdom awakened from its unconscious slumber in which it is indulging from time out of mind.

Analytically, purity of heart consists of sympathy and intelligence, and on this groundwork the structure of practical

Buddhism is founded. Sympathy is the tremulation of the spiritual cord which unites the hearts of all sentient beings; and it is intelligence that discovers the presence of the sacred cord in every one of us and keeps it from being entangled. The cord freely responds to cries of suffering.

The heart contrives to effect all the possible means to relieve sentient beings from misery and ignorance. The ten deeds of goodness, the eightfold path, the six virtues of perfection, and many other good things all flow from this one source of pure-heartedness.

It is, then, of unqualified importance in the ethics of Buddhism to have one's heart perfectly cleansed and free from the dust of egotism which has been accumulating through the want of enlightenment. In this sense "blessed are the pure in heart"; they may not see God as he is superficially and superstitiously understood, but they will surely come into personal touch with the ultimate authority of conduct and also perceive that the author is not residing outside of their being but within themselves. We read in the Dharmapada:

"Manopubbangama dhamma, manosettha, manomaya;

Manasa, ce padutthana bhasati va karoti va, Tato nam dukkham anveti, cakkara va vahato padam.

"Manopubbangama dhamma, manosettha, manomaya;

Manasa ce pasannena bhasati va karoti va, Tato nam sukhara anveti, chaya va anapayinî."

In this respect Buddhism can be said to have a decidedly idealistic tendency, since it fully recognizes the paramountcy of ideas in the moral realm. But we must not lose sight of the fact that Buddhism is not a system of metaphysics, but a religion which is practical more than anything else. What it teaches is the profound spiritual experience of every enlightened man, while the philosopher and theorist will speculate on the facts and offer whatever interpretation they may please or feel compelled to give to account adequately for them.

Buddhism is often charged with passiveness and quietism, lacking the "push" of some other religions; and the backwardness of Asiatic nations in the general march of humanity is sometimes ascribed to the influence of Buddhism. Though I am not here entering upon any lengthy polemics, a few words may not be altogether inopportune to refute such an erroneous opinion as this.

If there is anything passive in Eastern culture, which is often no more than tolerance or indifference or self-restraint, it is not due to Buddhism but to the racial idiosyncrasy of Asiatic peoples. Buddhism teaches contemplation and tranquillity and at the same time strenuosity, indefatigable energy in following truth and in destroying ignorance. We see many admirable examples among its believers who have fully illustrated these virtues in their person. The history of Buddhism, while perfectly free from bloodshed and inhumanity, evidences how far its moral teachings have been carried out. Buddhist ethics is not certainly passive or negative, unless the absence of arrogance, aggressiveness, intolerance, bigotry, and fanaticism could be called so.

Religion in its social aspect is not omnipotent, nor is it absolute, as is imagined by some. It is, like many other things created by man, a human institution; it has been discovered, shaped, developed according to the inner necessity of mankind; and as long as he is imperfect and steering his course through innumerable obstacles, religion also must share his imperfection and adapt itself to ever-changing surroundings. Instead of imposing its ideals upon man tyrannically and absolutely, religion reconciles itself to his needs, going through all the necessary modifications.

Therefore, one religion is diversely interpreted by different peoples among whom it may thrive. To suppose that religion could do anything it desires without regard to individual, national, racial peculiarities is far from the fact. The difference between Oriental and Occidental civilization is by no means due to the difference between Christianity and Buddhism. On the other hand, the difference between the two religions is due to the difference between the two great types of Civilization. Truth, be it religious or philosophical or scientific, is universal, and as such does not allow any modification or distortion. But it suffers modification in its practical application, for it is like a mathematical formula or figure. When conceived a priori, it is formal and not subject to any concrete individualization, which latter in fact is the condition of its particular forms.

In conclusion let me say most emphatically that the ethics of Buddhism is summed up in the purification of the heart, in keeping oneself unspotted even though living in the world; and from this eternal root must sprout such things of God as love, a heart of compassion, the virtue of strenuosity, humbleness of mind, longsuffering, forbearing one another, forgiving one another, and freedom from all evils. It is said that there were eighty-four thousand virtues of perfection practised by all Bodhisattvas, but they are no more than so many leaves and branches growing from the one stem of pure-heartedness.

BIBLIOGRAPHY

Allen, Ernst: *The English Novel: a Short Critical History*, London: Phoenix House, 1954.

Arthur Miller: *As a Critic of Drama*, New Delhi, Anmol, 2004.

Authors, Texts, Issues: *Essays on Indian Literature*, Delhi, Pencraft International, 2003.

Ball, M. J. : *Phonetics: The Science of Speech*, London, Arnold, 1999.

Bennett, J. A. W.: *Middle English Literature*, Oxford, Clarendon Press, 1986.

Beyond Borders: *An Anthology of SAARC Poetry*, Noida, Rainbow, 2002.

Bhattacharyya, Nath: *Indian Religious Historiography*, New Delhi, Munshiram Manoharlal Publishers, 1996.

Brown, J. M.: *Ireland in Fiction; a Guide to Irish Novels, Tales, Romances, and Folk-lore*, London: Maunsel, 1919.

Cahalan, M.: *The Irish Novel: a Critical History*, Boston, Twayne Publishers, 1988.

Cavanagh, John: *British Theatre: a Bibliography, 1901 to 1985*, Hampshire, Motley, 1989.

Classe, A.: *The Rhythm of English Prose*, Oxford, Blackwell, 1939.

Couper-Kuhlen, E.: *An Introduction to English Prosody*, London, Edward Arnold, 1986.

Courthope, John: *A History of English Poetry*, London, MacMillan and Co., 1903.

Crystal, D.: *Prosodic Systems and Intonation in English*, Cambridge, Cambridge University Press, 1969.

Davis, Brian L. : *Uniforms and Insignia of the Luftwaffe*, London, Arms and Armor, 1999.

Davis, Gwenn: *Drama by Women to 1900: a Bibliography of American and British Writers*, London, Mansell, 1992.

Dobree, Bonamy: *English Literature in the Early Eighteenth Century, 1700-1740*, Oxford, Clarendon Press, 1959.

Edmund Spenser: *A Critical Study*, New Delhi, Anmol Pub., 2005.

Ferrence, G.: *Deadly Fashion: the Rise and Fall of Cigarette Smoking in North America*, New York, Garland, 1989.

Francis, Russell: *The Scottish Novel: from Smollett to Spark*, Cambridge, Harvard University Press, 1978.

Halliday, M. A. K.: *Intonation and Grammar in British English*, The Hague, Mouton, 1967.

Harivansh R.B.: *In the Afternoon of Time: An Autobiography*, New Delhi, Penguin, 2001.

Hogan, Robert Goode: *The Modern Irish Drama: a Documentary History*, NJ: Humanities Press, 1975.

Jack, Ian Robert James: *English Literature, 1815-1832*, Oxford, Clarendon Press, 1963.

James, Ernest: *Principles of Textual Criticism*, San Marino, Huntington Library, 1972.

James, Runcieman: *English Literature of the Late Seventeenth Century*, New York, Oxford University Press, 1969.

Jhumpa Lahiri: *The Master Storyteller: A Critical Response to Interpreter of Maladies*, New Delhi, KPH, 2002.

John Milton: *A Critical Study*, New Delhi, Anmol, 2005.

Laver, J.: *Principles of Phonetics*, Cambridge, Cambridge University Press, 1994.

Logan, P.: *The Later Jacobean and Caroline Dramatists*, Lincoln, University of Nebraska Press, 1978.

Matricardi, Paolo: *Complete Book of World War II Combat Aircraft*, NY, Military Press, 1988

Naipaul, V.S. : *A House for Mr. Biswas: With an Introduction by Ian Buruma*, New Delhi, Penguin, 1992.

Nath, Narendra: *Indian Religious Historiography*, New Delhi, Munshiram Manoharlal Publishers, 1996.

Neil Bissoondath: *Indo-Caribbean-Canadian Diaspora*, New Delhi, Rawat, 2005.

Perkins, David: *A History of Modern Poetry*, Cambridge, Belknap Press of Harvard University Press, 1976.

Philip Roth: *A Novelist in Crisis*, New Delhi, Classical Publishing, 2001.

Rahilly, J.: *Phonetics: The Science of Speech*, London, Arnold, 1999.

Raja Rao: *The Fictionist*, Delhi, B.R. Publishing, 2003.

Rogers, H.: *The Sounds of Language: An Introduction to Phonetics*, Harlow, Longman, 2000.

Royle, Trevor: *The Macmillan Companion to Scottish Literature*, London, MacMillan Reference Books, 1983.

Seidlhofer, B.: *Pronunciation, Oxford*, Oxford University Press, 1994.

Stevenson, Lionel: *Victorian Fiction: a Guide to Research*, Cambridge, Harvard University Press, 1966.

Terence, P.: *The Later Jacobean and Caroline Dramatists*, Lincoln, University of Nebraska Press, 1978.

Underhill, A.: *Sound Foundations*, London, Heineman, 1994.

Vikram Seth: *Multiple Locations, Multiple Affiliation*, New Delhi, Rawat, 2001.

Wearing, J. P.: *The London Stage, 1890-1899: a Calendar of Plays and Players*, NJ, Scarecrow Press, 1976.

Wickham, Glynne William Gladstone: *Early English Stages, 1300 to 1660*, London, Routledge and Paul; 1959.

William Blake: *A Critical Study*, New Delhi, Anmol, 2005.

William, John: *A History of English Poetry*, London, MacMillan and Co., 1903.

Yeats, W.B. : *Poetry and Plays*, New Delhi, Atlantic, 2002.

INDEX

C

D

E

F

G

H

I

J

K

L

M

N

O

P

R

S

□□□